THE LONDON BOROUGH

Renewals

01159 293388

www.bromley.gov.uk/libraries

Please return this item ~~~~~ n which
it was borrowed.

Renewals
Any item may be renev~~~~~ ~~~~~ne or post, provided it is not
required by another customer. Please quote the barcode number.

Overdue Charges
Please see library notices for the current rate of charges levied on overdue
items. Please note that the overdue charges are made on junior books borrowed
on adult tickets.

Postage
Postage on overdue notices is payable.

03/06	2 9 NOV 2012 ~~Withdrawn~~
WESTMINSTER	~~from~~
2652743	1 5 NOV 2013 ~~stock~~
18.10.05	
	1 2 APR 2016
3 1 OCT 2006	
8 Dec KNX	
3 JAN 07 LNG	
CEN	
31/AY	

92.04

An Introduction to Rights

An Introduction to Rights is the only accessible and readable introduction to the history, logic, moral implications, and political tendencies of the idea of rights. It is organized chronologically and discusses important historical events such as the French Revolution. It deals with historical figures, including Grotius, Paley, Hobbes, Locke, Bentham, Burke, Godwin, Mill, and Hohfeld, and covers contemporary debates, including consequentialism versus contractualism.

Rights come in various types – human, moral, civil, political, and legal – and claims about who has a right, and to what, are often contested. What are rights? Are they timeless and universal, or merely conventional? How are they related to other morally significant values, such as well-being, autonomy, and community? Can animals have rights? Or fetuses? Do we have a right to do as we please so long as we do not harm others? Professor William A. Edmundson addresses these issues from both philosophical and legal perspectives.

As an undergraduate text, *An Introduction to Rights* is well-suited to introductions to political philosophy, moral philosophy, and ethics. It may also be used in courses on political theory in departments of political science and government and in courses on legal theory in law schools.

William A. Edmundson is Professor of Law and Philosophy at Georgia State University. He is the author of *Three Anarchical Fallacies* (Cambridge) and is co-editor of *The Blackwell Guide to the Philosophy of Law and Legal Theory.*

Cambridge Introductions to Philosophy and Law

This introductory series of books provides concise studies of the philosophical foundations of law, of perennial topics in the philosophy of law, and of important and opposing schools of thought. The series is aimed principally at students in philosophy, law, and political science.

Forthcoming

Liam Murphy: *The Limits of Law*

An Introduction to Rights

WILLIAM A. EDMUNDSON
Georgia State University

CAMBRIDGE
UNIVERSITY PRESS

PUBLISHED BY THE PRESS SYNDICATE OF THE UNIVERSITY OF CAMBRIDGE
The Pitt Building, Trumpington Street, Cambridge, United Kingdom

CAMBRIDGE UNIVERSITY PRESS
The Edinburgh Building, Cambridge CB2 2RU, UK
40 West 20th Street, New York, NY 10011-4211, USA
477 Williamstown Road, Port Melbourne, VIC 3207, Australia
Ruiz de Alarcón 13, 28014 Madrid, Spain
Dock House, The Waterfront, Cape Town 8001, South Africa

http://www.cambridge.org

First published 2004

Printed in the United States of America

Typefaces Minion 10.5/14 pt. *and* Stempel Schneidler   *System* LaTeX 2ε   [TB]

A catalog record for this book is available from the British Library.

Library of Congress Cataloging in Publication Data

Edmundson, William A. (William Atkins), 1948–
An introduction to rights / William A. Edmundson.
p.   cm. – (Cambridge introductions to philosophy and law)
Includes bibliographical references (p.) and index.
ISBN 0-521-80398-5 – ISBN 0-521-00870-0 (pbk.)
1. Civil rights.   2. Human rights.   I. Title.   II. Series.
JC571.E42   2004
323–dc22   2003059594

ISBN 0 521 80398 5 hardback
ISBN 0 521 00870 0 paperback

For Gloria Kelly, friend and guide

Contents

List of Tables

Preface

This book is an introduction to the subject of rights. I hope it will interest general readers, but it is aimed at upper-level undergraduates and postgraduates pursuing studies in ethics, moral philosophy, political philosophy, law, legal philosophy, jurisprudence, political science, political theory, or government. At a level of detail appropriate to an introductory book, it covers the history, formal structure, philosophical implications, and political possibilities and tendencies of the idea of rights.

It is impossible to understand what rights are without having a sense of their development over time, but the goal here is to bring current controversies into focus, and to indicate the likely direction of further discussion about the proper role of rights in our moral and political thinking. The most important of these controversies have been taking place on two planes: one plane being that of global politics and political philosophy in the widest sense, the other being a narrower plane on which legal philosophers have investigated the logic of the concept of rights. My aim has been to discuss the substantive concerns of political philosophy and the conceptual concerns of legal philosophy in a way that illuminates both.

One particular matter I hope this method illuminates has to do with understanding two different, though related, functions of rights – that is, rights as *prohibitions* and, contrastingly, rights as *permissions*. The former role of rights has predominated in traditional discussion: rights serve to endow individuals with a kind of "moral armor" protecting them from encroachments by political authority. The latter role, rights as permissions, emphasizes the importance of the moral "breathing room" that rights allow the individual, in which she may pursue projects of her own choosing, whether or not these are responsive to the demands that morality would otherwise impose upon her. The individual's antagonist here is not political authority so much as it is morality itself. In the former role, rights *prohibit* others from doing things to the individual for any reason whatever; in the latter, rights *permit* the individual to ignore demands that would be made of her from a disinterested moral viewpoint.

There are other dimensions of the subject of rights that I bring into the discussion here. One has to do with what could be called the metaethics of rights – that is, the philosophical presuppositions that underlie the very idea that rights exist. This dimension is capable of illuminating the other dimensions to at least some degree, as the book suggests. But an integrated understanding of these differing dimensions – much less, a complete understanding of any one of them – is beyond the grasp of this "Introduction to Rights." The Bibliographical Notes discuss my sources and suggest further reading.

I wish to thank the following: Andy Altman, Brian Bix, Clark Emerson, Martin Golding, Matt Kramer, Peter Lindsay, Chuck Marvin, Neil Kinkopf, Keith Poole, and two anonymous reviewers for Cambridge University Press, for commenting on the manuscript; participants in my rights seminars in 1999 and 2000, for their insights and patience; Jeremy Waldron, for strategic guidance at an early stage; and Terry Moore of Cambridge University Press, without whose encouragement this book would not have been possible. I am also grateful to my research assistants, Keith Diener, Wendi Armstrong, and Victoria Watkins, and to Christine Nwakamma, for help in preparing the final manuscript. The errors and omissions that remain in this book are my fault alone: but for the generous help of others there would have been more.

A Note on Citation Form

To facilitate smooth reading, I have not used footnotes or endnotes, and I have slightly modified the author-date system to document my sources. Wherever it is obvious in the text which work and what author I am quoting or citing, I have simply provided a page number in parentheses. Wherever the context leaves it unclear which work or what author I am referring to, I have given a full author-date citation, in accordance with *The Chicago Manual of Style* (15th ed.). I have also included a section of Bibliographical Notes before the References.

PART ONE

The First Expansionary Era

1

The Prehistory of Rights

Rights are universal, many people say. Everybody possesses certain fundamental rights simply by virtue of being human. But there are also many people who say that rights are a modern, Western invention. Rights are something made up, "constructed," by a certain historical culture – call it the modern, bourgeois West – that seeks, for its own purposes, to export its notions and even to impose them upon other cultures regardless of their traditional ways. And some people seem to want to say both that rights are something that modern Western culture made up and that rights belong to everybody simply by virtue of being human – ignoring the apparent inconsistency.

One way of trying to reconcile these conflicting opinions about the nature of rights is to trace the history of rights discourse, and see whether rights or something equivalent to rights are recognized in all human cultures at all times. If they are, then that would settle the question: rights, whatever else they are, are not simply a modern Western invention. If, on the other hand, rights are not universally recognized across cultures,

then the discovery may make us uneasy, for we will then have to face the
following dilemma: Should we say that the particular moral cultures that
do not, or did not, recognize rights are to that extent morally defective
cultures, or should we say instead that the fact that a given culture rejects
or ignores the idea of rights does not entitle us to draw any conclusions
about its moral worth? (I ignore for now a third possibility, of viewing
talk of rights as a decadent and defective mode of moral discourse.)

The dilemma has practical implications. If we are persuaded that
rights are not recognized in all cultures, the question then arises: What
posture should we adopt toward the cultures that do not recognize them?
If the culture in question is a historical one – ancient Greece, say – the issue
is whether we are to admire the ancient Greeks and even to emulate their
culture, or whether to regard them as morally primitive, even blamable.
If the culture in question is, on the other hand, a contemporary one –
say, China or Iran – the issue is whether or not to regard that culture as
a candidate for reform, censure, and sanctions by means of diplomatic,
economic, or even military pressure. For it would be remarkable if a
culture that did not recognize the existence of rights should nonetheless
be able to treat its members decently. Or is it possible that a culture
might treat its members decently without, by that very fact, exhibiting a
recognition of rights held by its members?

Finding that a culture recognizes the existence of rights will not, of itself, satisfy all of our possible concerns about that culture's treatment of
its members, for it is still possible that the kind of rights it recognizes, and
its distribution of rights, may be defective. For example, one culture might
tolerate religious nonobservance but not open dissent, or another culture
might allow certain rights to all but a despised minority of outcastes. But
we can appreciate that moral reform has a much surer opportunity within
a culture that recognizes that some of its members, at least, have some
rights, than it has within a culture to which the very idea of rights is alien.

Are rights a modern invention? Alasdair MacIntyre makes this observation about "natural" or *human* rights:

> It would of course be a little odd that there should be such rights attaching
> to human beings simply *qua* human beings in light of the fact . . . that
> there is no expression in any ancient or medieval language correctly
> translated by our expression "a right" until near the close of the middle
> ages: the concept lacks any means of expression in Hebrew, Greek, Latin,

or Arabic, classical or medieval, before about 1400, let alone in Old
English, or in Japanese even as late as the mid-nineteenth century. (67)

MacIntyre's account would explain why historians of ideas disagree about
which mediaeval thinker, writing in Latin, should be credited with having
introduced our modern concept of rights: some say William of Ockham,
some say Duns Scotus, others say Jean Gerson. The mediaeval thinkers
had to express themselves in a classical language, Latin, in order to convey an idea for which language had no expression. So it is only to be
expected that there should be disagreement, since none of the candidates
clearly announced: "I am introducing a concept without precedent in
this language."

Other writers have made similar observations about the concept of
rights. Benjamin Constant, writing in the aftermath of the French Revolution, thought rights to be a modern innovation, and the twentieth-
century classical scholar Kenneth Dover has written:

> The Greek [of classical antiquity] did not regard himself as having more
> rights at any given time than the laws of the city into which he was born
> gave him at that time; these rights could be reduced, for the community
> was sovereign, and no rights were inalienable. The idea that parents have
> a *right* to educate . . . their children . . . or that the individual has a *right*
> to take drugs . . . or a *right* to take up the time of doctors and nurses in
> consequence of not wearing a safety-belt, would have seemed to a Greek
> too laughable to be discussed. (157–58)

But here we should pause and consider carefully what to make of these
claims. Assuming for the moment that we have before us a correct account of the linguistic resources and commonsense beliefs of, say, classical
Greece, what conclusions would this warrant with respect to the nature
and existence of rights?

The presence or absence of a word or concise phrase or locution
in another language, with which to translate a word we use, is hardly
conclusive as to the *availability* of an idea to speakers of another language.
The Greeks had no word for *quarks*, but the idea of what a quark is could
surely have been conveyed to them as a kind of constituent of certain
subatomic particles – after all, we have borrowed the Greek terms *atomos*,
electron, *proton*, and so on in order to describe these very things. So, if the
argument is that the concept of rights cannot be attributed to a linguistic

culture lacking a precisely equivalent term, the argument is not a very good one.

But perhaps the argument is more subtle. MacIntyre admits that his linguistic observations do not show that there are no human rights: "It only follows that no one could have known that there were" (67). What might this tell us? It might tell us something very important if the existence of rights is somehow dependent upon their being known. Certainly some kinds of entity are dependent upon being known. *Headaches*, for example, have no existence whatever apart from being felt and known as such. We could imagine an isolated tribe of people who had the good fortune of never suffering headaches. Naturally, their language would lack an expression for headache. Would we then conclude that the concept of headache was simply inapplicable within this culture? We might hesitate before drawing this conclusion, because there are two possible ways of introducing the concept to this tribe.

One way would be by analogy. If the tribe knew what *aches* were – maybe from the occurrence of stomachaches among them – and it knew what heads were, we could explain headache as a stomachache of the head. Another way would be to simply introduce the concept by banging tribespeople "upside" their heads and thereby introducing them to the thing itself. Similarly, the concept of rights could be introduced either by analogy or by the institution of rights among the members of a culture unfamiliar with them. But both methods require some further examination.

Introducing the concept of rights by analogy would first require our getting clear about what rights are and what they are analogous to. And here comes a worry: If rights are not closely analogous to anything else, any analogy will fail; but if rights are too closely analogous to something else, then rights would seem to reduce to that something else. If, to suggest one example, rights are like *privately enforceable legal duties not to harm*, and another culture is familiar with *privately enforceable legal duties not to harm*, but not with rights, the worry might arise as to whether we would be better off abandoning our talk of rights except insofar as it was a shorthand for *privately enforceable legal duties not to harm*. Rather than introduce our concept to another culture, perhaps we should eliminate it from ours. Call this worry the *reductive worry*.

The other way of introducing the concept – by instituting it within the other culture – creates a separate but equally serious worry. Just as it would be objectionable to teach someone what a headache was by hitting him on the head, it may seem objectionable to teach another culture what human rights are by forcing it to respect them. This kind of imposition may seem especially objectionable in the case of rights, which exemplify a moral concept. It may seem to be hypocritical to try to force a moral concept upon another culture. Call this the *imperialism worry*.

Having looked ahead at the dilemma we will face should it turn out that rights are not found among the conceptual resources of all people at all times, let us return to the question: Are rights universal? That is, can we attribute a grasp of the idea of rights, or something very close to it, to every culture? It will help us to focus this question if we look at two particular points of dispute, the first having to do with mediaeval Europe, the second with India.

Mediaeval Europe, and the Possibility of Poverty

The first of these disputes involved the Franciscan monastic order. St. Francis lived a life of poverty, and his example galvanized the order that bears his name. Worldliness (that is, attachment to this world and a coordinate neglect of the world to come after death) was a vice for the Franciscans, and poverty a sign that one was free of it. But how is perfect poverty possible? Surely even St. Francis had to eat, and in so doing did he not exercise dominion over what he ate? This fact posed a disturbing problem for the Franciscans, for it seemed that even St. Francis had to have been a proprietor, even if only on a small scale, and that "apostolic" poverty (the austere practice the Franciscans attributed to the apostles) was not a pure state isolated from worldly concerns at all. The solution for the Franciscans was put forth by Duns Scotus, a member of the order. Scotus emphasized the distinction between *dominium* or dominion (what we can simply call property rights), on the one hand, and use or mere possession of a thing ("imperium"), on the other. Although in order to live it is necessary to use things, it is not necessary to own them or to exclude others from using them. Property is not natural, and the world belongs in common to humanity, at least before civil society arises and draws most of us into the network of artificial relationships that constitute property holding. Apostolic poverty is possible, after all, and the Franciscan view was for a time the official view of the Roman Catholic Church.

The Franciscan view was in an important sense consistent with the theory of the ancient Roman jurists, who were of the opinion that property was not something that occurred in nature, but only came into existence with human institutions that define and enforce it. The Romans (Cicero aside) did not typically conceive of rights as preexisting or possibly opposing and limiting the enacted or "positive" law (and they notoriously did not harbor our worries about imperialism). Christians, on the other hand, took very seriously the idea that God administers a moral kingdom that stands apart from and above any merely temporal institution or convention, and that the "natural" design God made for the world is what ought to be consulted for guiding our lives.

But apostolic poverty was not a doctrine that appealed to all within the Church. It had the inconvenient implication that we all ought to follow St. Francis's example, and live in a condition of humble communism. Thomas Aquinas, a member of the rival Dominican order, had already seen the matter as at least ambiguous: Although material things are subject, in a sense, only to God's moral powers, they are, in another sense, subject to at least de facto human power whenever they are used or consumed. The dispute was finally settled in the year 1329, when Pope John XXII issued a papal bull flatly declaring that human dominion over material things is, though in miniature, precisely like God's dominion over the universe. The Church's official position, reversing a half-century of Franciscan-inspired precedent, became this: Property is natural and inescapable, apostolic poverty is impossible and, moreover, primitive communism is impossible – God has made us as individual shareholders, however small, *ab origine* – that is, from the very first. Even in the Garden of Eden, Adam was already exercising moral as well as physical power over the fruits he gathered – at least over those that were not forbidden to him.

Although that battle was now over, a number of conceptual issues crystalized in the Franciscan William of Ockham's rebuttal to John XXII (if not earlier – who is to be credited with these refinements, and when, is a matter of controversy into which we need not enter). One crucially important distinction was by this time generally appreciated – that between what has been called *objective right* and *subjective right*. The objective sense of "right" is that which is expressed by the formula "It is right that p" – where p stands for a proposition describing an actual or possible fact, as in "It is right that promises are kept," or "It is right that there be a Palestinian state," or "It is right that Palmer inherit Blackacre." The job done by any expression of the form "It is right that *p*" could equally well be done by the expressions "It ought to be the case that *p*" or "It is just that *p*" or perhaps "It is fitting that *p*." The formula "It is right that *p*" expresses what logicians would call a *sentential operator*: it operates on a sentence expressing proposition *p* to yield another sentence, and in this case the truth of the resulting sentence, "It is right that *p*," happens not to be a function of the truth of *p*. In other words, depending upon what proposition *p* we pick, *p* may be false while "It is right that *p*" is true, and vice versa. For example, it is false that children are never abused, but it is nonetheless true (if awkward) to say that it is right that children are never abused.

Subjective right is different in that it expresses a relationship between *a person* and a state of affairs. The canonical form is "*X* has a right to a thing or to do something" – where *X* stands for an individual person, or perhaps a group of individuals. The crucial difference is that the concept of objective right is a global moral evaluation of a state of affairs, while the concept of subjective right is a moral *relationship* between a person (typically) and a thing or action or state of affairs. One question that rights theory must decide is whether moral reality is fully describable in terms of objective right: that is, by filling out the formula "It is right that the world be as follows . . . ," followed by a description. The Decalogue can be understood as an example of a moral code stated solely in terms of objective right – these are the Ten Commandments: "Thou shalt not do this and thou shalt do that, and so on," or (translating), "It is right that this be done and it is right that that not be done, and so on."

Subjective right adds something that objective right might very well do without: subjective right refers to individuals and defines moral facts that essentially involve them. Suppose I take St. Francis's sandals without his permission. "Thou shalt not steal" – I have violated objective right, I have transgressed God's commandment. But where does St. Francis come into the picture? We want to add, "St. Francis has a right to his sandals." It isn't enough to say "It is right that St. Francis has his sandals back," because that way of putting it leaves St. Francis on the sidelines, so to speak. There is more to the situation, somehow, than the fact that St. Francis needs sandals and I have an extra pair that I wrongfully got from him. We want to say that *St. Francis has a right* to those sandals, and saying it that way puts the focus on him in a way that merely stating that my wrongful action caused him to be in need does not. If we worked at it, we might be able to avoid using the language of subjective right, but it would be cumbersome to do so, and probably pointless as well. We don't have to come to a decision about the precise logical relationship between objective and subjective right to appreciate the fact that subjective right puts a right-*holder* in the foreground, in a way that objective right does not.

The terms for subjective right and objective right are unfortunate, in a way, because they misleadingly suggest that there is something more real about objective right, and that subjective right is somehow in the eye of the beholder. This is not what is meant at all. The "subject" in subjective right is the right-holder, not the right-*be*holder. And the "object" in objective right is not any particular object – natural, material, or otherwise – but is, if anything, the global object of moral assessment or prescription.

Let us assume that the language of rights as we know and understand it has not taken hold until the subjective right/objective right distinction is operating. What implications follow? If the concept of subjective right has to have emerged in a culture before we can say that the concept of a right has emerged, what does that tell us about, say, contemporary and traditional cultures in Asia?

Third-Century India and Tolerance

The former Prime Minister of Singapore, Lee Kuan Yew, has argued that the imposition of the concept of human rights upon Asian nations is insensitive to the cultural values of the East, and so represents a kind of cultural imperialism. Singapore is typically thought of in the West as a prosperous but authoritarian, even repressive, regime, where the chewing of gum is a crime and petty vandalism is punishable by flogging. Ought Singapore to align itself with Western thinking about human rights, or ought the West learn to respect the more authoritarian traditions of the East? The Nobel Prize–winning economist Amartya Sen has taken issue with Lee's premise that the traditions of the East are monolithically indifferent or hostile to human rights. The imperialism worry, in other words, is misplaced if rights already have gotten a foothold in Eastern traditions.

But have they? Sen adduces evidence that liberty and toleration – if not for all, then at least for some – have been valued by powerful leaders in India's past. The third-century B.C. emperor Ashoka, for example, decreed that "a man must not do reverence to his own sect or disparage that of another man without reason. Depreciation should be for specific reason only, because the sects of other people all deserve reverence...." (Sen 1999). Ashoka intended edicts such as this to guide citizens in their daily lives, as well as public ministers in their official acts. A convert to Buddhism, Ashoka dispatched missionaries beyond India, thus projecting an influence throughout Asia.

Much as we may approve of Ashoka's promotion of tolerance and diversity, is it a sufficient basis for attributing to him a concept of rights? More pointedly, is Ashoka's attitude one that necessarily reflects an appreciation of subjective right – that is, of the rights *of persons* to worship as they see fit? Or might Ashoka equally well be understood as declaring as a matter of objective right that tolerance is to be extended by each to all – announcing, as it were, yet another "Thou shalt...?"

If it is granted that the concept of rights that interests us is a subjective conception, what would that do to address the relativism worry? Some will say that there is far more built into a distinctively modern conception of rights than what the idea of a subjective right captures. Rights are "trumps" over political majorities, or over considerations of aggregate social welfare, others have argued. Nothing in the subjective notion, standing alone, guarantees that rights are taken seriously enough to match our modern notion of them, some would argue, along with MacIntyre. Others have pointed to aspects of the Roman Code of Justinian, or of Aristotle's *Politics*, that go beyond a bare-bones notion of subjective right, and they have gone on to argue on this basis that ancient Greece and Rome employed a vigorous conception of rights that is essentially continuous with the one that we use today.

Deciding these kinds of controversies is beyond the scope of this book. We will take it as granted that the concept of rights is a subjective one, but we have now to consider carefully what else is distinctive of the concept. To do this, it is necessary to trace some further intellectual history. The language of rights has attained the importance it has because it answers somehow to the needs that people have felt to express themselves in certain ways rather than others. These felt needs can be better understood if we have at least a loose grasp of the historical circumstances and practical problems that were before the minds of those who have made most articulate use of the language of rights. The concept of rights is a *practical* one, and we must not lose sight of this central fact about rights: By their very nature they have a bearing upon how we are to conduct ourselves and order our affairs.

Two Expansionary Periods of Rights Rhetoric

If we were to draw a time line running from left to right, representing the prevalence of rights rhetoric across history, we should show two periods of time during which "rights talk" was so prevalent that its very prevalence became a matter of comment and criticism. For convenience, I will refer to these as "expansionary periods," without meaning to imply thereby that any sort of deflationary reaction was or is justified. I simply want to call attention to the peculiarity that rights rhetoric, as a historical fact, has had its ups and downs and, looked at in schematic profile, resembles a Bactrian camel – it has two humps.

The first hump appeared in the late eighteenth century, approximately between the American Declaration of Independence in 1776 and the end of the French Reign of Terror in 1794. The 1790s produced several important skeptical examinations of the concept of rights, which we will look at in some detail after a brief look at some of the philosophical writings that preceded, and fed, the first "hump" – that is, the first expansionary period. To say that that expansionary period ended is not to say that the clock was turned back or that rights ceased to be important: it is only to suggest that as a result of an accumulation of skeptical doubts and practical worries, rights rhetoric became more guarded and ceremonial than exploratory and provocative.

We are living today somewhere in the midst of the second hump, or second expansionary period of rights rhetoric. The second period began with the Universal Declaration of Human Rights in 1948, in the aftermath of the Second World War. We do not know whether the second expansionary period will end, or has ended, or when. There was increasing concern during the last decade of the twentieth century that "rights talk" had gotten out of hand, or was being debased or devalued, or was muddleheaded, misleading, or dispensable. Some of the deflationary reaction to the second period of inflation recapitulates, as we shall see, the reaction to the first.

There are two important differences between the two expansionary periods. One is that the second period has so far shown little tendency to lead to the chaos and bloodshed that accompanied the French Revolution. The expansion of rights rhetoric since 1948 has had mainly good consequences, and its excesses (if any) have been merely rhetorical. But every demand (and there are many) that reality match rhetoric is a challenge to the status quo, and the perception that rights are being denied can engender deep resentment and violent passion. This is particularly so because positions on matters of distributive justice and economic equality are now routinely debated in terms of rights rather than (mere) aspirations. People are generally readier to fight to keep what is theirs than to get what is not yet theirs – social psychologists call this the "endowment effect." When aspirations are expressed as entitlements the chances are greater that delivery will be demanded.

The second difference between the two expansionary periods is a difference in the underlying intellectual and cultural background of rights. Moral skepticism and nihilism are today eminently thinkable alternatives to moral theories of any sort. Such was not the case at the end of the eighteenth century, which, though rightly called an age of reason, was not one of disenchantment. During the first expansionary period, there was close to universal agreement that there was some moral order to the universe, and there was dispute about whether and how rights fit in to that order. During the second expansionary period, however, there is increasing doubt that there is any cosmic moral order; and the difficulty of reaching agreement about whether there are rights, and about what rights are, and about how they are distributed, tends to fuel that doubt. There is no reason to suppose that people cannot live peaceably and harmoniously together in the absence of an objective moral order. It may even be possible to live in harmony without any shared belief in the existence of such an order. But it is more difficult to conceive how we might live *justly*, apart from such an order, or a shared belief in one. If the language of rights is an essential part of any adequate account of justice, then that language (like the notion of justice itself) has to situate itself somehow within a larger account of how people fit into the natural order. What is it about us that can make it true that we hold rights against others even though those rights are contrary to all established conventions? What is it about us that can make it true that we hold rights against others even though it might please those others to violate our rights? These and similar questions about rights are especially poignant now that rights have again thrust themselves to the forefront of moral discourse.

Although we cannot fully answer these questions in a book of this kind, we can get clearer about what rights are and what are the minimum presuppositions of rights talk. We can also get a bearing on the question whether rights discourse, if it is in fact a historical innovation, represents moral progress, and, if so, what further progress (if any) the fulfillment of rights commits us to.

2

The Rights of Man
The Enlightenment

The concept of rights first became unmistakably prominent during the period of modern intellectual history known as the Enlightenment, which for our purposes had its beginnings in the early seventeenth century and ran to the end of the eighteenth. It was a period in which both the Church and the ancient Greek authorities (which had been recovered during the Renaissance) began to be questioned, and the order of the natural world began to be seen as capable of being understood by means very different from those that Renaissance scholars and church scholastics had hitherto been accustomed to using. Francis Bacon's turning away from scholastic to experimental methods of investigating the world marks the beginning of this period, and we can think of it as ending with (if not culminating in) two political revolutions: the American and the French, which defined the first expansionary period. What began as a new, antidogmatic and inquisitive approach to the study of nature was applied to human affairs, and with consequences that are still unfolding.

A subjective concept of rights – subjective in focusing in an important but as yet unspecified way upon the right-*holder* – had already emerged at least as early as the late Middle Ages, in disputes among Catholic clerics. It would be a mistake to regard this emergence as an unambiguous mark of moral progress, however. One of the more curious and least reputable chapters in the history of rights concerns the role of the concept of rights in the defense of human slavery. Rights in the sense we have called subjective had had a key role in the Dominican answer to Franciscan communism. That which we use we acquire a right to exclude others from using, and if we wish, we may transfer our right of exclusive use to another in gift or exchange. But implicit in the Dominican answer is the further question: If using things naturally gives the user property in them, does a person not then acquire property in his own body? And if a person has property in himself, why may he not give or trade it away, or put it at hazard? In other words, if people can naturally acquire property in what they use – which they may then trade or risk – why can they not naturally enslave themselves, by trading away or staking their persons and their liberty?

As Richard Tuck has pointed out, the discovery of the New World made this question far from academic for Spanish and Portuguese clerics. The Dominican answer to the Franciscans seemed capable of providing a straightforward defense of exploiting Africans and American Indians. Slaves could be assumed to have hazarded or traded away their dominion over themselves, just as anyone might trade away or chance any chattel acquired by use. Some Spanish Dominicans recoiled from this implication, and argued that God's law forbade men to exchange their liberty for anything short of life itself. But others, such as the Spaniard, Silvestro Mazzolini and the Portuguese, Luis de Molina, were entirely comfortable with making man the natural master of his own liberty to such an extent that he might surrender, lose, or bargain it away.

The emergence of a subjective conception of right was, in itself, not necessarily an instrument of moral progress. It is against this suggestive but murky background that we turn to the first, and perhaps most important, figure in Enlightenment political, legal, and moral theory, Huig de Groot, now usually referred to by his Latinized name, Hugo Grotius.

Hugo Grotius

Grotius is best known for his treatise *De Iure Belli ac Pacis* ("Of the Law of War and Peace") published in 1625 in the midst of the Thirty Years War, which involved all of the European powers and was to an important degree a religious war pitting Catholics, Lutherans, and Calvinists against each other. Holland, then as now, was heavily dependent upon sea trade for its economic welfare. Grotius, a Dutch lawyer, had a professional as well as a philosophical interest in establishing international law and the law of war as serious subjects. The Netherlands, as a trading nation, had to contend with the superior maritime might of Spain and Portugal. It is not surprising that a representative of a weaker power would wish to invoke justice to resolve disputes with the stronger. Although there was already a venerable tradition devoted to the study of "municipal" law – that is, the law of particular nations (especially the law of the Roman republic) – Grotius had to overcome an even older tradition of skepticism about the very idea of justice between nations rather than within a nation. According to the skeptics, there is no "law" of nature other than the imperative of self-preservation. But such skepticism, Grotius argued, ignores man's "impelling desire for society" (1646, 11) and for orderly and peaceful society, at that.

Grotius thought that humans have a social nature. Even animals and children are, to a degree, capable of restraining themselves to benefit others; but mature humans uniquely have powers of speech and understanding. Sociability and understanding combine in humans to make justice, as contrasted to mere sympathy, possible. Justice is therefore an expression of a human nature that Grotius believed to be sufficiently determinate to allow him to speak of *laws* governing that nature. Moreover, this conception of natural law would have "some degree of validity even if we should concede that which cannot be conceded without the utmost wickedness, that there is no God. . . ." (13). With this mild-seeming phrase, Grotius introduced the possibility of separating the study of morality from theology, departing from the centuries-old Christian tradition that insisted that the latter must subsume the former of the two subjects. Grotius evidently saw such a separation as essential if there were to be a basis for peacefully resolving disputes between nations of different religions. (Grotius himself was not a skeptic on theology: the title of his most widely circulated book is translated as *Of the Truth of the Christian Religion.*)

Grotius was innovative in another way. He was determined, as no one had been before, to analyze the whole subject of justice as a matter of *rights*. A right, in the sense Grotius wanted to emphasize, "has reference to a person." It is in fact "a moral quality of a person, making it possible [for that person] to have or to do something lawfully" – that is, to have or do it justly (35). Grotius's conception is recognizably one of subjective right: "To this sphere," he wrote, "belong the abstaining from that which is another's, the restoration to another of anything of his which we may have . . . the obligation to fulfil promises, and the inflicting of penalties upon men according to their deserts" – all, in his analysis, matters of respecting or exercising rights (12–13). Governments could be understood as pacts among men, formed to further the aims of sociability. War itself, he concluded, was typically occasioned by rights violations and "ought not to be undertaken except for the enforcement of rights" (18).

The preeminence Grotius gave to subjective rights represented a new turn in intellectual history. Rights, in Grotius's theory, were not limited to property, but extended presumptively to the whole range of an individual's *actions* as well, in which she enjoyed a natural liberty. How are these rights to be known? Grotius was almost gleefully optimistic on this point:

> [T]he principles of the law of nature, since they are always the same, can easily be brought into a systematic form; [unlike] the elements of positive law, [which,] since they undergo change and are different in different places, are outside the domain of systematic treatment. . . . . I have made it my concern to refer the proofs of things touching the law of nature to certain fundamental conceptions which are beyond question, so that no one can deny them without doing violence to himself. For the principles of that law . . . are in themselves manifest and clear, almost as evident as are those things that we perceive by the external senses. . . . I have, furthermore, availed myself of the testimony of philosophers, historians, poets, finally also of orators . . . [for] when many at different times, and in many different places, affirm the same thing as certain, that ought to be referred to a universal cause. . . . (21–23)

He went on to compare the truths of natural law to those of arithmetic, which not even God could alter or deny without absurdity. Grotius thus invoked three channels by which rights may be known: by a vivid sort of quasi-sensory perception, by a purely intellectual power akin to logical and mathematical reasoning, and by the consensus of testimony in varied places and times.

Rights, so conceived, would seem capable of setting limits to the authority of government, in that a sovereign monarch who was ignorant or mistaken about human nature could easily issue morally incorrect decrees. But Grotius rejected the idea that rights check the just powers of the sovereign, and made a suggestion that may seem as surprising now as it did in the seventeenth century:

> To every man it is permitted to enslave himself to anyone he pleases for private ownership, as is evident both from the Hebraic and from the Roman Law. Why, then, would it not be permitted to a people having legal competence to submit itself to some one person . . . in such a way as plainly to transfer to him the legal right to govern, retaining no vestige of that right for itself? (103)

Although Grotius cautioned against interpreting actual legal systems as founded upon a pact of *abject* submission to a sovereign, he admitted the logical possibility and legitimacy, and even the possible rationality of it. *Alienability* – the power to irrevocably transfer something to another – is built into the notion of a right as Grotius conceived it. Grotius, in effect, transposed the Dominican idea of the essential alienability of rights from the context of justifying slavery to that of justifying government itself. The natural sociability and presumed good sense of right-holders are ultimately what will determine the shape of the distribution of rights in the various nations that people build for themselves. But is there not some ideal of the state against which to measure such distributions? Grotius rejected the idea of a single, best form of government:

> Just as, in fact, there are many ways of living, no one being better than another, and out of so many ways of living each is free to select that which he prefers, so also a people can select the form of government which it wishes; and the extent of its legal right in the matter is not to be measured by the superior excellence of this or that form of government, in regard to which men hold different views, but by its free choice. (104)

Here, Grotius made another break with the past. Whereas earlier thinkers from Plato to St. Augustine had concerned themselves with the problem of specifying the ideal political state, Grotius tersely rejected the possibility of solving it. The problem is insoluble for the simple reason that there is no single best type of life for people of all kinds to lead, and therefore there is no single best kind of political state to facilitate a best life. Grotius is, in modern terms, a *pluralist* about values.

This pluralism, if combined with the idea that governments are essentially compacts among diverse persons holding diverse views of the good life, had more revolutionary implications than what Grotius was willing to draw. The free choice that people have by nature was to be understood to have been already exercised, and governmental forms already to have been decided, leaving in the people no residual right of choice. Grotius's intentions were pacific and conservative rather than revolutionary, but the potentially explosive conception of rights that he employed proved to be both a challenge and a temptation to later thinkers.

Grotius's three great innovations were: (1) to regard justice as a matter of respecting and exercising individual rights; (2) to separate the study of rights from theology; and (3) to turn political philosophy away from the quest for the ideal form of government by admitting the possibility of different, equally legitimate forms, derived from different peoples' exercise of rights in differing circumstances. Looking only at these three aspects of his thought would be misleading, however, if it obscured Grotius's regard for the sociability of humanity. Nature ordains not only the laws of justice but a "law of love," which though not "perfectly" obligatory or enforceable, is praiseworthy to follow and perhaps blameworthy not to. Grotius thus distinguished between *perfect* and *imperfect* rights – perfect rights being enforceable by legal process or self-help, imperfect rights not being enforceable titles to what is "one's own," but rather like one's worthiness to receive assistance or esteem.

How should we understand the distinction between perfect and imperfect rights? Grotius revealingly considered the question whether an innocent citizen may be sacrificed to save the state from calamity. He thought it clear that the sacrifice may be imposed, but confronted this problem: If the innocent citizen has entered political society solely to secure his own advantage, how can he be *obligated* to sacrifice himself? And if the citizen has no obligation to sacrifice himself, how can it be permissible for the state to sacrifice him over his protest? Or, to put the question in terms of rights, if the state has no right to demand that the innocent citizen sacrifice himself, what right can it have to sacrifice him against his will, which would be a "perfect" right?

The response Grotius gave is subtle. From the fact that "a citizen is not bound to surrender himself by law properly so-called; it does not follow also that love permits him to do otherwise. For there are many duties which are not in the domain of justice properly speaking, but in that of affection, which are not only discharged among praise . . . but cannot even be omitted without blame." But, having invoked love and affection as the basis of a duty, Grotius immediately added: "Such a duty seems quite clearly to be this, that a person should value the lives of a very large number of innocent persons above his own life" (579). The basis of the duty now seems to lie not so much in the actual affection felt by the person called upon to sacrifice as in the numbers on each side of the ledger. The "law of love" is in this sense an impersonal law, and one that commands us regardless of what value we, individually, might place upon sacrificing for others.

These steps lead to a duty not of strict justice, but of love, to make the sacrifice. But, Grotius pointed out, "there remains the question whether he may be compelled to do that to which he is morally bound" (580). If, as Grotius allows, a rich man cannot be compelled to give alms to a beggar, how can an innocent man be forced to sacrifice his life to save the many? An imperfect or unenforceable right is the most that the law of love yields. Yet Grotius agreed with the ancient authorities that the sacrifice of the innocent to save the state may properly be compelled even though other imperfect rights, such as the right to receive charity, may not. What is the basis of this crucial distinction? Grotius made this observation:

> [T]he relation of parts among themselves is one thing, and that of superiors, when they are contrasted with those subject to them, is quite another. For an equal cannot be compelled by an equal, except to perform what is owed in accordance with a right properly so called. But a superior can compel an inferior to do other things also, which some virtue demands, because this is embraced in the proper right of the superior as such. (580)

If a "superior" may compel contributions to a common granary in time of famine, so also may an innocent be forcibly sacrificed to save the many, or so Grotius concluded. What remains mysterious, though, is how what in other hands would be an unenforceable imperfect right becomes an enforceable perfect right in hands of the "superior" authority of the state. The mystery need not worry anyone who is content with the idea that there are rights that are unenforceable, period, full stop. But Grotius was not one of those contented people, and it is a problem that we will return to. In one respect, at least, Grotius was unwilling to accept the superior authority of the state; for, rather than serve a sentence of life imprisonment for having taken the wrong side in a religious controversy (one concerning predestination, ironically enough), Grotius had himself smuggled to freedom in a basket of books.

Thomas Hobbes

The Spanish sea power that was to stimulate Grotius's thinking had provoked such wide alarm in England in the year 1588 that Thomas Hobbes's mother, on hearing talk of the approaching Armada, went into labor and delivered him prematurely into the world. Hobbes was, as he said himself, "born of fear." He later studied at Oxford, and then spent most of the rest of his life employed as a personal secretary at two of the stateliest homes of England, Chatsworth and Hardwick, punctuated by several nervous trips to the Continent to escape persecution.

Hobbes dispensed with Grotius's belief in the natural sociability of humanity. Without the constraints government imposes, life would be "solitary, poore, nasty, brutish, and short" in Hobbes's estimation (89). In his view, a sovereign power is necessary in order to avoid the dismal circumstances of a "state of meer Nature" (140), which is a condition of war "of every man, against every man" (88). Hobbes's great idea was to elaborate the Grotean thought that states and their municipal laws, and their legitimacy, are somehow derived from a pact among their subjects. Although this idea is a radical one, Hobbes's purposes were – like Grotius's – conservative. He wrote during a period of political tumult occasioned by disputes about the succession to the English crown. Hobbes saw that appeals to the divine right of kings were an invitation to perpetual conflict, and that therefore the legitimacy of the regime had to have a foundation less permeable by religious and dynastic controversies.

The idea of rights figured into Hobbes's theory in the following way. In a state of nature, everyone has a right to everything he judges to be necessary to his survival:

> The RIGHT OF NATURE . . . is the Liberty each man hath, to use his own power, as he will himselfe, for the preservation of his own nature; that is to say, of his own Life; and consequently, of doing any thing, which in his own Judgement, and Reason, hee shall conceive to be the aptest means thereunto. (91)

If you and I both judge that we need, for example, the fruit from an apple tree in order to survive, we both have a right to it, and in pursuing our respective rights we come into conflict. The rights a person holds are not naturally tailored to be compatible with the rights held by others. In Hobbes's own words: "[B]ecause the condition of Man . . . is a condition of Warre of every one against every one. . . . It followeth, that in such a condition, every man has a Right to every thing; even to one another's body" (91). If I judge that my survival requires my enslaving you, and you likewise judge that yours requires your enslaving me, we are at war, a war that no appeal to natural rights, as Hobbes conceived them, can settle. Conflicts of rights are inescapable in a world of limited abundance, like ours, unless people agree to surrender their rights to a sovereign who is capable of adjudicating conflicts and apportioning the scarce resources of a commonwealth. Persons in a state of nature do have the power to surrender rights and, seeing the necessity of doing so to secure themselves, they create the state, a sovereign "LEVIATHAN," an "Artificiall Man" (9) possessing just those moral rights and powers that have been transferred to it.

Do the people retain no rights, once the sovereign has been created? Hobbes's answer was that they retain only the natural right to resist being killed or confined, for that is the only right it would be absurd to suppose they did not retain. People make governments in order to escape the state of nature and the uncertain prospects they enjoy there for survival. They must be understood to have surrendered all, but only, those rights necessary to escape a condition of such insecurity. But if the sovereign sentences me to hang, I have no duty to submit to the hanging. Survival being the very reason for the surrender of rights, I cannot have surrendered the right to resist the hangman.

This does not, however, mean that the sovereign has a duty not to hang me; it only means that the sovereign does me no wrong by hanging me, nor I by resisting. I must, however, be understood as having surrendered *every other* right against the sovereign (and if the sovereign sentences *you* to hang, I may not resist the execution of your sentence). Hobbes recognized no other "retained" natural rights that would be good against the sovereign, and any "civil" rights the sovereign chose to extend to subjects (a right to a fair trial, for example) would depend entirely upon the sovereign's prerogative to withdraw them. The sovereign is *incapable* of injustice, in Hobbes's view; although the sovereign may be answerable to God, she is not answerable to her subjects.

Hobbes's theory exasperates many because it begins with assumptions that have an undeniable appeal: a bracing unsentimentality about human nature, a recognition of natural rights belonging to each and all, and a determination to understand government as resting upon a compact among the governed. Yet Hobbes makes these assumptions yield conclusions that seem to legitimate the severest authoritarianism. In a manner strikingly parallel to the Dominican's use of subjective rights to justify chattel slavery, Hobbes's theory uses the idea of rights to justify a possibly quite tyrannical government. It would not be an exaggeration to say that the history of political philosophy since Hobbes has been a story of troubles taken to disentangle the attractive from the repulsive elements in his theory.

Samuel Pufendorf

The Thirty Years War, which had prompted Grotius and Hobbes to think about politics in terms of rights, was concluded in 1648 by the Treaty of Westphalia, instituting in Europe a system of sovereign nation-states and, with it, (relative) peace. Pufendorf was the first major thinker to take up the challenge of giving coherent intellectual shape to the resulting international order. Although Pufendorf's first writing was done while he was imprisoned during hostilities between Sweden and Denmark, his most influential work was done while he held a series of academic posts in Holland, Germany, and in Sweden, where he later became an advisor to King Charles XI. Pufendorf thought carefully about Grotius and Hobbes, and challenged and corrected them in numerous matters of detail, but in many respects his task was one of consolidation and systematization rather than innovation.

One point on which Pufendorf challenged Hobbes had to do with Hobbes's careless attribution of rights to men in a state of nature. Pufendorf argued that "it must be recognized that not every natural faculty to do something is properly a right, but only that which concerns some moral effect. . . ." Horses may graze in the meadow, he wrote, but it would be fanciful to describe horses as exercising a right to graze. A "natural faculty," such as the ability to gather or to graze, becomes a "real right" only when it has a moral effect upon other creatures of the same kind. Nothing a horse can do has such an effect on other horses, so it is merely fanciful to attribute to horses a right to graze. But, similarly, it makes no sense to attribute to a human being a right to gather acorns unless his gathering alters the moral situation of other humans so "that other men may not hinder him, or compete with him, against his will, in using such objects . . . [and] of course it is absurd to try to designate as a right that faculty which all other men have a right to prevent one from exercising." What sort of effect, then, is necessary before the exercise of a faculty gives rise to a right? Pufendorf's answer is that nothing "properly called a right" can arise without others' coming under an obligation to the putative rightholder (1672, 391).

Pufendorf thus was one of the first to notice an important aspect of rights – at least of "real" or "properly called" rights – which we can characterize as the *correlativity of rights and duties*. No right can be attributed to one person without at the same time attributing certain correlative duties of noninterference to others. With respect to property rights, the question immediately arises: Whence comes this burdensome duty of noninterference? Pufendorf's answer was that because of the "natural equality of men" such a duty or obligation cannot arise without the others' consent, "express or presumed." Therefore, "nature does not define what particular things belong to one man, and what to another, before they agree among themselves on their division and allocation" (1672, 391). The initial division is to be regarded as consensual and conventional, rather than natural, and, after that, further appropriation of things not already divided is subject to a rule of first occupancy, which is itself a conventional rule rather than a natural law.

Pufendorf also took up and elaborated Grotius's distinction between *perfect* and *imperfect* rights. For Grotius, the difference lay in the enforceablity of perfect rights and the unenforceability of imperfect ones. Pufendorf argued that there are also characteristic differences in the degree of specificity and the functions of the two types of right. Perfect rights are rights that are honored by others' performing or omitting specific types of act. For example, my (perfect) right to my life correlates with your duty not to kill me, and my (perfect) right to expect you to keep your promise correlates with your duty to do as promised; but my (imperfect) right to gratitude or to assistance in dire need does not correlate with a duty so specific as to raise the question whether its performance "is equal to, or less than, that which was [its] reason" (1672, 119). This difference reflects a further, underlying difference between laws "which conduce to the mere existence of society" – that create perfect, exact, and enforceable rights – and those that conduce merely "to an improved existence" (1672, 118).

Whereas Grotius found humans to be sociable by nature, Pufendorf, like Hobbes, took a darker view. But Pufendorf saw our human desire for safety as a corrective to our innate viciousness, for "in order to be safe, it is necessary for man to be sociable." This conclusion furnished a basis for what he called the "fundamental natural law: every man ought to do as much as he can to cultivate and preserve sociality . . . all that violates sociality is understood as forbidden" (1673, 36). In addition to the natural duties each human owes to himself, three fundamental duties each owes to every other have been ordained by God. The first is a duty not to harm others (this is the easiest of the three to observe since it requires "mere omission of action"), the second is a duty that each "value and treat the other as naturally his equal," and the third is that "everyone be useful to others, so far as he conveniently can" (1673, 56, 61, 64). All the other duties to which we are subject arise by agreement and arrangement. It is by a series of such agreements that "regular" states arise, in which "all have subjected their own will to the will of those in power in matters affecting the state's security, so that they are willing to do whatever the rulers wish." Once installed, it is for the government to determine – both by general enactments and in the course of adjudicating particular disputes – "what each must regard as his own and what as another's; what is to be taken as lawful in that state, what as unlawful;

what as good, what as bad; [and] what remains of each man's natural liberty . . ." (1673, 139). Pufendorf also made a case for a stronger, more centralized state, as opposed to smaller, looser, and more local associations. This position, taken together with his emphasis on the natural duties to respect the equal dignity of each and affirmatively to cultivate sociality, would ultimately form the intellectual foundation of the modern European welfare state.

John Locke

The physician John Locke was drawn into philosophy by his interest in the foundations of science, but into *political* philosophy by events not of his choosing. Impatient with teaching at Oxford, and finding that he had no calling to the ministry, he took a job as physician in the household of Lord Shaftesbury. This led, with Shaftesbury's appointment as Lord High Chancellor, to Locke's becoming secretary to the Council of Trade and Plantations. As a result of conflict between Protestants and Catholics over the line of succession to the English throne, Shaftesbury's fortunes fell, and Locke's with them. Locke was obliged to flee England for Holland. He returned to England upon the accession of William and Mary, which completed the "Glorious Revolution" that promised to settle the crown on a basis that was immune to religious controversy.

Locke wanted to refute both of two very different arguments favoring absolute monarchy. Both arguments rested on an appeal to the idea of rights. One was Robert Filmer's argument that the legitimacy of the English monarch derived from a divine right invested in Adam that had descended by inheritance to the then-present king. The other argument from rights to absolutism was Hobbes's. Setting aside Locke's refutation of Filmer, let us focus on his answer to Hobbes, which Locke advanced in *The Second Treatise of Government* (1690). Although Locke does not name Hobbes, it is clear that Hobbes was one adversary he had in mind. Where, in Locke's view, had Hobbes gone wrong about rights?

Locke employed Hobbes's idea of a state of nature, and the idea of legitimating the state by explaining it as an improvement upon the state of nature. Locke, like Hobbes, defines the state of nature partly in terms of rights distributed equally to all humans. Locke crucially departs from

Hobbes in his specification of what those "natural" rights are, and how they are distributed.

In Locke's account, the state of nature involved much greater moral complexity than Hobbes recognized. For Hobbes, the inhabitants of the state of nature had the right to do whatever they judged to be necessary for their individual survival. Locke's state of nature is different. It is a state of "reciprocal" liberty, "yet it is not a state of licence." Each has a natural right to preserve himself but not a right to harm others in order to do so (except in self-defense against a violent attacker). Each has a natural right to private property, moreover, which must be respected by others. Although God originally gave the earth to humankind in common, the "law of nature" permits each, without needing another's consent, to appropriate such lands, crops, herds, and game as he sees fit, by the simple expedient of "mixing labour" with it. So long as one leaves "enough and as good" in common for others to appropriate, and does not allow what one has taken to spoil, one has a natural right to such private property. Each also has a natural right to compensation for injuries, and a "natural executive right" to punish anyone who violates the "law of nature" (4–7, 17–19). Locke, in other writings, also recognized a natural right to liberty of conscience.

Because of these moral features, the state of nature is not, for Locke, necessarily a state of war – but it is attended with inconveniences, chiefly the obscurity of natural law to those blinded by interest, and the absence of a settled "positive" law and impartial judges to decide disputes and enforce decisions, leaving one only an "appeal to heaven." These inconveniences so undermine the security of "property" – and Locke deliberately conscripts this term to refer compendiously to the natural rights to "life, liberty, and estate" – that joining together into a commonwealth looks attractive to rational people. Rather than appeal to heaven, a member of organized society may turn to an earthly power, an umpire, to decide controversies and impose relief. "Political or civil society," as Locke terms it, comes into being when a number of individuals, perceiving the advantage of doing so, give up their natural executive right – while retaining others – to the public with whom they unite (14, 48–50).

This brace of natural rights restricts the ways in which government may legitimately originate, the ends that government, once in being, may legitimately seek, and the measures it may legitimately take to achieve those ends. The background of natural rights, and the paths of their transference, control governments throughout their careers. As Locke puts the point: "Men being . . . by nature all free, equal, and independent, no one can be put out of this estate and subjected to the political power of another without his consent" (54). Those who withhold their consent remain in a state of nature, but those who do consent therewith confer a legislative power on the majority of those consenting, or on a number of representatives – conceivably, on only one, who would in that case be their monarch.

Consent need not be express; it may be, and more typically is, tacit – that is, it is given by "having possessions or enjoyment of any part of the dominions of any government," perhaps only "barely traveling freely on the highway . . . in effect, it reaches as far as the very being of anyone within the territories of that government." How lasting is one's consent? Those who tacitly consent, by being in the territory or having possessions within it, may free themselves by ending their "enjoyment" and "by donation, sale, or otherwise, quit the said possession." Those who give express consent, however, are bound in perpetuity, and may not resume the state of nature "unless by any calamity the government . . . comes to be dissolved, or else, by some public act, cuts him off. . . ." (68–69).

Locke allowed that people might consent to a monarchical government, but in his view (as in Grotius's), it would be irrational to submit to an absolute *arbitrary* power, for that would be to expose one's "property" (in his expansive definition of the term) to greater insecurity than exists in a state of nature. Moreover, it is *impossible* to convey a greater right than one possesses, and because one does not possess absolute arbitrary power over oneself, much less over anyone else, one cannot transfer to government such power. So, absolute arbitrary government cannot be legitimate, *pace* Hobbes, for the same reason that voluntary enslavement is impossible, *pace* Mazzolini and de Molina. The consent of the governed is the only legitimate basis of government, but it would be irrational to consent to arbitrary absolutism. And it is impossible to consent to it, because one cannot by consent convey to another what one does not rightfully possess.

In a way that answered the exigencies of seventeenth-century England, Locke showed how a monarchy – even a monarchy exercising a broad prerogative "of doing public good without a rule" (95) – could be constructed by the transference of natural rights, while an arbitrary absolutism, such as a tyrannical monarchy, could not. Rights, properly understood, led neither to anarchy nor to tyranny, but explained and justified the outcome of the Glorious Revolution that had brought William and Mary to the English throne.

But how, precisely, do natural rights affect the relationship between the state and the individual, once government is in business? If one is aggrieved by government, what may one do for a remedy, if government itself offers none that seems adequate? Reverting to a state of nature is not an option for those who have expressly consented to government, nor is it a practical option for those whose consent was merely tacit, who according to Locke must liquidate their estates and leave the territory if they wish to cease being subjects. But the state must respect rights, and when it does not, it acts *ultra vires* – beyond its proper powers – and imposes no duty of obedience. Moreover, a persistently abusive government is always subject to the natural right vested in the majority of citizens to remove or alter the legislative authority. "May the commands, then of a prince be opposed? May he be resisted as often as any one shall find himself aggrieved, and but imagine he has not right done him?" Locke had to face the objection that rights tend not to "government and order . . . but anarchy and confusion." (115)

His answer is a complicated one that emphasizes that resistance and revolution are matters only of the very last resort, but Locke concluded that "if a long train of abuses . . . all tending the same way, make the design visible to the people" (126) that the government intends systematically and without redress to violate their natural rights, then the people do indeed recover their natural right to install a new government and to resist and overthrow the incumbent, who may be regarded as having instigated a state of war. Locke thus cleared a path that aggrieved subjects of a monarch might take: They might legitimately dissolve their political bonds and form new ones, which, should they so choose, might be republican rather than monarchical.

The American Declaration of Independence

History realized the possibility that Locke's writings described. In 1776, representatives of the North American colonies of Great Britain declared their independence of the sovereignty of King George III. The Declaration of Independence was chiefly the work of Thomas Jefferson, who was deeply influenced by Locke. Rights figured prominently in the colonists' justification of their apparently treasonous break with the Crown:

> We hold these truths to be self-evident, that all men are created equal, that they are endowed by their Creator with certain inalienable Rights, that among these are Life, Liberty and the pursuit of Happiness – That to secure these rights, Governments are instituted among Men, deriving their just powers from the consent of the governed, – That whenever any Form of Government becomes destructive of these ends, it is the Right of the people to alter or abolish it, and to institute new Government, laying its foundation on such principles and organizing its powers in such form, as to them shall seem most likely to effect their Safety and Happiness. . . .

The Declaration went on to itemize the "long train of abuses" to which the colonists had been subjected by the government of George III, just as Locke had prescribed as the prerequisite to a people recovering its natural right to form a government afresh and to overthrow a tyrant. Rights were on the march.

Immanuel Kant

Unlike earlier contributors to the development of the idea of rights, Kant was rarely involved in any direct way in political, religious, or even domestic turmoil. He lived the entirety of his years in or near Königsberg, East Prussia, earning a living first as a tutor and later as a professor in the university where he had gotten his own degree. He spurned opportunities for academic advancement and travel, but read and corresponded widely, and was involved in lively discussions among friends and visitors. His interests were of almost unlimited scope, and his intellectual influence on the Enlightenment made him one of its leading figures. He and Aristotle are generally considered to be our two greatest philosophers.

Because of their connections with his overall philosophical system and methodology, Kant's contributions to the theory and practice of rights can only be rendered superficially here. Perhaps his most significant practical influence today flows from a proposal he advanced in 1795 for an international organization resembling the United Nations. What is of the greatest and most enduring theoretical interest is the foundation that Kant proposed for rights and for all of moral philosophy, which was set out in his *Grundlegung zur Metaphysik der Sitten* ("Groundwork for the Metaphysics of Morals"), published in 1785. Under the influence of Pufendorf, Kant recognized that the content of rights is tied to that of our duties, thus the immediate focus of the *Grundlegung* is on the basis of duty, which Kant located in "reason alone" – that is, apart from our wants, desires, passions, and appetites. Unlike Grotius, who argued that insight into the nature and content of our rights and co-ordinate duties is available through various channels – reason, intuition, and historical authority – Kant believed that rights and duties could not properly involve any experiential or emotional element *at all*. Therefore any approach such as utilitarianism, which would link rights and duties to the amounts of pleasure and pain people would experience, is profoundly mistaken. Kant's reason for taking this stern position was largely tied to his understanding of the person. Ours is a divided nature – we have a double aspect as *phenomena* (appearances to the senses, whether our own senses or others') and as *noumena* (as "things-in-themselves," nor given to us in any sense experience, even to introspection). As phenomena, we are determined to act as we act, and have no more freedom than any other physical object. But as noumena, we are not determined by physical law, but only by such laws as we give to ourselves. Freedom, for Kant, is not lawless, but consists in living by *self-given* laws.

For Kant, our duties and rights are fixed by laws we give to ourselves as rational beings, rather than by those physical and psychological laws that pertain to us as creatures determined by physical forces, appetites, and sense perceptions. Reason itself, in other words, must be practical – otherwise morality, which presumes freedom, would be an illusion. It is our knowledge of moral law that in fact demonstrates that freedom for us is real. But what are these laws, and how are they known? Kant's answer is that they are known not by their content but by their form, and that the form of such laws is that of a *categorical imperative*: "So act that the maxim of your will can at the same time be a universal law" (Ak 4:402). This formulation makes it clear that the moral law is not founded on the pursuit of any particular goal (such as happiness, well-being, or pleasure).

The categorical imperative stands in contrast to any merely hypothetical imperative of the form "If you want X, then do this to get it." Hypothetical imperatives have a "heteronomous" character in that they assume that the agent has some antecedent goal that determines her will. But the moral law demands an unconditioned or autonomous will, for only such a will is capable of treating *others* as rational beings who are equally capable of autonomy. Hence, Kant's second and equivalent formulation of the categorical imperative: "Treat all humans as ends in themselves rather than as mere means" (Ak 4:429). The second formulation makes it clear that the moral law is founded on regard for the humanity of others as well as one's own, rather than on any merely self-centered ethic of excellence or virtue. The duties that the moral law prescribes are, by their very form, coordinate with the rights of others. Further underlining this feature of the moral law, Kant provided a third formulation of the categorical imperative that is equivalent to the first and second: "Conduct yourself as a member of a kingdom of ends" (Ak 4:439) – a kingdom of ends being, for Kant, the community of all rational beings who to themselves give laws that respect all others as ends in themselves.

I have merely sketched here the foundation Kant laid for rights. It is an elementary sketch, and the interpretation it offers is both vague and contestable. We will return to the possibility of a Kantian foundation for rights later, in Chapter 6, in the context of the second expansionary period. In application to key problems of political and legal philosophy, Kant's views were distinctive but not quite as novel. Unlike Locke, Kant believed (as did Hobbes) that abandoning the state of natural liberty and entering civil society was not merely advantageous and optional, but was rationally compelled. Kant's view on the question whether property rights might arise in a state of nature was consistent with Locke's: They could arise. But, siding with Pufendorf, Kant argued that on entering civil society the nature and dimension of all property holdings become subject to definition by the state. Kant also firmly denied any right to resist the sovereign. Even so, on hearing of the declaration of the French Republic, he exclaimed that he had witnessed "the glory of the world" (Kuehn 2001). Although he closely followed the course of events in France and continued to write almost until his death in 1804, nothing he published responded to the skepticism about rights that resulted from the tumultuous course of the French Revolution.

William Paley

The fact that Locke had so influenced events in America, and that Jean-Jacques Rousseau's ideas were having similar influence in Europe, caused the English prelate William Paley to treat moral and political philosophy together, in a work entitled *The Principles of Moral and Political Philosophy* (1786). Paley (like Kant) was after much bigger fish than the arcana of the law merchant or the Justinian Code, or even the legitimation of government; his design was nothing less than "a system of ethics –, [for the] direction of private consciences in the general conduct of human life" (xi). Paley's work grew out of notes he kept over years of tutoring students, and his aptitude as a pedagogue is attested to by the fact that his *Principles* was adopted for instruction at Cambridge, and consequently directed the thinking of generations of leading figures in British political, theological, and academic life.

Morality, in Paley's account, is a matter of following God's rules. But not all of these rules appear in Scripture; there are simply too many kinds of issue to be dealt with in any manageably sized code of rules. Moreover, Scripture was intended only to emphasize moral truths that are known to everyone in another way, by "principles of natural justice" (8). But how are these principles known? One proposal that Paley discarded is that humans are endowed with a special *moral sense* that enables them intuitively to reach correct conclusions in circumstances not within a Scriptural rule, or where a Scriptural rule is of ambiguous application. Following the arguments of Locke and David Hume, which emphasize the diversity and conflict between moral rules observed in different times and locales, Paley concluded that an appeal to intuition or to the perceptions of a moral sense was not a safe way to reach moral truth. If the issue were, for example, the justice of African slavery, what was there to discuss, if the only sources of evidence are Scripture (which is ambiguous) and intuitions (which differed)? Aristotle had found it intuitively obvious that some were meant for slavery – must we who oppose slavery claim to be more acute receptors of moral intuition than Aristotle? Calling the moral sense "conscience" does not answer the difficulty, if everyone is deemed to be the final authority in interpreting what his conscience delivers.

The way to determine God's will, in Paley's view, is discovered by considering God's nature. God is good without limitation, and so:

> The method of coming at the will of God, concerning any action, by the light of nature, is to inquire into 'the tendency of the action to promote or diminish the general happiness.' This rule proceeds upon the assumption, that God Almighty wills and wishes the happiness of his creatures; and, consequently, that those actions which promote that will and wish, must be agreeable to him. . . . (67)

God's will is in accord with Grotius's "law of love" – God's goodness guarantees His love, and His love determines Him to will His creatures' happiness. But happiness is not to be equated with enjoying pleasure and avoiding pain, Paley argues; rather, it is a matter of being engaged with others, exercising our powers to pursue chosen ends, developing sound habits, and staying healthy. Personal happiness may be had in the simplest ways: the happy man is

> easy and satisfied, taking up his book or his pipe, as soon as he finds himself alone; ready to admit any little amusement that casts itself up, or to turn his hands and attention to the first business that presents itself; or content, without either, to sit still, and let his train of thought glide indolently through his brain, without much use, perhaps, or pleasure, but without hankering after anything better . . . . (39)

What, then, does morality demand of us? "Whatever is expedient, is right. It is the utility of any moral rule alone, which constitutes the obligation of it" (72). For Paley, expediency and utility are synonymous with "productive of the greatest happiness"; but utility creates obligation not of its own power, but through the medium of God's will: "Right and obligation are reciprocal; that is, wherever there is a right in one person, there is a corresponding obligation upon others . . . Now, because moral *obligation* depends . . . upon the will of God; *right*, which is correlative to it, must depend upon the same" (84). Here, Paley (as Pufendorf and Locke had before him) embraced a *sanction theory of duty* – that is, the theory that duty and obligation cannot exist unless some authority stands ready to enforce them by imposing a sanction of some kind. Because rights imply duties, rights too imply sanctions.

Does God endow us with rights? Indeed He does, even though they are not mentioned in so many words in Scripture. But if what is right to do is simply what is expedient to do, that seems to mean that there are no rights sturdy enough to oppose the claims of utility. God in fact appears to be ready to impose sanctions on anyone who chooses to respect another's right when greater utility would be gained by ignoring it:

> There are many occasions, in which the hand of the assassin would be very useful. The present possessor of some great estate employs his influence and fortune, to annoy, corrupt, or oppress, all about him. His estate would devolve, by his death, to a successor of an opposite character. It is useful, therefore, to dispatch such a one as soon as possible out of the way; as the neighborhood will exchange thereby a pernicious tyrant for a wise and generous benefactor. It might be useful to rob a miser, and give the money to the poor.... What then shall we say? Must we admit these actions to be right, which would justify assassination [and] plunder ... or must we give up on our principle, that the criterion of right is utility? (72–73)

Paley here faced a dilemma that had been pointed out earlier by Bishop Butler, in his widely influential sermon, *Dissertation on the Nature of Virtue* (1736), which warned of the perils of any direct pursuit of what Grotius had called the "law of love" (and which we may term the *principle of beneficence*), which enjoins that we always act so as to maximize good consequences. Paley escapes the dilemma in precisely the way Butler suggested: by stipulating that what is relevant to determining the utility of an action is not particular but general consequences – that is, the consequences of violating the *general rule* against assassination or against plunder. It does not matter what the particular consequences of an action are, if its general consequences – that is, the consequences of admitting such actions as a general rule – are contrary to utility. Paley thus embraced what has come to be known as *rule utilitarianism*, a doctrine we will return to later.

Rights are simply protections conferred by rules of general utility that God enjoins us to respect. Paley went on to distinguish between natural and "adventitious" rights, alienable and inalienable rights, and (following Grotius) perfect and imperfect rights. Natural rights are those people enjoy regardless of the existence of civil institutions, while adventitious rights depend upon them. Adventitious rights include the monarch's right to rule, and rights of this description are no less binding than natural rights; God enjoins us to follow general rules that maximize happiness regardless of their derivation. The mode of derivation is relevant, however, to the question as to whether a certain right is alienable – all rights are alienable except those originating from contracts stipulating a personal performance. Thus, a master may not transfer his right to a servant's performance, nor may a king transfer his kingdom. Civil rights are not of this kind, however: "The right to civil liberty is alienable; though in the vehemence of men's zeal for it, and the language of some political remonstrances, it has often been pronounced to be an unalienable [sic] right" (90).

What, then, of the enslavement of Africans in the English colonies? The Dominicans had at one time defended the institution of slavery by invoking alienable subjective rights. Paley did not find even a pretense of consent backing the justifications then currently offered for slavery. Scripture was silent as to the justice of slavery, the colonial regime was merciless and brutal, and the conditions of the slaves cruel and miserable, "but necessity is pretended; the name under which every enormity is attempted to be justified . . ." (235). Paley dismissed the argument from necessity, but did not invoke or derive any right on the part of Africans to liberty. Rather, he looked forward to the disappearance of the "odious institution" by the "gradual emancipation" of the slaves. Like many of slavery's opponents, Paley chose to frame his opposition in terms of the *duties* of the slaveholders and slaveholding societies, rather than in terms of the *rights* of the slaves.

The rights of the destitute to the bounty of the wealthy were imperfect rights, for Paley as for Grotius and Pufendorf.

> It may be at first view difficult to apprehend how a person should have a right to a thing, and yet have no right to use the means necessary to obtain it. This difficulty, like most others in morality, is resolvable into the necessity of general rules. . . . The answer is, that by reason of the indeterminateness, either of the object, or of the circumstances of the right, the permission of force would, in its consequence, lead to the permission of force in other cases, where there existed no right at all. (91–92)

Thus, for example, though the poor have a right to relief from their better-off neighbors, they may not steal or extort what they need if it is denied them:

> [A] poor man has a right to relief from the rich; but the mode, season, and quantum of that relief, who shall contribute to it, or how much, are not ascertained . . . [and] to allow the poor to ascertain them for themselves, would be to expose property to so many of these claims, that it would . . . cease indeed to be property. (93)

Likewise, the duty of beneficence toward others, imposed by the law of love, is an imperfect one, but not on that account any less serious – Paley in fact believed that some omissions to perform imperfect duties would be a "greater crime" than to violate a positive duty. Failing to assist a needy vagabond might be much worse, for example, than stealing his bandana.

A pleasing structure can be seen, Paley thought, underlying this variety. "Positive" duties – that is, duties to take affirmative action – are "often indeterminate in their extent," and are therefore imperfect duties. Rights that impose positive duties on others are thus imperfect rights – that is, rights that the right-holder is not permitted to employ direct force to ensure the performance of. "Negative" duties – that is, prohibitions – are "generally precise," and therefore are perfect duties which, when correlated with a right, the right-holder is permitted to enforce. Thus, for example, parents have an imperfect right to their children's respect, but a perfect right not to be killed by them. Paley neatly summarizes: "Religion and virtue find their principal exercise among the imperfect obligations; the laws of civil society taking pretty good care of the rest" (95).

The French Declaration of the Rights of Man and the Citizen

While Paley was putting rights into the textbooks, the current of human events was quickening across the Channel in France, where royal expenditures in support of the Americans had contributed to the amassing of an enormous national debt. The American Revolution had excited widespread sympathy and support in France for reasons much deeper than the fact that American independence weakened England, France's longtime rival. Under the Bourbon kings France had generated a culture that combined the relentlessly iconoclastic rationalism of the *philosophes* – Diderot, Helvetius, D'Alembert, Voltaire, and (for a time) Jean-Jacques Rousseau – with a social structure that supported an opulent court, an arrogant nobility, and a prosperous clergy upon the backs of lower orders, which were practically voiceless in affairs of the state. The extravagance, ineptitude, and insensitivity of the court of Louis XVI led to a financial, then a governmental, crisis that culminated in a series of unprecedented events in 1789. In hopes of finding a way to resolve the crisis, the King summoned the Estates General to Versailles. The Estates General was composed of three parts, representing the nobility, the clergy, and a "third estate" corresponding to the remainder of propertied society. Intrigues abounded, with the result that the Third Estate broke away from the Estates General, presumed to constitute itself as a National Assembly, invited members of the other estates to join it, and swore allegiance to the nation as a whole. Food shortages and efforts by the King's party to intimidate the National Assembly by a show of arms combined to provoke disorder in the streets of Paris, culminating in the storming of the Bastille, the execution of its warden and the Mayor of Paris (their heads were subsequently paraded on the points of pikes), and the King's being forcibly taken from Versailles to Paris to deliver assurances to a mass of aroused Parisians hard to describe except as a "mob."

A revolution was in progress, and in its midst the French National Assembly issued a Declaration of the Rights of Man and of the Citizen, described for the first time as "human rights" and said to be "natural, imprescriptible, and inalienable." The primary author of the Declaration was the Marquis de Lafayette, hero of the American Revolutionary war, in collaboration with none other than Jefferson himself. The Declaration consisted of seventeen numbered provisions, the most central being the first three:

I. Men are born, and always continue, free, and equal in respect of their rights. Civil distinctions, therefore, can be founded only on public utility.

II. The end of all political associations is the preservation of the natural and imprescriptible rights of man; and these are liberty, property, security, and resistance of oppression.

III. The nation is essentially the source of all Sovereignty; nor can any INDIVIDUAL, or any BODY OF MEN, be entitled to any authority which is not expressly derived from it.

The fourteen further provisions state, inter alia: that political liberty consists of "the power of doing whatever does not injure another," and that therefore "the law ought to prohibit only actions hurtful to society"; that arrests are to be according to lawful process; that no punishments should be imposed beyond what is necessary, and only for a previously defined offense; and that accused persons are presumed innocent at trial. There are further guarantees of freedom of religious opinion (though not of expression, if disruptive), of the right to free speech and press (subject to legal process "for abuse"), and of the right to indemnity for any taking of property for public necessity.

The brave beginnings in France rapidly went wrong, however. The revolutionaries fell into factions, and the one that emerged as dominant – the Jacobins – had to govern France in the face of threats of intrigue and secession within, and of invasion by monarchical armies without. Continuing food shortages aggravated matters, and it became a fair – if unutterable – question whether the bulk of the French people had not been better off under Louis XVI. By August of 1792, the guillotine – devised by a deputy of the National Assembly as a humane, dignified, and egalitarian method of capital punishment – was busily ending the lives of citizens who had been deprived, all the way from their arrest to execution, of the rudiments of due process. "The hot hand," or "the blade of the law," was to claim Louis, his Queen, Marie-Antoinette, and tens of thousands of other victims before the Reign of Terror at last abated – among them the chemist Lavoisier and the radical Jacobin leaders themselves, Danton, Desmoulins, Robespierre, and Saint-Just. Guillotin himself perished on the machine he invented. The Marquis de Lafayette failed to get a "look through the republican window" only because he was in Austrian captivity, and the brilliant Marquis de Condorcet took his own life to preempt republican justice. What had become of the Rights of Man and the Citizen? As the theatrical figure and Jacobin revolutionary Collot d'Herbois expressed it, "The rights of man are made, not for the counter-revolutionaries, but only for the *sans-culottes*" – the sans-culottes being, literally, the "untrousered," those whose lives of honest toil did not permit them to wear the fancy pants favored by the *riches égoïstes* whom they suspected of conspiring to drive up bread prices.

3

"Mischievous Nonsense"?

By the close of the eighteenth century, the rhetoric of rights had proven its capacity to inspire and to motivate individuals strongly enough to undermine the established political and moral order. But it had not succeeded in establishing itself as a coherent and well-founded mode of discourse. In Britain's former American colonies, the Bill of Rights completed a charter of government that, though experimental, ultimately proved to be one of the most successful in human history. But in France, the Declaration of the Rights of Man and the Citizen proved incapable of preventing the Revolution from degenerating into a Reign of Terror. If the American and the French Revolutions were to be considered as experiments in the practical value of making the concept of rights central to our understanding of our political arrangements, the results were decidedly mixed.

Even many of the British friends of the cause of the American colonists, such as Edmund Burke, Jeremy Bentham, and John Austin, deplored the rhetorical emphasis upon rights. As for wholesale political and moral reform in England, Burke was not in favor, and utilitarians such as Bentham and Austin looked not to the idea of rights but to that of utility as the conceptual key to remaking society.

Edmund Burke

From the standpoint of England, the events of 1789 in France were as alarming to some as they were inspiring to others. A number of the inspired formed a Revolution Society, which was determined to apply the principles of the French Revolution to England. Those who were alarmed, rather than inspired, found a spokesman in Edmund Burke, a member of Parliament who had been a champion of the cause of the American colonists and supporter of their independence. In his *Reflections on the Revolution in France* (1790), Burke denounced the French Declaration of the Rights of Man in strong terms. The *Reflections* created a sensation in England and in France, and drew almost immediate rejoinders from incensed English friends of the French revolutionaries. If rights were good enough for the Americans, why did Burke not think them suitable for the French or, for that matter, the English?

The answer is that Burke's sympathies for the Americans, and for the colonized people of Ireland and India, were not derived from a regard for their rights as "metaphysical abstractions," but from a regard for the integrity and value of their respective traditions. Moreover, Burke did not deny that there were rights: "Far am I from denying in theory; full as far is my heart from withholding in practice . . . the *real* rights of men. . . . If civil society be made for the advantage of man, all the advantages for which it is made become his right" (56). Burke then enumerated a list of "real" rights, which (given the tenor of his attack upon the French Declaration) may seem surprisingly generous. The list includes a right to be governed by the rule of law, a right not only to the "fruits" of one's labor, but also to the means of making it fruitful, a right to inherit, a right "to the nourishment and improvement" of children, a right to do whatever does not trespass upon others, and a right to a "fair portion," although not necessarily an "equal dividend" of the "joint stock," civil society itself being "an institution of beneficence," and law itself "only beneficence acting by a rule" (56). Burke's list seems if anything to extend, rather than contract, the list propounded by the National Assembly. Where is the disagreement?

Burke's disagreement had to do with the basis and orientation of rights. For the Revolution Society and the authors of the French Declaration, rights are natural, and furnish an "Archimedean point" outside established governments, by which governments may be moved, even overthrown, by the holders of rights. This is simply the nature of rights conceived on Lockean lines. What Burke denied is that rights can have this character:

> [A]s to the share of power, authority, and direction which each individual ought to have in the management of the state, that I must deny to be amongst the direct original rights of man in civil society; for I have in my contemplation the civil social man, and no other. It is a thing to be settled by convention. (56–57)

Here, without citing David Hume (1789), Burke availed himself of Hume's critique of the idea of a social contract, and his alternative analysis of the "artificial virtue" of justice as a matter of *convention*. Hume derided Locke's understanding of the social contract as a historical event. Institutions owe their origins and their stability to interlocking habits and expectations not by any formula or declaration, although once they have arisen it is always possible to interpret them in terms of rules. Burke's application went like this:

> If civil society be the offspring of convention, that convention must be its law. That convention must limit and modify all the descriptions of constitution which are formed under it. Every sort of legislative, judicial, or executory power are its creatures. They can have no being in any other state of things; and how can man claim, under the conventions of civil society, rights which do not so much as suppose its existence? Rights which are absolutely repugnant to it? (57)

Burke's point was that the specification of any plausible kind of right presupposes the existence of a background of social convention. Rights cannot intelligibly function as an external Archimedean point available to revolutionary critics as a fulcrum for unseating those very conventions. Then, without signaling a transition, Burke argued that even if the Lockean story is taken at face value it must fail as an account of a *stable* society.

> One of the first motives to civil society, and which becomes one of its fundamental rules, is, *that no man should be judge in his own cause.* By this each person has at once divested himself of the first fundamental right of uncovenanted man. . . . He abdicates all right to be his own governor. He inclusively, in great measure, abandons the right of self-defence, the first law of nature. Men cannot enjoy the rights of an uncivil and of a civil state together. (57)

Burke then repeated the Hobbesean reason that motivates the surrender of natural rights: "[H]aving a right to every thing, they want [i.e. come to lack] everything," and so set up government, "a power out of themselves," as the necessary means to furnish those wants. But why does Burke suppose that *all* natural rights have to be surrendered to society? Even Hobbes believed that the right of self-preservation could not rationally be given up. Burke continued:

> The moment you abate anything from the full rights of men, each to govern himself, from that moment the whole organization of government becomes a matter of convenience . . . a matter of the most delicate and complicated skill. . . . The rights of men in governments are their advantages; and these are often in balances between differences of good; in compromises sometimes between good and evil, and sometimes between evil and evil. Political reason is a computing principle; adding, subtracting, multiplying, and dividing, morally and not metaphysically or mathematically, true moral denominations. . . . Men have no right to what is not reasonable. . . . (58)

However one conceives "full" natural rights, the moment these are surrendered in order to achieve a benefit, every issue about the substance and dimension of rights – be they surrendered or be they retained – is drawn into a general discussion in terms of benefits and reasonableness. And that's what the discussion is really about. Rights are the *output* of that discussion; they are not parameters or boundary conditions or external "side" constraints to that discussion. For example, even if we agree with Hobbes and Locke that the right of self-preservation is retained, not surrendered, we are forced on reflection to admit that any legally and socially recognizable counterpart of that retained right is to be understood as shaped by social considerations and context. Rights are "incapable of definition, but not impossible to be discerned." Their discernment is not by reasoning *a priori* but is a matter to be learned by experience, and "no short experience" at that:

> [E]ven more experience than any person can gain in his whole life, however sagacious and observing he may be, [therefore] it is with infinite caution that any man ought to venture upon pulling down an edifice which has answered in any tolerable degree for ages the common purposes of society, or on building it up again, without having models and patterns of approved utility before his eyes. (58–59)

Burke was making two different types of attack on the Lockean understanding of rights. The first emphasizes the *indeterminacy* of rights, if rights are understood abstractly rather than as conventionally defined "positive" rights grounded in law or at least in local or national tradition. The second is a moral attack on the idea that what rights there are might be *opposed to* the standards of reasonableness and utility. In short, Burke's critique combines (perhaps confuses) a conventionalistic critique of rights and a utilitarian critique. (Interpreting Burke is further complicated by the fact that in other passages he seems to mount a sentimentalistic, even irrationalistic, attack on the modern age and all things associated with it, rights included.) There is a degree of affinity between the two critiques, however. Burke's regard for the past as furnishing "models and patterns of approved utility" puts him in company with *rule* utilitarians, such as Paley. Rule utilitarians believe utility or "the greatest happiness of the greatest number" to be the ultimate moral standard, but do not apply that standard directly to individual acts, but instead to categories of acts. Rule utilitarianism approves those rules that pick out the categories of acts that promote the greatest utility. Tradition and convention were important in two ways for Burke: They summarize the wisdom of ages on the subject of what does and what does not promote the welfare of all, and they are capable of inspiring an *affection* for what has that tendency – and without affection, people are unlikely to be moved consistently to action.

This way of regarding Burke's critique is not the only one possible. Another would emphasize the conventionalistic aspect of his thinking, and would have him deny that there could possibly be rights apart from a particular social setting. In particular, this kind of conventionalism might deny the possibility of embedding locally defined conventional rights within any generally applicable moral framework. Looked at this way, Burke might be seen as a moral relativist about rights or, looking forward, as a harbinger of what has been called the communitarian critique of rights, which we will briefly examine later.

William Godwin

Almost as soon as it appeared, Burke's impassioned *Reflections* drew forth equally impassioned rebuttals. Thomas Paine, in *The Rights of Man* (1791) offered the most widely read defense of the French Revolution, and devastated Burke's claim that any natural right that might be asserted by British subjects against the Crown had been surrendered in the settlement that had brought William and Mary to the throne. Paine hammered home the point that rights are *individual*, and that earlier generations cannot surrender the natural rights of their progeny, who hold them as individuals, not as inheritors. Otherwise, however, Paine had little of substance to say in answer to Burke's critique of rights. Nor did Mary Wollstonecraft, in her *Vindication of the Rights of Men* (1790). The most thorough, if now less-read, defense of the revolutionary spirit was offered by William Godwin in his book *Enquiry Concerning Political Justice* (1793), of which the English essayist William Hazlitt wrote, "No work in our time gave such a blow to the philosophical mind of the country" (1825, 202).

Godwin, like Burke, was attuned to the broadly utilitarian approach to moral thinking that was becoming dominant in England. But in almost every other respect it is hard to conceive a more polar opposition between contemporaries. As a utilitarian, Godwin held that justice, as well as morality generally, reduced to a calculation of the relative consequences, in terms of pleasure and pain, to be anticipated by alternative actions. But Godwin's understanding of the utilitarian principle was without deference to conventional wisdom or common sentiment. If, for example, one were faced with the alternatives of saving one's own father from a fire or saving instead a philanthropic stranger (Godwin's example was Archbishop Fénelon, who influenced Rousseau, beside whom he rests in the Panthéon), one ought morally to save the philanthropist – "What magic is there in the pronoun 'my,' that should justify us in overturning the decisions of impartial truth?" By the same logic, the needy have a right to assistance from those with means, and property generally is held only "as a trust" for the greater benefit of humankind. Not even our lives belong to us: "We have in reality nothing that is strictly speaking our own" (170, 194).

Similarly, promises have no binding force in themselves; the duty to fulfil a promise ceases as soon as a conflicting opportunity to do greater good presents itself. Although Godwin later tried to palliate some of the more shocking inferences drawn from his book, the unsettling tendency of utilitarian principles applied to acts (eventually to be termed "*act utilitarianism*") was unmistakable. Because we are almost always capable of acting, and are practically never faced with morally indifferent alternatives, there is at every moment of our lives some act that we are duty-bound to do – the one that will maximize the balance of pleasure for humanity. Although it has been disputed whether Godwin's overall doctrine was act-utilitarian, there is no dispute either that his doctrine, however described, was a strenuous one, or that act-utilitarianism is a strenuous doctrine, whether or not it was Godwin's.

What of rights, in Godwin's view? He was largely in sympathy with the French Revolution, and had exposed himself to some personal risk by facilitating the publication of Paine's *Rights of Man*. He was eventually to marry Mary Wollstonecraft, author of *A Vindication of the Rights of Women* (1792) as well as her response to Burke, *A Vindication of the Rights of Men*. Nevertheless, Godwin's critique of rights was unsparing and severe:

> The rights of man have, like many other political and moral questions, furnished a topic of eager and pertinacious dispute more by a confused and inaccurate statement of the subject of enquiry than by any considerable difficulty attached to the subject itself.
>
> The real or supposed rights of man are of two kinds, active and passive; the right in certain cases to do as we list; and the right we possess to the forbearance or assistance of other men.
>
> The first of these a just philosophy will probably induce us universally to explode.
>
> There is no sphere in which a human being can be supposed to act, where one mode of proceeding will not, in every given instance, be more

reasonable than any other mode. That mode the being is bound by every
principle of justice to pursue. . . . (191–92)

[A]s it has been before shown that it cannot be their duty to do
anything detrimental to the general happiness, so it appears with equal
evidence that they cannot have a right to do so. There cannot be a more absurd proposition, than that which affirms the right of doing wrong. (196)

An "active" right, in Godwin's view, is a nullity. Any action is either one's
duty, contrary to duty, or indifferent. Doing one's duty is not "doing what
one's lists," so there is no active right here. A right to act contrary to duty
would amount to a right to do wrong – an absurdity, in Godwin's view.
Although there might be a right to choose between indifferent actions,
or between indifferent means to an end, such instances are vanishingly
few, in Godwin's estimation, and are presented only due to the ignorance
of the actor:

[I]f anything remain to the active rights of man . . . it will be, first, . . . not
an absolute right, the offspring of ignorance and imbecility; and, sec-
ondly, it will relate only to such insignificant matters, if such there be,
as, after the best exercise of human judgement, can not be discerned to
have the remotest relation to the happiness of mankind. (193–94)

What, then, of "passive" rights, rights to forbearance and assistance, by
his definition? Godwin turns to them:

[Man] is said to have a right to life and personal liberty. This proposition,
if admitted, must be admitted with great limitation. He has no right to
his life, when his duty calls him to resign it. Other men are bound (it
would be improper in strictness of speech . . . to say they have a right)
to deprive him of life or liberty, if that should appear in any case to be
indispensably necessary to prevent a greater evil. (197–98)

Godwin bites not just a bullet, but an entire bandolier. The principle of
utility dissolves rights both active and passive, or so it seems. But Godwin
goes on:

The passive rights of man will be best understood from the following
elucidation. . . . Every man has a certain sphere of discretion, which he
has a right to expect shall not be infringed by his neighbours. This right
flows from the very nature of man. . . . it is necessary that every man
should stand by himself, and rest upon his own understanding. For that
purpose each must have his sphere of discretion. No man must encroach

upon my province, nor I upon his. He may advise me, moderately and with out pertinaciousness, but he must not expect to dictate to me. He may censure me freely and without reserve... [and] may exercise a republican boldness in judging, but he must not be peremptory and imperious in prescribing. Force may never be resorted to but, in the most extraordinary and imperious emergency. I ought to exercise my talents for the benefit of others; but that exercise must be the fruit of my own conviction.... (198–99)

So for Godwin there is at least one right: the passive right against being compelled to act contrary to one's judgment. It is, in a sense, a "right to do wrong," though not an "active" right to do wrong – it is a passive right against interference within the "sphere of discretion," in which the actor must be permitted to choose by his lights. So unqualified and complete is Godwin's elevation of the value of individual judgment that it is impossible to classify him with full confidence as a utilitarian – mental independence sometimes seeming to be for him not a mere means to pleasure but of value in and of itself. Even this right must yield in emergencies, however. Moreover, it is not a right to exercise judgment free of advice and censure. In fact, it is subject to the *duty* of all to encourage others to do what is best:

As we have a duty obliging us to a certain conduct respecting our faculties and our possessions, so our neighbour has a duty respecting his admonitions and advice. He is guilty of an omission in this point, if he fail to employ every means in his power for the amendment of our errors, and to have recourse for that purpose, as he may see occasion, to the most unreserved animadversion upon our propensities and conduct. It is absurd to suppose that certain points are especially within my province, and therefore he may not afford me, invited or uninvited, his assistance in arriving at a right decision. (194)

The "sphere of discretion" thus is not one that concerns the actor alone, or one as to which what one does is nobody else's business. It is a sphere in which others may, and must, encourage the actor to do what is best, but may not ordinarily compel the actor to act. Moreover, in the small communities that Godwin thought ideal, moral error would be checked by "the inspection of all exercised upon all" and the application of relentless social pressure, "the censure of every beholder" (717, 794).

Godwin also recognizes a second sort of passive right, "the right each man possesses to the assistance of his neighbour." For Godwin, wherever the principle of utility imposes on others a duty to assist me, I may be said to have a right to that assistance. The right is simply the "flip side" of the duty.

> I have a right to the assistance of my neighbour; he has a right that it should not be extorted from him by force. It is his duty to afford me the supply of which I stand in need; it is my duty not to violate his province of understanding whether he is to supply me, and, secondly, in what degree. (735–36)

The passive right to receive assistance, which Godwin admits, hovers in the twilight zone between what Grotius called perfect and imperfect rights. Recall that, for Grotius, a perfect right is one that is enforceable, and an imperfect one, not. Godwin's view is that the passive right to receive assistance is not one that the right-holder may compel another to respect, and in this sense it is imperfect. But the right-holder, and others, may bring withering social pressure to bear upon those who withhold needed assistance, and, in this respect, the right seems almost a "perfect" or enforceable one, in Grotius's sense.

One telling wrinkle in Godwin's system is his theory of property. Property in the strictest sense is apportioned by the utility principle, and things are simply distributed to whomever would get the most pleasure from their possession. But there is property in a less-strict sense, which arises roughly along Lockean lines, by the mixing of labor. Once someone has appropriated something in this sense, she becomes its "steward," and her right of individual judgment comes into play when others make demands of what she is steward of.

But what good, then, is the property right in the strict sense, held by the needy, if it cannot be enforced (is "imperfect")? Godwin has a difficulty to deal with, one that William Paley had avoided by the simple expedient of pointing to God's readiness to impose a posthumous sanction upon the stingy. Godwin's atheism denies him this "out," however, and so his first move is to remind us that actions to enforce rights are subject to the utility principle, just as all actions are; therefore, enforcing a right is forbidden where doing so would create a net deficit of pleasure. This reminder seems unworthy of Godwin's principles, however, because it seems to require that the needier defer endlessly to the stinginess or obstinacy of the Lockean owner. Godwin's further answer goes this way. First, we must remember that the utility of respecting the right of private judgment can itself, in extraordinary cases, be overbalanced by the utility principle. If a fire threatens to destroy the town, all have permission to destroy another's house if doing so would prevent greater destruction. Second, we have to recall the power that right-thinking people retain of shaming the stingy or obstinate steward into sharing: "[E]very individual would then live under the public eye; and the disapprobation of his neighbours, a species of coercion not derived from the caprice of men, but from the system of the universe, would inevitably oblige [the wrongdoer] to reform or to emigrate" (644). Godwin did not consider the inconvenient case of the wrongdoer who chooses neither to reform nor to emigrate.

Godwin took as narrow a view of governmental authority as he did of conventional moral doctrines, and he is read today chiefly as an advocate of philosophical anarchism. His influence rapidly waned after the French Revolution descended, as Burke had foreseen it would, into a reign of terror. Although Godwin was avowedly in favor of "many reforms, but no revolutions" (252), he had become too much identified with extremism, utopianism, licentiousness, and anarchism to be safely cited either as an authority or a serious contributor in the subsequent development of the theory of rights. Nonetheless, as we shall see, aspects of his analysis, like an underground stream, tend to spring up again and again.

Jeremy Bentham

Like Burke, Jeremy Bentham was a friend of the American colonists' independence, but quite unlike Burke, he was also a tireless (and perhaps at times tire*some*) champion of reform. He is credited above all others with making utilitarianism a force in society, and his influence is today greater than ever before. Anyone who discusses issues in terms of *cost/benefit analysis* owes an intellectual debt to Bentham. He was neither a respecter of institutions, nor a utopian in the way Godwin was, but shared with Godwin and Burke a suspicion of the emerging rhetoric of natural rights – "mischievous nonsense" as he characterized the idea (501). Not that Bentham was hostile to the idea of rights, generally. In fact, the language of rights in legal contexts could be made perfectly good sense of, as we shall see. But outside the "positive" context of law the language of rights was a mere fiction. Because Bentham was unwilling to assign any sense to the idea of a natural right, or of any moral right standing apart from a legal setting, he of course had nothing to say on the subject of utilitarian moral rights (in contrast to legal rights recommended by the principle of utility). So Bentham is an important figure in the history of rights for two reasons: first, for his negative critique of the very idea of natural rights; second, for his positive account of "positive" – that is, legally recognized, rights.

Both Bentham's negative and positive critiques operate by application of a general methodology he used to determine the meaning of terms. Bentham personified the increasing sensitivity of philosophers (at least some of them) to the importance of avoiding confusion and obscurity by paying careful attention to the meanings of words. But word-meanings are often not to be found in isolation; the important test was whether a word in the contexts in which it was found could be paraphrased in ways that "cashed out" in experiential terms. Bentham was working in the empiricist tradition in philosophy, and in that tradition knowledge is knowledge only to the extent that it relates to people's experiences, actual or possible. "Rights," like "miracles" or "witches" or "causes" or what-have-you have to be put to this test, and are meaningful only if they survive it – otherwise they are literally "non-sense," noises without reference or truth-value. One need not accept the adequacy of the empiricist test of meaning to be curious about what it might turn up in the case of rights.

Bentham's Negative Critique of Natural Rights

The grist for Bentham's analytical mill was the French Declaration, the very document that had gotten Burke going. The Declaration had been undergoing a process of evolution, a fact that Bentham noted with dry satisfaction:

> Compare the list of rights, whoever they belong to, whether to the man and the citizen, or the man in society, we shall find, that between the year 1791 and the year 1795, inalienable as they are, they have undergone a change. Indeed, for a set of inalienable rights they must be acknowledged

to have been rather unstable. [In] 1791, there were but two of them – liberty and equality. By the time the second article of [the 1791] declaration was framed, three new ones had started up . . . viz. property, security, and resistance to oppression: total, four . . . not five; for in the same interval an accident had happened to equality, and somehow or other it was not to be found. In the interval between 1791 and 1795 it has been found again . . . [but l]ooking for resistance against oppression, we shall find it kicked out of doors. (525)

But Bentham saw worse than inconsistency; there was an anarchical tendency at work in the Declaration, compounded with Gallic impertinence: "Hark! ye [British] citizens of the other side of the water! Can you tell us what rights you have belonging to you? No, that you can't. It's we that understand rights: not our own only, but yours into the bargain. . . . " (497). After laying down a barrage of charges – abstractness, incitement to selfish passion, confusion, falsity, meaninglessness – Bentham excoriated the very idea of natural rights:

How stands the truth of things? That there are no such things as natural rights – no such things as rights anterior to the establishment of government – no such things as natural rights opposed to, in contradistinction to, legal: that the expression is merely figurative; that when used, in the moment you attempt to give it a literal meaning it leads to error, and to that sort of error that leads to mischief – to the extremity of mischief. (500)

Without mentioning Grotius, Bentham denied that any of Grotius's three ways of knowing natural rights – experience, intellectual intuition, or consensus of variously situated observers – delivered any knowledge at all.

Bentham was willing to accept a broadly Hobbesian rendition of the pre-political state as one of "perfect" liberty against nonexistent government but without any liberty at all against "the mandates of stronger individuals," and thus no security, no property, but plenty of keen anxiety, and "consequently in point of happiness below the level of the brutal race." In such a state, rights would be a highly desirable innovation, "But reasons for wishing there were such things as rights, are not rights; – a reason for wishing that a certain right were established, is not that right – want is not supply – hunger is not bread. . . . *Natural rights* is simple nonsense: natural and imprescriptible rights, rhetorical nonsense, – nonsense upon stilts" (501). Nonetheless, for Bentham there was something that may meaningfully be said without dragging the disreputable language of natural rights into the discussion:

> What is the language of plain sense upon this same subject? That in proportion as it is *right* or *proper*, i.e. advantageous to the society in question, that this or that right – a right to this or that effect – should be established or maintained, in that same proportion it is *wrong* that it should be abrogated: but that is there is no *right*, which ought not to be maintained so long as it is upon the whole advantageous to the society that it be maintained, so there is no right which, when the abolition of it is advantageous to society, should not be abolished. (501)

Here, Bentham permitted only the "objective" sense of right distinguished by the mediaeval jurists; but even right in this sense is subjected to a utilitarian construction. What is right is simply what is advantageous for society. It follows that there is nothing imprescriptible here – when advantage ceases, right ceases also. "Right" and "advantageous to society" are coextensive terms, and it is only on this basis that Bentham was willing to admit any talk of "right" external to the law. And there was yet a further stricture, if what is under discussion is the advantage of "maintaining or abolishing" a legal right: "To know whether it would be more for the advantage of society that this or that right should be maintained or abolished . . . the right itself must be specifically described, not jumbled with an undistinguishable heap of others, under such vague general terms as property, liberty, and the like" (501). This seems meant as a prudential observation about the terms in which it might be profitable to frame proposals on the subject of which recognized legal rights it would be advantageous to "maintain or abolish" – for it would be mischievous and false to so much as suggest that there were legal rights of such dramatic breadth.

Bentham made two further points: First, imprescriptible rights, if there were any, would tie the hands of societies forever, regardless of utilities – an advantage, some might think, but not he; second, no account is available of how such natural rights might have come to be. The French National Assembly made "a pretence of finding them ready made. Made by what? Not by a God – they allow of none; but by their goddess, Nature." And Bentham further found the idea of origination in a social contract an insupportable fiction; "Contracts came from government, not government from contracts" (501, 502). Since natural rights can have come from no place, they cannot be. (Bentham did not tarry over the question, "Whence the principle of utility?")

Bentham made a particular point against the purported right to liberty: "[A]ll rights are made at the expense of liberty. . . . [there is n]o right without a correspondent obligation" – that is, without a corresponding restriction of everyone else's liberty (503). Liberty is nothing unless there is some protection against interference with it, and this protection is necessarily a constriction of the liberty of others. Natural-rights theory thus faces a dilemma: Ignore this fact about liberty and forbid government to restrict it in any way, and accept anarchy; or acknowledge this fact about liberty, and qualify the right to it to permit precisely the legal restrictions needed to secure it against invasion by others. But if the latter horn of the dilemma is seized, Bentham challenges natural-rights theorists to specify the needed qualification of the supposed natural right. The same type of restriction must apply to the right to property – "what is every man's right is no man's right" – ; the idea of an imprescriptible right of all to property renders property insecure rather than secure, unless the limitations of the right are specified. The implication his argument suggests is that these limitations can *only* be described in terms that presuppose an existing political framework. Bentham simply ignored Locke and his natural-rights account of property.

Bentham had yet another argument against the sweeping rights to liberty and to property (the right to security and to resist oppression collapse into these, he showed). The argument goes like this: Suppose *it is right that* I have liberty and property – Bentham seems willing to allow this supposition, taking it as a summary expression of a consideration of utilities subject to revision and qualification in the face of circumstances. But now allow the transition from the objective sense of right to the language of "anti-legal rights of man" – that is, from "it is right that I should possess all these blessings," of liberty and property, to "I have a right to all of them" in the anti-legal, natural-rights sense (522–23). It would then follow, if this transition were sound, that I had a right to do whatever I thought necessary to protect my liberty and property from interference – but this is an absurd result, which would leave me and everyone, who are supposed to enjoy equal rights, in a state of anarchy and war. Anti-legal rights are nothing other than "the rights of anarchy." Therefore the transition from objective right to a subjective, anti-legal right has to be rejected.

Bentham, again, had chosen perhaps too easy a target. Grant that rights to liberty and property entail that the right-holder also enjoys the further right to protect that liberty and property from interference; Bentham fails altogether to engage Locke's fairly subtle account of how one would surrender these associated natural rights of self-help. By choosing to attack the loose and hyperbolic Declaration of rights in imprescriptible form, Bentham avoided the more formidable structure of argument erected by Locke. This is not to say that Locke's account is without defects, even fatal ones; but it illustrates one of the less happy aspects of what I have called the first expansionary period of rights rhetoric: the more enthusiastic and inflated expressions of the "rights of man" tended to obscure the better arguments to be made on their behalf.

Of the proposition that all ought to have "equal rights," Bentham pointed out that it could not be understood literally and generally without its having radical consequences: "If all men are equal in rights, there will not exist any rights; for if we all have the same right to a thing, there will no longer be any right for any one" (533). The institution of property is incompatible with a general equality of rights.

Might the needy have a right to assistance, as was proposed to the French National Assembly? Against whom would such a right be held? – Bentham asked. If against all of the better-off, this would "overturn every idea of property; for as soon as I am unable to provide for my subsistence . . . I have a right to what you possess . . . – it is mine; you rob me if you keep it from me." Even Godwin was not quite ready to accept this conclusion. Or is it that the needy's right is held not against the better-off, severally, but only against the community? All very well, if the community has provisions in store, but what if it does not? Granted that there is a duty of beneficence, what follows if it is regarded as conferring a right? "This would be to give the indigent class the most false and dangerous ideas; it would not only destroy all gratitude on the part of the poor towards their benefactors – it would put arms in their hands against all proprietors" (533–34). This and similar discussions show that Bentham was well able to work out the consequences of various asserted natural rights, even though his official attitude is that such assertions are nonsensical.

Bentham's Positive Account of Legal Rights

Bentham's work on legal rights, as opposed to the "ante-legal and anti-legal" natural rights of the French Declaration, was done more cooly; much of it, however, was unpublished until long after his death. In accordance with his general methodology, Bentham treated legal rights as fictions, which to be meaningful have to be related to "real entities," the relevant ones being *person, command*, and *prohibition*. When persons act in certain ways they can be seen as commanding or prohibiting, and so we are in the realm of real entities.

To be subject to a legal duty is simply to be subject to the command or prohibition of a person or class of persons acting in an official capacity. Legal *rights* have existence only in virtue of the existence of legal duties. Who has a legal right? The person or class of persons who benefits from the existence of a legal duty. This is what we mean when we speak of rights: duties that benefit. Here is how Bentham expressed the point:

> An act is a real entity: a law is another [a law being the command or prohibition of a suitably situated person]. A duty or obligation is a fictitious entity conceived as resulting from the union of the two former. A law commanding or forbidding an act thereby creates a duty or obligation. A right is another fictitious entity, a kind of secondary fictitious entity, resulting out of a duty. Let any given duty be proposed, either somebody is the better for it or nobody. If nobody, no such duty ought to be created: neither is there any right that corresponds to it. If somebody, this somebody is either the party bound, or some other. If it be himself, then the duty, if such it may be called, is a duty he owes himself: neither in this case is there any *right* that corresponds to it. If it be any other party then it is a duty owing to some other party: and then that other party has at any rate a right: a right to have this duty performed: perhaps also a *power*: a power to compel the performance of such duty. (1970, 293–94)

Bentham here took an important step. He isolated the "subjective" element of "having a right" and specified that *it consists in the benefit conferred*, or at least intended to be conferred, to the right-holder. To have a legal right is, in essence, to be the beneficiary of someone else's legal duty. But that is all there is to the essence of legal rights; such rights may or may not be "barren" – that is, they may or may not be coupled with a power of enforcement in the rightholder – but they are always enforceable by official authority because legal rights entail legal duties, and legal duties are *always* backed by official punishments of some sort or another. In short, Bentham's theory of legal rights could be called a benefit theory or, as we shall call it, an *interest theory* of rights, and it is coupled with a *sanction theory* of duty. Any legal duty that benefits me gives me a right, but it may be a barren right, in which case the duty is enforceable not by me but only by an official, who may have discretion to choose not to enforce that duty.

Bentham further analyzed legal powers into legal rights and duties, and introduced a number of interesting classifications of and distinctions among these various elements. What is most remarkable about Bentham is that his work on rights combines an innovative *interest theory* of legal rights with a *nonsense theory* of natural, or as he put it, "anti-legal" rights. Why, one is bound to wonder, did he not consider the possibility of an interest theory of *natural* rights? The obstacle most likely lay in his sanction theory of duty. Bentham shared Paley's sanction theory of duty without sharing Paley's belief in a divine sanctioner. Legal rights grow out of beneficial legal duties. Legal duty is a legal fiction tied to real entities: persons, commands, prohibitions, punishments; benefit is a real entity, comprising our "sovereign masters: pleasure and pain." Why cannot natural moral rights analogously grow out of beneficial natural moral duties? The only missing element seems to be the enforcer – unlike government, with its apparatus of officials, nature furnishes no enforcer of moral duty other than pleasure and pain (supposing, as Bentham did, that God was out of the picture). In that case, why could Bentham not invoke society (if not our "sovereign masters," pleasure and pain, themselves) as possessing the relevant enforcing power? Perhaps Bentham would have been repelled by any suggestion that might smack of an appeal to a Rousseauvian, Frenchified notion of *volunté commun*, or general will. Most likely, Bentham thought that utility, rather than rights, was the better notion in which to frame the discussion of the best constitution of government.

One other aspect of Bentham's thought has to be mentioned. For Bentham, the good to be considered in moral calculation is nothing other than the net quantity of pleasures and pains, the "sovereign masters" that nature has placed us under. Whereas Paley spoke of the "greatest happiness" in terms not reducible to pleasures felt and pains avoided, Bentham believed that this very reduction was the only way to avoid mystification and to make morality scientific. If working out moral questions is a matter of calculating the net sum of pleasures and pains, then the experiences of any creature capable of experiencing pleasure and pain become relevant, whether that creature is human or not. As to the moral importance of animals, "the question is not, Can they *reason*? nor, Can they *talk*? but Can they *suffer*?" Bentham foresaw that "The day *may* come, when the rest of the animal creation may acquire those rights which never could have been withholden from them but by the hand of tyranny" (1996, 282–83, n.1). The question whether rights can be possessed by animals or only by humans is one to which we will return.

4

The Nineteenth Century
Consolidation and Retrenchment

The Reign of Terror in revolutionary France marked the end of the first expansionary period of rights discourse. The Terror discredited free-wheeling rights claims as proper rhetorical tools in the service of reform. The Declaration of the Rights of Man and the Citizen remained and still remains an object of veneration for most of the French people, but no French thinker since Rousseau has had a major influence on our understanding of rights. Beyond France, the post-Terror reaction against rights rhetoric was far more pronounced in England than in the United States. This is not surprising, since the affinity between France and the United States was undiminished, and the Americans – unlike the British – had little reason to fear an adverse spillover from the further course of French developments. Accordingly, the career of rights took different paths on different sides of the Atlantic. But these paths were not entirely diverse, in large part because in both places the issue of slavery came to dominate the moral agenda.

The Utilitarian Formula: Rights as Rules

At the beginning of the nineteenth century, utilitarianism was already becoming the dominant moral theory in England, but it was not without its own difficulties. The challenges that utilitarians faced included that of explaining how the pursuit of the greatest utility could somehow be self-limiting. Rule utilitarianism was designed to answer this challenge, but it required further elaboration, as we shall see. The nineteenth-century utilitarians preferred, where possible, to *reconstruct* rather than to contradict the rules of commonsense morality. Utilitarian reconstruction was a process of showing how a given commonsense rule could be justified by means of the "greatest happiness" principle.

It could not have been clear how far this preference for peace with commonsense required utilitarians to elaborate a theory of rights. Rights in the "anti-legal," *rights-of-man* sense were perceived as latecoming, unsettling, radical ideas themselves. Moreover, an answer had to be given to the philosophical objections to the idea of natural rights. But English utilitarians were generally persons of a progressive frame of mind, and to the extent that *rights* had served as an opening wedge in the attack on privilege and custom, the possibility of twinning rights with utility in a common effort to unseat the tyranny of the past must have held promise.

John Austin

A detailed defense of utilitarianism deploying the idea of rules was offered by John Austin. Austin was a neighbor and friend of Bentham's, and his views were deeply influenced by Bentham's. Although Austin shared Bentham's and Burke's distaste for the rhetoric of natural rights, Austin did not dismiss them as nonsense, as Bentham had. Moreover, Austin's analysis of *legal* rights departed from Bentham's in ways that, though subtle, would prove to have important implications. Austin set out his views in a series of lectures published as *The Province of Jurisprudence Determined* (1832), which was, as the title suggests, an attempt to define the law as a distinct object of study, but was also much more than that. Austin's celebrated definition of law as the *command of the sovereign* became the founding precept of what is known as *legal positivism*, although in this basic idea he was obviously indebted to Bentham. Austin repeatedly expressed his unwillingness to give an exhaustive definition of rights, but he nonetheless had a good deal to say on the subject. In answer to an objection to his definition of law as the sovereign's imperative, he wrote:

> There are laws, it might be said, which *merely* create *rights*: and, seeing that every command imposes a *duty*, laws of this nature are not imperative. But . . . there are no laws *merely* creating *rights*. There are laws, it is true, which *merely* create *duties*: duties not correlating with rights, and which, therefore may be styled *absolute*. But every law, really conferring a right, imposes expressly or tacitly a *relative* duty, or a duty correlating with the right. If it specify the remedy to be given, in case the right shall be infringed, it imposes a relative duty expressly. If the remedy to be given be not specified, it refers tacitly to pre-existing law, and clothes the right which it purports to create with a remedy provided by that law. Every law, really conferring a right is, therefore, imperative. . . . (34)

Not a word here about benefit. Bentham had briskly laid it down that a law that benefitted no one should not be supposed, but, in a careful departure from Bentham, Austin avoided supposing that law was even presumptively beneficial. The holder of a right need not even have been intended to benefit, so far as Austin's analysis goes; but being a legal right-holder implies *something* – namely, having a remedy. That remedy may be expressly stated in the law creating the relative duty, or the remedy may merely tacitly refer the right-holder to a remedy in preexisting law, but for Austin there is no legal right without a legal remedy. This remedy is presumably one the right-holder may choose to invoke or to waive, and therefore Austin's analysis is the forebear of what has come to be known as the *choice theory* of rights.

Both the *interest theory*, which we find the beginnings of in Bentham, and Austin's nascent *choice theory* offer a way of resisting the reduction of legal rights to legal duties. All legal rights entail legal duties, but not vice versa. Therefore there is something to rights talk that talk about duties cannot fully capture, and what we earlier called *the reductive worry* can be put to rest, at least within the realm of legal rights. A legal right is a legal duty plus something more, and that something more has to do with the person or class singled out as the *right-holder*. This is why "having a right," in the subjective sense that the mediaeval theorists first identified, differs from it merely being "right," in the objective sense, that some duty be performed. So far, Bentham and Austin are at one, but now their thoughts take different paths. For Bentham and the interest theory, the distinguishing "something more" is the benefit the duty conveys to the person or class that we identify as the right-holder. But for Austin and the choice theory, the "something more" has to do with who has access to a remedy, and who may choose to pursue it or not to pursue it.

What, then, of natural rights? Austin disliked the term "natural law" because it misleadingly suggested an analogy to the laws of nature, such as the laws of physics. Accordingly, the term "natural" was to be avoided. If an appeal to "natural" rights is simply an appeal to morality, then natural rights are simply moral rights. But "morality," too, is an ambiguous term: As Austin saw it, it can refer either to the positive, conventional moral code of the community, or instead to the ideal moral code promulgated by God. If the appeal is one to the *as yet still developing* moral conscience of the community, it is to be understood as an appeal to a "right divine." *Right divine* is of two sorts: revealed and unrevealed. Revealed rights divine would be found in revealed divine law – that is, in some commandment or Scriptural deliverance of divine inspiration.

For the purpose of identifying *revealed* rights that subjects might have against their sovereign, nothing in Scripture seems to answer, unless Christ's advice to "render therefore unto Caesar the things which be Caesar's" (*Luke* 20:20) is apposite. But God's revealed commandments are not all there is to divine law or right divine. Austin was persuaded, as were generations of English thinkers, by Paley's demonstration that, in addition to the revealed specific commandments found in the Bible, there is an *unrevealed* divine law, "the Divine law as known through the principle of utility" (238). God's perfect goodness assures us that He wishes the highest happiness for His creatures, and enjoins them to seek it. Seeking the greatest happiness of the greatest number is therefore a principle commanded by divine law.

Unlike Bentham and many of Bentham's other followers, Austin believed, with Locke and Paley, that the binding force of moral duty rests ultimately on sanctions administered by God. God revealed rather little regarding the specifics of political justice, but his unrevealed will is discoverable by application of the principle of utility. So understood, when we speak of what it is just or unjust of government to do, or of rights government has or does not have against its subjects, we must be understood to be speaking of what is "*generally useful or pernicious*" that government do or not do. Therefore, for example,

> assuming that the government sovereign in Britain was properly sovereign in the colonies, it had no legal right to tax its colonial subjects; although it was not restrained by positive law, from dealing with its colonial subjects at its own pleasure or discretion.... But it had not a Divine right to tax its American subjects, unless the project of taxing them accorded with general utility.... (238, 239)

And what of the colonists' rights against Britain? Austin presumably would treat the colonists' assertion of a right against Britain in the same way he treated Britain's right against the colonists: to say that the tax violated the colonists' rights could only mean that the tax was either contrary to a revealed commandment *or* was not generally useful. No revealed right divine appears in Scripture; in fact, the injunction to render to Caesar what is Caesar's apparently contradicts any thought that God has issued some specific command to the sovereign that could be the basis of a right divine that colonists not be taxed. But it is nonetheless a fair question whether the colonists being taxed is generally useful. No nonsense here, Bentham notwithstanding. The inflammatory "anti-legal" rhetoric of natural rights can be understood as an appeal to the principle of utility as a standard against which to measure the positive law.

Does this mean that the principle of utility is to be applied by each individual colonist to the question of the general utility of his paying *his* tax bill? Austin resisted any such Godwinian, act-utilitarian approach:

> [W]e must not consider the action as if it were *single* and *insulated*, but must look at the class of actions to which it belongs.... The question to be solved is this: – If the acts of the *class* were *generally* done, or *generally* foreborne or omitted, what would be the probable effect on the general happiness or good? Considered by itself, a mischievous act may seem to

be useful or harmless. Considered by itself, a useful act may seem to be pernicious.... But suppose that [acts of the kind] were general ... and mark the result....

If I evade the payment of a tax imposed by a good government, the specific effects of the mischievous forbearance are indisputably useful. For the money which I unduly withhold is convenient to myself; and, compared with the bulk of the public revenue, is a quantity too small to be missed. But the regular payment of taxes is necessary to the existence of government. And I, and the rest of the community, enjoy the security which it gives, because the payment of taxes is rarely evaded. (42–43)

Austin recognized that there are cases "wherein the specific considerations balance or outweigh the general" to so great a degree that "the evil of observing the rule might surpass the evil of breaking it," in which case we must "dismiss the rule; resort directly to the principle upon which our rules were fashioned; and calculate specific consequences to the best of our knowledge and ability" (53–54). Even if in difficult cases appeal must be made to the utility of particular acts – Austin instances the rule of obedience to a sovereign who turns tyrant – this direct appeal to utility is superior to the mysticism he finds infecting any *direct* appeal to rights, which simply touches off a "war of words" between contending parties, each invoking a right contrary to that of its opponent.

Austin's main contribution to the theory of rights was to propose that the existence of a remedy available to the right-holder is an essential part of what it means to say that a *legal* right is in existence. This makes his a "choice" theory of what defines legal rights. But Austin also revived the utilitarian project of understanding *natural* or moral rights as *rules* of general utility (or, more precisely, as protections established by rules). Rights in this "anti-legal" sense are not nonsense, as Bentham had charged; nor are they contrary to considerations of expediency, as Burke had feared. But, as rules of general utility, rights were in Austin's view always subject to being "dismissed" when the utility of following the rule was less than that of ignoring it. The question that Austin's view raises, but which Austin himself did not confront, is whether rights have any power to resist calculations of utility in concrete cases. As much as Austin the rule utilitarian might like to create a secure place for rights, his utilitarianism keeps the reductive worry alive. If rights are simply guideposts to general utility, the utilitarian seems, in consistency, to have to "dismiss" them whenever "specific considerations" of utility favor doing so.

John Stuart Mill

John Stuart Mill is a pivotal figure both in giving direction to the development of the theory of rights and in clarifying and popularizing utilitarianism. His 1859 essay *On Liberty* and the series of magazine articles collected under the title *Utilitarianism* in 1861 were influential on both scholarly and popular thought to a degree that perhaps has never been matched. Although the details of Mill's position are beyond the scope of this book, it is worthwhile to review some of the main points. Mill was dedicated to reforming society, and was very much a disciple of Bentham, via the influence of his father, James Mill, and another mentor, the just-discussed John Austin.

Bentham had brought scientific method into the reform effort, to his eternal credit in the younger Mill's view, but the enactment of Bentham's effusion of practical proposals rested on the mechanism of majority rule. Ensuring that rulers were responsible to the majority was a great advance, given the feudal background of most British institutions, but what was to be feared – though overlooked by Bentham – was the threat of majority tyranny over the individual, and particularly over the gifted individuals to whose efforts so much of mankind's achievements were due. The enlightened condition of those rulers was no consolation, Mill believed, because there is no limit to the progressive improvement of human culture. But improvement can be stifled by "the despotism of Public Opinion" (1838, 114), however enlightened that opinion may appear by comparison with what had earlier prevailed.

Mill thus echoed Bishop Butler's concern that the principle of beneficence (i.e., the law of love, secularized) could be invoked to justify persecution, whether directly or via majoritarian institutions otherwise properly responsive to the principle of beneficence in its utilitarian form. The Reign of Terror was an ever-present reminder that a reign of republican virtue could be a tyranny, but Mill was even more alive to the soul-killing conventionalism of English society. (By Mill's autobiographical account, he suffered a nervous breakdown when, in his early twenties, he realized that what made for the greatest happiness of the greatest number would not make for his own.) How to respond? Mill proposed "one very simple principle":

> The sole end for which mankind are warranted, individually or collectively, in interfering with the liberty of action of any of their number, is self-protection . . . the only purpose for which power can rightfully be exercised over any member of a civilised community, against his will, is to prevent harm to others. His own good, either physical or moral, is not a sufficient warrant. . . . The only part of conduct of any one, for which he is amenable to society, is that which concerns others. In the part that concerns himself, his independence is, of right, absolute. (1859, 13)

Mill's qualifications and elaboration of what has come to be referred to as his "Harm Principle" need not detain us. The important points for our purposes are two. The first is that what Mill proposes can be, and came to be, identified as a moral *right to liberty*. The second is that Mill claims that this right is consistent with – is even derivable from – the principle of utility, "the ultimate appeal on all ethical questions" (1859, 14).

The right to liberty encompasses the rights of conscience and free speech, but it is of much wider scope – as wide, apparently, as the rights contended for by the pamphleteers of the late eighteenth century. Although Mill acknowledged no debt to Godwin, the similarity between Mill's right to liberty and Godwin's passive right to be free of interference within one's "sphere of discretion" is striking. But Mill's right to liberty is more extensive, in that it requires

> liberty of tastes and pursuits, of forming our own plan of life to suit our own character, of doing as we like, subject to such consequences as may follow, without impediment from our fellow-creatures, so long as what we do does not harm them – even though they should think our conduct foolish, perverse, or wrong. (1859, 16)

That it is a moral, rather than a merely political, right is plain from Mill's exposition, as well as from the fact that it limits the conduct of society and individuals within society, as well as the conduct of the state. Moreover, this right is not one that individuals surrender at the threshold as they enter civil society making the Hobbesian or Lockean transition from a state of nature.

Second, the right to liberty is supposed to be supportable on utilitarian principles. How can this be? Godwin suggested that such a right "flows from the very nature of man" (113), but consistency would require a utilitarian to tie any such appeal to empirical facts about what gives humans the greatest pleasure. The obvious way of working this out would rest on the empirical claim that it is always the case that people are better judges of their own interests than others. But such a claim seems at least as doubtful as the claim that it is always best that promises not be broken, or that lies not be told. Yet, as we have seen, there is another way to take the utilitarian principle. Rather than have the actor apply it directly to the set of possible *actions* she faces at the moment of decision, have her apply the principle to the set of *rules* that purport to govern action, and then have her act according to the best rule. This approach is the one Paley suggested and Austin outlined, and which we have been referring to as rule utilitarianism (sometimes called *indirect* utilitarianism).

In contrast to the direct- or act-utilitarian approach that Godwin favored, rule utilitarianism offers the possibility of making peace with a number of objections to the utilitarian approach to ethics. One recurring objection was that the consequences of any action, like those of any event, run into infinity, and so are incalculable: a utilitarian would never be able to complete the computations necessary to choose which was her best option, and as a result would never act at all! Another objection was that utilitarianism logically led to conclusions too discordant with ordinary moral understandings to be plausible; Godwin might embrace them, but even Godwin, notoriously, chose to marry the pregnant Mary Wollstonecraft rather than cohabit with her on an entirely conditional, act-utilitarian basis.

Rule utilitarians, unlike Godwin, could answer both sorts of objection. If the agent's deliberations are limited to choosing the best rules, rather than the best act in each case as it arose, then the amount of time spent in deliberation would be drastically reduced. Rather than, say, decide the optimal amount of falsehood to allow into each of our utterances, we may decide that the optimal consequences overall flow from our following the rule, "Do not lie." In applying the rule, the actor will "rule out" any option that involves her lying; although she must still decide among the remaining options, that is what she must do anyway, on any account of morality.

How is the actor to know, however, that the best consequences flow from following the rule, "Don't lie"? Mustn't she at least experiment with lying, and won't her experiments, if pursued widely, turn up some instances in which the greater happiness was gotten by lying rather than telling the truth (especially if, as Austin indicated, she is free to dismiss the rule where "special circumstances" exist)? Here, the rule utilitarian could invoke the social dimension of scientific enquiry. Science is cumulative; later researchers build on the results of earlier ones. Although results are always open to rechecking, and are always subject to correction, an individual's having scientific knowledge does not entail her having to re-run every experiment and check every result in scientific history. She is entitled to rely on the cumulative wisdom of a scientific community, which differs from the supposed wisdom of a superstitious community in that its doctrines ultimately rest on experiences which *can* be reproduced anytime, for the benefit of any inquirer.

Morality, the rule utilitarian may continue, is like science in precisely this way. The received moral wisdom of the ages is like the accumulated experience of a scientific community. The observed beneficial effects of various types of conduct are reported to us via the maxims we are taught in the nursery. These maxims are not sacrosanct because they are always subject to the check of experience, and the accumulating experience of humankind may require some of them to be revised or rejected – as in the cases of human sacrifice and slavery, for example.

In *Utilitarianism*, Mill expressly seized the opportunity of explaining moral rights as utility-grounded moral rules, and went still further, in the spirit of Grotius, to explain justice generally as a matter of respecting moral rights:

> The idea of justice supposes two things; a rule of conduct, and a sentiment which sanctions the rule.... There is involved, in addition, the conception of some definite person who suffers by the infringement; whose rights (to use the expression appropriated to the case) are violated by it.... I have, throughout, treated the idea of a right residing in the injured person, not as a separate element in the composition ... but as one of the forms in which the other two elements clothe themselves. These elements are, a hurt to some assignable person or persons on the one hand, and a demand for punishment on the other ... these two things include all that we mean when we speak of the violation of a right....

> To have a right, then, is, I conceive, to have something which society ought to defend me in the possession of. If the objector goes on to ask, why it ought? I can give him no other reason than general utility. If that expression does not convey a sufficient feeling of the strength of the obligation, nor to account for the peculiar energy of the feeling, it is because there goes to the composition of the sentiment, not a rational only, but also an animal element.... (1861, 65–66)

The "animal element" is the retaliatory impulse connected with our basic survival instinct. This instinct, though rationally to be considered only as a utility, "gathers feelings around it so much more intense than those concerned in any of the more common cases of utility, that the difference in degree (as is often the case in psychology) becomes a real difference in kind" (1861, 67). Here, Mill was walking a tightrope between two very different ways of regarding popular feeling about rights. One way would be to take a tough line and dismiss such feeling as an irrational atavism – pleasures are pleasures, and they differ only in duration, intensity, purity, propinquity in time, and probability of occurring, just as Bentham had said. But Mill rejects this line and chooses instead to take the strength of the feeling associated with self-preservation as indicating that a utility of an incomparably different order is at work.

This is not Mill's only deviation from the strictest utilitarian line; he elsewhere distinguishes higher-order from lower-order utilities – for example, the utility derived from poetry is of a higher order than that derived from "pushpin" (a children's game). Mill was subjected to considerable criticism for this innovation, both from friends of utilitarianism and foes. Allowing a distinction between qualitatively different types of pleasure or utility in this way might make the utilitarian philosophy more appealing to those who were offended by its apparent philistinism, but the cost of this concession is considerable.

As the eminent Victorian moral philosopher Henry Sidgwick argued, allowing qualitative distinctions between kinds of pleasure would weaken utilitarianism. It would reintroduce controversial intuitions about which is the higher pleasure and which the lower, and, in so doing, abandon utilitarianism's ability to arbitrate between conflicting moral claims. Instead of reducing contending claims to common, commensurable terms, a utilitarian would have to acknowledge the possibility of appealing to something other than utility to decide moral questions, and if on some one moral issue utility is not conclusive while intuition *is*, why not on all?

So, Mill is on the verge of making a rather large adjustment in his utilitarianism when he tells us that the difference in degree between ordinary utilities and the utility of self-preservation amounts to a difference in kind. There is another question to be answered: Does this difference in kind confer on rights an absolute priority over the demands of utility? Mill is unwilling to go so far.

> Justice is a name for certain moral requirements, which, regarded collectively, stand higher in the scale of social utility, and are therefore of more paramount obligation, than any others; though particular cases may occur in which some other social duty is so important, as to overrule any one of the general maxims of justice. (1861, 78)

Thus Mill, like Austin and Godwin, acknowledges that a character of *defeasibility* attaches to rights on a utilitarian account, and that this will in some circumstances justify, even require, measures such as stealing food or drugs or kidnapping a physician to save a life (these are Mill's examples). So, on Mill's account some rights rest on a kind of utility different in kind from ordinary utilities, but such rights nonetheless may be overbalanced by greater utilities of the same kind (but presumably not by utilities of the ordinary kind).

Mill's view, then, is that "certain interests . . . either by express legal provision or by tacit understanding, ought to be considered as rights" (1859, 91). Self-preservation is such an interest, but there are perhaps others. In *On Liberty*, Mill had advanced an argument for a right to liberty; that argument had been grounded on the (contestable) proposition that it would be better if individuals were allowed to learn from their own mistakes regarding their own interests: "Mankind are greater gainers by suffering each other to live as seems good to themselves, than by compelling each to live as seems good to the rest" (1859, 17). The analysis in *Utilitarianism* provides the material for grounding the right to liberty differently, on *the individual's* interest in spontaneous self-development, once that is recognized, like self-preservation, as a higher-order utility. Mill thus appropriates Bentham's interest theory of legal rights and transforms it in order to characterize an "anti-legal" *moral* right to liberty, which is grounded on a higher-order individual interest in spontaneous self-realization.

A question now arises that will have great significance for the further development of theories of rights. Mill seems to be concerned to create a space for individuals in which they may be free of social interference in their spontaneous pursuit of what seems most pleasant or useful to pursue. (At one point he goes so far as to state that "it is desirable . . . that people should be eccentric" (1859, 81)). At other points, however, Mill seems to be rather stern in his attitude toward those who are slack in their efforts to promote the general welfare, and is willing to compel us "to perform certain acts of individual beneficence, such as saving a fellow-creature's life, or interposing to protect the defenceless against ill usage . . ." (1859, 15). Are there, on Mill's view, any "active" rights, in Godwin's phrase, rights to "do as we list" regardless of the general utility? The better understanding of Mill's view has him answer "Yes," there is an "active" right to liberty; rule utilitarianism makes it possible, as act utilitarianism does not.

Rule utilitarianism opens up the possibility that we may often find ourselves in situations in which no moral rule demands of us any affirmative act while, at the same time, the totality of moral rules leaves open to us genuine *moral options*. To recall Paley's example, it is possible that as I sit puffing on my pipe, while a train of thought glides indolently through my brain, no moral rule positively commands that I seek out and perform the act most productive of general happiness. It is logically possible that the principle of utility warrants only a more relaxed rule, which requires that each of us do what makes for the greatest general happiness some of the time. Whether this possibility is actual will depend on empirical facts, and if the empirical fact is that people do more good if they do not try to do good everywhere, on every occasion, and without regard to their social and geographical relationship to their beneficiaries, then the properly utilitarian rule of beneficence will not require me to maximize the net sum of human happiness at every moment of my life. My simply sitting in my armchair, by turns drowsing or staring at the ceiling, may thus entail no violation of any affirmative duty. And if my lying there violates no other duties, I have an active right to slouch in my armchair doing nothing even though I may know full well that there are better things I might do.

Godwin's act utilitarianism might permit me to lie for a while on my couch, doing nothing, but only in case I were faultlessly ignorant of any possibility of creating a greater net sum of happiness by other means – a rare occasion, on Godwin's account. In any case, this would not be an instance in which I had an active right to "do as I list" contrary to the demands of justice – it would be a case in which act-utilitarian justice would *demand* that I slouch in my armchair! "You! Hold still there; you're now maximizing happiness. Don't get up until the beneficence principle tells you to!" Mill would have objected to the utilitarianism of the embarrassing Godwin as excessively Calvinistic.

By interposing rules between actors and a principle of beneficence, rule utilitarianism exploits a possibility that had also existed under the older divine-command moralities. As long as morality was understood in Ten Commandment fashion – enumerating certain "thou shalts" and "shalt nots" – its demands were limited. But once the Levitical and New Testament injunction to "love thy neighbor as thyself" – Grotius's "law of love" – is taken to enjoin us to follow the principle of (maximum) beneficence, morality becomes a much more demanding affair, seeming to require sainthood. Theological interpretations varied, but if the Gospel is understood to require us to measure each of our acts by the principle of beneficence, that would be a vivid way of emphasizing our inability to deserve salvation. As Nietzsche and others were to complain, the Christian law of love had transformed a livable Judaic code of "Shalts" and "Shalt nots" into an inherently unlivable and totalitarian quest for sainthood.

American Developments: From The Bill of Rights to the Abolition of Slavery

The career of rights took a more benign and, for a while at least, a less dramatic course in the United States of America than in France. In France, the inflationary rhetoric of rights contributed to, or at the very least failed to resist, the Reign of Terror, and although the Declaration was never repudiated, there was a sense that somewhere a terrible theoretical as well as practical mistake had been made. Writing decades after the event, Benjamin Constant diagnosed this mistake as a failure on the part of his fellow revolutionaries to appreciate the difference between the rights or liberties dear to the ancients and those that had come to be dear to the moderns (1820). The difference was this: The Greeks valued political participation, and, given political rights of participation, were willing to follow the decision of the *polis* wherever it led. Pericles' oration to the Athenians was the summation of the rights of the ancients: having a part in the politics of the city is the highest good, and those who disagree with that assessment should leave.

We moderns, according to Constant, are different. We don't necessarily care about politics: we have our own projects, businesses, and interests, and we don't mind if the state maintains conditions in which we are free to pursue them, but on the other hand we don't want political decisions to interfere with them. We moderns are satisfied if politics doesn't get in the way of our personal lives. (Understandably, Constant, while a member of the Revolutionary Tribunal, had decided to postpone a projected translation of Godwin until calm returned.) The error of the French Revolution, according to Constant, was to try to force the rights of the ancients onto moderns.

The Americans had not made this error. The Framers of the U.S. Constitution took care to ensure that the federal government they created was incapable of dominating the states or the societies within the states. Rights of political participation were guaranteed (to propertied adult white males only, of course), but the Americans never attempted to set out in any exhaustive way (as the French had) an enumeration of the rights of citizens. In fact, the U.S. Constitution was ratified despite the objection of its "anti-Federalist" opponents that it lacked a Bill of Rights. "So what?" had in essence been the answer of its "Federalist" proponents, for many of the states' constitutions lacked bills of rights as well. As Alexander Hamilton argued in the tract known as *Federalist #84*, the mere listing of specific rights is to invite the argument that others, not listed, are denied. Even those listed become targets for those who would urge exceptions and ingenious qualifications. Better, Hamilton argued, to leave rights unstated, with the understanding that no powers are conveyed to the Federal sovereign other than those enumerated in the founding document. Everything else remains with the people. "Here," Hamilton declared, "in strictness the people surrender nothing; and as they retain everything they have no need of particular reservations" (Rossiter, 481). This was perhaps intentionally hyperbolic of Hamilton, especially in light of John Jay's uncontroversial remark, in *Federalist #2*, that "the people must cede to it [viz., the federal sovereign] some of their natural rights, in order to vest it with requisite powers" (5).

When a Bill of Rights was later adopted in 1791, in the form of ten amendments to the Constitution, it included one that explicitly disclaimed any ambition of exhaustiveness:

Amendment IX

The enumeration in the Constitution of certain rights shall not be construed to deny or disparage others retained by the people.

The God-given, "unalienable rights" of "life, liberty, and the pursuit of happiness" set forth so prominently in the Declaration of Independence are presumably among those meant.

Unlike the French, the Americans were never tempted to re-create the Athenian *agora* or the Roman forum on a national scale, and so America avoided the kind of political convulsion that wracked the French. But America's hour of trial was to come nonetheless, and the concept of rights was very much involved in it. The great controversy that consumed the new American republic between 1791 and 1865 centered upon slavery.

The United States united, in almost equal number, slaveholding Southern states and "free" states in the North. The "peculiar institution" of slavery was acknowledged and approved in the Constitution itself, a fact that led abolitionist William Lloyd Garrison to denounce it as a "pact with the devil." Political struggles between the North and the South intensified as new territories in the West sought admission into the Union as states. Abolitionist sentiment in the North grew throughout the period, and in equal measure the slaveholding South stiffened its spine and, under the leadership of Senator John C. Calhoun of South Carolina, strenuously refused even to allow discussion of slavery on the floor of the United States Congress. In 1836, the House of Representatives resolved, by a lopsided majority, "That slaves do not possess the right of petition secured to the people of the United States by the constitution."

Had the slaves *no* rights? Indeed, did black Africans – free or slave – enjoy *any* of the rights, enumerated or not, in the Bill of Rights? Both abolitionists and apologists for slavery appreciated the fact that, if African slaves held the very same natural rights to "life, liberty, and the pursuit of happiness," that the white colonists had held, then the far greater "train of abuses" to which the Southern planters (and, before them, the Yankee shipowners) had subjected the Africans gave them at least as much a right to revolt as the colonists had ever had. Between the stark alternatives of "no rights for African slaves" and "full rights for African slaves, including the right to make bloody revolt," many whites in the North (and some in the South) wished to find a moderate middle ground in which slaveowners were duty-bound, as Christians, gradually to ease and ultimately to release the bonds of servitude, while the African slaves were duty-bound patiently to suffer the inconvenience of temporary, but necessary, bondage. To speak the language of rights in this close atmosphere was too inflammatory, too explosive, for those who sought to locate a middle position between Calhoun and Garrison. But the foundational position occupied by the idea of natural rights in the American constitutional edifice made any evasive, gradualist position hard to sustain.

In 1841, the Supreme Court of the United States decided the case of *The Amistad,* so called after a vessel of that name, which had been commandeered by captive black Africans who sought to return to Africa after having been kidnapped there and taken to Cuba, a colony of Spain. The United States was a party to the case but asserted only the claims of Spanish subjects to ownership of the Africans as their slaves. The United States was opposed by the Africans themselves, who claimed the rights of free men. Spain had outlawed slavery by this date, and Justice Story, writing for the Court, might have rested the decision on the narrow ground that, under the municipal law of Spain, these Africans were not slaves and hence not the property of the Spaniards suing for their return. But Justice Story went further:

> It is also a most important consideration . . . that, supposing these African negroes not to be slaves, but kidnapped, and free negroes, the treaty with Spain cannot be obligatory upon them; and the United States are bound to respect their rights as much as those of Spanish subjects. The conflict of rights between the parties under such circumstances, becomes positive and inevitable, and must be decided upon the eternal principles of justice and international law. . . . The treaty with Spain could never

have been intended to take away the equal rights of all foreigners, who should contest their claims before our Courts, to equal justice.... Upon the merits of the case, then, there does not seem to be any ground for doubt, that these negroes ought to be deemed free; and that the Spanish treaty interposes no obstacle to the just assertion of their rights. (40 U.S. 15 *Peters* 595–96)

The Court here indicated a willingness to give Africans a hearing even if the municipal law of a foreign state recognized slavery; and the Court explicitly referred to Africans' rights under "eternal principles of justice," as well as under the law of nations.

But in the 1857 case of *Dred Scott v. Sandford*, the United States Supreme Court declared that black Africans, having been "regarded as beings of an inferior order" by Europeans for centuries, therefore "had no rights which the white man was bound to respect...." (60 *Howard* 393, 407) and that, slave or free, they were incapable of being citizens of the United States. Black Africans were not second-class citizens (like women or children); they were not citizens of the United States at all. But what of the Declaration of Independence – "We hold these truths to be self-evident: that all men are created equal ... endowed by their Creator with certain unalienable rights"? The Court made this observation:

The general words quoted above would seem to embrace the whole human family, and if they were used in a similar instrument at this day would be so understood. But ... the enslaved African race were not intended to be included, and formed no part of the people who framed and adopted this declaration; for if the language, as understood in that day, would embrace them, the conduct of the distinguished men who framed the Declaration of Independence would have been utterly and flagrantly inconsistent with the principles they asserted.... (410)

The Court decided that the intention of the Founders, rather than the plain meaning of the language they used, was to control its interpretation; and that the intention of the Framers was to be gauged not by the high aspirations that they professed, but by their practices. The practices of the slaveholders among the Founders were certainly at odds with their principles, and they were aware of that fact, as the correspondence of Jefferson, for example, amply shows. But the Court in *Dred Scott* curtly determined that the Founders were not the inconsistent idealists we now know them to have been, but rather men of honor and learning "incapable of asserting principles inconsistent with those on which they were acting" (410). The Constitution was to be interpreted in the same way: not in terms of *natural* rights but in terms of what was intended by the draftsmen, ratified, and made *positive* law. In other words, the Court chose to reconcile the Constitution not with the theory of rights nurtured by Grotius and Locke, but with the compromise that was necessary to bring the Southern states into the Union.

No one – not Justice Taney, writing for the Court, nor the dissenting Justices – even mentioned *The Amistad.* But that case would have been easy for a lawyer to distinguish anyway. What Congress intended in ratifying a treaty with Spain is one thing; what the people of the slave states and free states intended in forming a federal union is another. The treaty with Spain did not – according to *The Amistad* – express the intention of the United States to deny the rights of black Africans to a hearing in a case arising under the federal courts' admiralty jurisdiction; but the Constitution of the United States did – according to *Dred Scott* – express the intention of "the people" to deny blacks of African ancestry the status of citizens of the United States.

The *Dred Scott* decision created a public furor in the United States that did not subside until a civil war had claimed 700,000 lives and devastated the South. The defeat of the Confederate States of America represented the end of a period consolidating the defensible gains that rights rhetoric had unlocked. Settled, at least for the time, was the issue: Who are the holders of natural rights? The answer was: All humans do, and equally, in virtue of their common humanity. This hard-won answer did not even begin to resolve the further questions that had been raised by Godwin, Burke, and Bentham. Nor did it answer the further challenge to the idea of natural rights, made by Karl Marx: "None of the so-called rights of man goes beyond egoistic man ... an individual withdrawn behind his private interests and separated from the community" (147). The concept of rights, in Marx's analysis, was not so much an instrument of liberation as a tool of oppression wielded by an emerging *bourgeoisie* seeking to legitimate its dominion over the means of industrial production, thereby (a charge that would be seconded by American philosopher John Dewey (1927)) promoting selfish individualism at the expense of community.

In fact, the consolidation that followed the first expansionary period left in disarray the whole matter of settling what specific moral rights there are. The British utilitarian Sidgwick, writing in 1874, put it this way:

> There is a wide-spread view, that in order to make society just certain Natural Rights should be conceded to all members of the community, and that positive law should at least embody and protect these . . . but it is difficult to find in Common Sense any definite agreement in the enumeration of these Natural Rights, still less any clear principles from which they can be systematically deduced.
>
> There is, however, one mode of systemizing these Rights and bringing them under one principle. . . . It has been held that Freedom from interference is really the whole of what human beings, originally and apart from contracts, can strictly be said to *owe* to each other. . . . All natural Rights, on this view, may be summed up in the Right to Freedom. . . . (274)

Having given it a name, Sidgwick said little more about this supposed right to freedom from interference, and almost a century would pass before philosophers would engage in significant further discussion about the concept of moral, natural, or human rights.

American Developments: From The Civil War Amendments to the Right of Privacy

The seeds of the second expansionary period of rights are to be found not in scholarly or philosophical disquisitions but among legal developments in the United States in the aftermath of the Civil War. This is a complex story that we can only barely sketch here. A main theme of the post-Civil War developments has to do with the *civil rights* guaranteed to the newly emancipated slaves. These civil rights included access to courts to protect property and contract rights, as well as rights to participate in the political process. The practical guarantee of civil rights to African-Americans took another century to be fulfilled but, for our purposes, this effort was not strictly speaking "expansionary" for it did not expand the scope of rights: it merely acknowledged entitlements that had been implicit at least since the eighteenth century, and had been made explicit in the constitutional amendments enacted in the wake of the Civil War.

Among these "Civil War Amendments" was the Fourteenth Amendment, enacted in 1868, which provided for the first time a federal guarantee that no state shall "deprive any person of life, liberty, or property, without due process of law. . . ." These "vague and majestic" phrases (as the U.S. Supreme Court has termed them) seeded the second expansionary period of rights in which we live today. The "due process" clause came to be interpreted as incorporating into American law a moral check on the power of government, and of the electoral majorities that direct it. One landmark was the 1905 case of *Lochner v. New York* (198 U.S. 45) in which the U.S. Supreme Court held that the State of New York had violated the "due process" rights of bakers by limiting their hours on the job. The right to liberty guaranteed by the Constitution encompassed the liberty to contract to work long hours, the Court held, and therefore the states cannot by mere legislation restrict that right even if the intention were to benefit the bakers.

The Court later backtracked from the *Lochner* understanding of the right to liberty, but nonetheless, in the spirit of *Lochner*, recognized a right to educate one's children privately, a right to procreate, a right to buy contraceptives, and a right to abort a first-trimester fetus – perhaps as aspects of what Justice Brandeis, dissenting in *Olmstead v. U.S.*, called "the most comprehensive of rights and the right most valued by civilized men . . . the right to be let alone" (277 U.S. 438, 478 (1928)), or, as it is more commonly termed, the *right to privacy*. (The difference between the right to be let alone, and the right not to be interfered with that Sidgwick thought summarized all other rights, may be merely verbal.) These judicial decisions and others like them have been highly controversial, and much of the controversy stems precisely from the fact that they represent determinations of legal rights contrary to the popular will manifested by acts of the legislature, and bottomed upon judicial declarations of the existence of one or another "fundamental" right not mentioned in any legal instrument.

It is difficult to avoid the conclusion that in its fundamental-rights jurisprudence, the U.S. Supreme Court is giving legal effect to what are, in essence, moral rights – in fact, to instances of the moral or natural right to liberty Sidgwick mentioned – and in so doing is overriding the

legislative process. Such an immunity against ordinary legislation is rem-
iniscent of the "imprescriptible" nature of moral rights, as the French
Declaration described it, and as objected to by Bentham. If a moral right
exists and is in conflict with a legislative stipulation of legal right, then the
moral right presumably enjoys a position of greater dignity in the conflict.
(Antigone acts morally rightly in burying her brother, we think, even if
legally she acts wrongly.) Fundamental-rights jurisprudence does not,
however, simply note that legislation has encroached on an abstractly superior moral right: it declares that legislation to be legally invalid because
it violates an implicit *legal* right. In a legal system that immunizes constitutional rights from legislative abridgement, and whose courts consult
moral rights in order to *define* legal rights, it is simply a legal mistake to
declare the existence of a law contrary to an (incorporated) moral right –
no matter how hard the legislature might try to do so, or how formally
impeccable the processes it follows, or even how faithfully it reflects the
popular will.

This sketch of how American fundamental-rights jurisprudence has
transformed the "anti-legal" natural rights of the first expansionary period into fully legal rights is no more than a very rough one. It misleadingly suggests that the judiciary – in effect, a current majority of the U.S.
Supreme Court – regards itself as in the business of making its own independent inquiries into moral truth – specifically, into whether or not
certain putative natural moral rights exist or not. In fact, the Court avoids
doing so almost whenever possible, and manages this avoidance by the
use of a number of limiting devices. Some of these are inherent in the
judicial role – the Court must wait for cases to come to it, for example;
it cannot declare the existence of rights unless some party is properly
before the Court invoking its remedial powers – but other devices are
self-imposed, such as various "abstention," "standing," and "political
question" doctrines.

U.S. citizens hold fundamental, though "unenumerated," rights
against the states in which they reside, but what are they, and how is a
Court to tell? One test by which the U.S. Supreme Court has tried to determine whether a putative right is "fundamental" is to ask whether it is "implicit in the concept of ordered liberty" (*Palko v. Connecticut,* 302 U.S. 319,
325 (1937)). This test seems plausible to adopt, but in application it would
not seem to uncover many, if any, of the fundamental rights the Court

has discovered. The problem is that the balance of order and liberty does not lend itself to conceptual line-drawing; it is far from obvious, for example, that a state's prohibiting private schooling, or a state's excluding German language instruction from public and private schools, tips so far toward order and away from liberty as to be logically inconsistent with "the concept of ordered liberty."

Another test identifies fundamental rights as ones that are "deeply rooted in this Nation's history and tradition" (*Moore v. City of East Cleveland*, 431 U.S. 494, 503 (1977)). But how is a court to tell whether a purported right is rooted deeply enough in tradition? And why should it matter anyway? Whether or not a candidate fundamental right is deeply rooted or not turns largely on the level of generality or specificity with which it is described. Is there a fundamental right to buy and use contraceptives? As of 1965, when the U.S. Supreme Court decided *Griswold v. Connecticut* (381 U.S. 479), it could hardly be said that such was a traditionally recognized right in America, for it emphatically was not. Nonetheless, the Court was able to derive that right as one of the "emanations" from the "penumbras" (484) of other, more general, textual rights having to do with privacy. A right to privacy was manifest in a number of more specific protections of the Bill of Rights (including, for example, the Third Amendment right not to have troops quartered in one's home), and – by analogy – a right to possess and use contraceptive devices could be located under the umbrella of privacy as well – despite the absence of any explicit language in the Constitution saying so.

The decision in *Griswold v. Connecticut* is a landmark of the second expansionary period of rights. Its affinities to the 1905 *Lochner* case have been widely remarked, and *Griswold* was the precedent on which the Court based its 1973 decision in *Roe v. Wade* (410 U.S. 113), which held that a woman's right to privacy forbade the states from prohibiting first-trimester abortions. The constitutional right to privacy seemed surely to be expansive enough to prohibit the states from criminalizing consensual sex acts between adults, but the Court held to the contrary in *Bowers v. Hardwick* (478 U.S. 186), a 1986 case challenging a state sodomy statute. Justice White (who had dissented in *Roe*) wrote for the *Bowers* majority that the suggestion that a right to engage in homosexual sodomy was "deeply rooted" in American tradition was "at best, facetious" (194). But why would that suggestion be any more facetious than the suggestion, in 1973, that a right to abort a fetus was "deeply rooted" in tradition? The Court's recourse to history as a brake on expansive readings of constitutional rights has seemed to many commentators to be selective and tendentious, at best.

The Court overruled *Bowers* in 2003 in *Lawrence v. Texas* (123 S.Ct. 2472), noting that "history and tradition are the starting point but not in all cases the ending point" (2480), of its inquiry; but the right-of-privacy decisions raise a deeper question: Why should tradition matter at all? Slavery had, after all, been a traditional practice, at least until the American Civil War – but surely the Supreme Court's decision in the *Dred Scott* case was a mistake. Why should moral rights not stand against tradition just as steadfastly as they stand against contrary state and national legislation? If the answer is that tradition offers clues about what moral rights there are, the question simply becomes: Why assume that moral rights are knowable by consulting entrenched conventions, which is all that tradition is? Moral rights are supposed to offer a vantage point from which entrenched convention can be challenged and overturned – to require that they be "tradition friendly" is to gut them.

At this point in the debate, it is often said that if moral rights are not anchored in convention or traditional practice of some kind, then it is simply anybody's guess as to what they are, and the entire question becomes a matter of each person deciding for herself, based upon her own moral views. The dilemma seems to be this: Either moral rights are tied in some strong way to actually established human practices, or they are not knowable at all unless by some mysterious process of intuition that may vary from individual to individual. If the tie to conventional practices is too strong, then moral rights collapse into specialized conventions; if it is too weak, then discourse about what moral rights there are loses focus, and threatens to degenerate into what Austin called a mere war of words, and Bentham castigated as "nonsense upon stilts."

Appreciation of the difficulty of this dilemma helped to bring an end to the first expansionary period of rights rhetoric, at the close of the eighteenth century, and it should come as no surprise if the dilemma remains to be resolved today, in the midst of the second expansionary period. In what follows, we will explore more recent work that may help to clarify the nature of rights. In particular, there have been advances in clarifying the conceptual structure of rights-talk. Some have argued that careful attention to the logic of rights can, in and of itself, cut down on the number of extravagant and fanciful rights-claims that others have made. We will take a look at this conceptual work and try to evaluate the claims made for it.

5

The Conceptual Neighborhood of Rights

Wesley Newcomb Hohfeld

Bentham had argued that talk about rights made sense only within a legal framework. Within such a framework, to say that someone had a right of a certain kind was simply to say that he stood to benefit from a legal duty imposed on someone else. Legal rights correlate with legal duties, and if we wished, we could dispense with talk of rights altogether and simply speak in terms of legal duties and their beneficiaries. Bentham's view calls for a rigorous moral critique of law, but in his view, that critique cannot sensibly be phrased in the terminology of rights. The moral critique, for the Benthamite, must be in terms of utility. As we saw in the last chapter, Bentham's reasons for disallowing an external critique of law and political institutions in terms of rights were inconclusive. Some modern utilitarians have taken Mill's line, which is to attempt to reformulate the idea of moral rights in utilitarian terms, whereas others have tried to avoid using the notion of rights altogether.

But was Bentham correct about the analysis of *legal* rights? Specifically, was Bentham correct in suggesting that a legal right is simply the correlate of a legal duty? Wesley Newcomb Hohfeld, an American law professor who wrote in the early twentieth century, found this sort of analysis simplistic and misleading. Bentham's account of legal rights is more subtle than his writings attacking the French Declaration suggest, but his more subtle account was scattered through a prodigious body of manuscript, much of which is still being edited, and which employs technical terminology that has never caught on. Consequently, Hohfeld rather than Bentham is widely credited with having first taken the analysis of rights to a level deeper than that reflected in the simple reduction of having a legal right to benefitting from another's legal duty.

Hohfeld's work did not stem from his involvement in tumultuous events but from a scholarly interest in the law of trusts – a *trust* is a legal arrangement by which one person, the *trustee*, holds legal title to property, but does so solely for the benefit of another, the *beneficiary*. Analyzing the relationship in vulgar Benthamite (though not Bentham's considered) terms, we would say that the beneficiary's rights in the trust consist in her standing to benefit from the duties the trustee owes her – for example, a duty to preserve the trust assets and manage them carefully. But suppose the trustee violates that duty by, say, carelessly selling an asset to a third party for far less than it is worth. Assume that the third party is innocent in all this, and that the asset in question is something irreplaceable, with great sentimental value, such as the beneficiary's great-great-grandfather's cavalry sabre. How do matters then stand between the beneficiary and the third party? Can the beneficiary demand that the sale be rescinded? After all, the beneficiary can argue, the trustee had no right to sell it. The third party will reply that the trustee did indeed have a right to sell it – but now, what account can be given of this alleged right of the trustee? What is the correlative duty, and whom does it benefit? The best we can do would seem to be this: The trustee's right to sell the asset correlates with a duty imposed on all the world not to upset the sale, and this duty benefits the third-party purchaser and, indirectly, the beneficiary. But this account seems strained and artificial: if the whole world has a duty not to upset the sale, then so does the beneficiary, and it seems odd in the extreme to say that the beneficiary wrongs the trustee by challenging a sale that, we assumed at the outset, was in violation of the trustee's duty to the beneficiary!

The outcome in a court of law would be that the sale stands, and the beneficiary is limited to whatever remedy he has against the trustee. The trustee seems paradoxically both to have had a right to sell the sabre, and yet no right to sell it. Consider another example. We all enjoy a legal right of freedom of speech. On a vulgar Benthamite analysis, this means that certain others are under duties that benefit us. But suppose that our legislature passes what it styles an "Anti-Sedition Act" that criminalizes speech that is disrespectful of government officials. This enactment, surely, violates our right to free speech. But are we not, nonetheless, under a legal duty not to speak disrespectfully of government officials? After all, the trustee was able to convey good title to the innocent purchaser despite the fact that by selling carelessly the trustee violated the duty of care owed to the beneficiary – mustn't we conclude, in parallel fashion, that the legislature validly criminalized disrespectful speech despite the fact that, in doing so, it violated a duty to the public to respect free speech? And what is our remedy, other than to try to oust our representative at the next election unless he promises to work to repeal the Anti-Sedition Act? In the meantime, if we want to exercise what we believe is our legal right to speak disrespectfully of government officials, will we simply have to face the legal consequences of doing so? This line of thinking seems not to capture the full nature of the legal right to free speech. The correct legal analysis would show that the Anti-Sedition Act was void, unconstitutional, from the outset because it violates the right of free speech. But a simple, straightforward, vulgar Benthamite analysis does not uncover this conclusion, at least not in any obvious way.

Hohfeld saw that the terminology of rights had been used in the law to cover a range of different legal relationships, and that the simple correlation of right and duty failed to capture the essential nature of some of them. What was called for was a more complex analysis. Luckily, as it turned out, the family of legal relationships covered by the term "right" was manageably small. Moreover, as Hohfeld described it, this family had a pleasing, logically coherent structure, which is readily described with reference to Table 5.1, a table of what he termed "jural correlatives" (36).

The first thing to notice about this arrangement is that the upper row sets out four logically distinct notions, each of which had been referred to in cases at law and in legal commentary as a right. Confusion abounded in legal argument, Hohfeld believed, to the extent that these four notions

Table 5.1. Hohfeld's jural correlatives

right (or *claim-right*)	privilege (or *permission*, liberty)	power	immunity
duty	no-right (or no duty not to)	liability	disability

were not carefully distinguished. Immediately below each of the four notions in the upper row is its direct Hohfeldian correlative. Notice that
only one of these four notions of legal rights – "claim" rights, or rights in
what he calls the "strictest sense" – are directly correlated with a duty. (To
avoid confusion here, I will speak of "claim-rights" to refer to rights in
his "strictest sense.") To say that a claim-right is *directly* correlated with a
duty is simply to say that if X has a right, with respect to Y, to perform the
action P (or, as philosophers write, "to φ," where φ stands for a verb),
that fact entails that Y has a duty to X not to *interfere* with X's φ-ing. A
privilege, on the other hand, correlates with a "no-right" – which is simply to say that if X has a privilege, with respect to Y, to φ, that fact entails
that Y has no right against X that X not φ. (In what follows, I will use
the term *permission* instead of privilege.) If I have a permission to
thumb my nose at you, you have no right that I not thumb my nose
at you.

The connection between a power and a duty, and between an immunity and a duty, is less direct. A power correlates with a liability, which
is to say that if X enjoys a legal power with respect to Y, that means
that some legal right, duty, or other "jural relation" (26) of Y is apt to
be created, altered, or extinguished by X's exercise of that power. Similarly, an immunity correlates with a disability, which is to say that if X
has an immunity with respect to Y, Y is disabled from altering (has no
power to alter) X's legal relations in some relevant respect. Powers and
immunities have a "second-order" character in the sense that they cash
out in terms of changes in the array of first-order rights and permissions
and their correlative duties and "no-rights" (and, conceptually, there can
exist powers to alter powers, and so forth). To say that X has a power is
not to say that X or anyone else *has* a duty, but it is to say that someone
might incur a duty if X exercises the power. This is the sense in which the
correlation of powers (and immunities) to duties is *indirect*.

Let us now reconsider the trustee's sale of the cavalry sabre and
the Anti-Sedition Act in light of Hohfeld's distinctions. Recall that the

third-party purchaser gets to keep the sabre (that's the correct legal outcome) even though reaching that conclusion seems to involve saying that the trustee had a right to sell it. Hohfeld would analyze the issue of the trustee's right into the separate issues of the trustee's *duty* to conserve trust assets and the trustee's *power* to dispose of, even to squander, trust assets. The trustee's violation of the duty to conserve trust assets is perfectly compatible with his validly exercising his power (we don't want to say "right" if we want to speak of right in its "strictest sense") to dispose of trust assets. The trustee's exercise of the power both conveyed good title to the purchaser and violated his duty to the beneficiary to conserve trust assets. We thus avoid the paradoxical result that the trustee both had a right and had no right to sell the sabre.

In the case of the Anti-Sedition Act, the right to free speech is to be understood as involving a Hohfeldian immunity. To say that citizens enjoy a right of free speech is to say that they are immune from certain alterations of their legal duties, and this is in turn to say that the legislature is disabled from imposing certain legal duties. This renders in a more transparent way the path to the conclusion that citizens have no legal duty not to speak disrespectfully of government officials despite the passage of the Anti-Sedition Act. Unlike the trustee, who had the power to sell trust assets, and thus did convey good legal title, the legislature is *disabled* – that is, has no legal power to impose a legal duty not to speak disrespectfully of government officials.

Hohfeld believed that he had identified the fundamental legal relationships, and that all other legal relationships could be analyzed into these fundamental elements. Moreover, the precise logical properties of these fundamental elements were, he thought, now made evident. To complete the exposition, here is a complementary table (Table 5.2) of "jural opposites" (36).

The upper row is the same as in the table of correlatives, but the lower row contains the denial of the item immediately above it. Having a legal permission to scratch my nose, for example, is the opposite of having

Table 5.2. Hohfeld's jural opposites

right (or *claim-right*)	privilege (or *permission*, liberty)	power	immunity
no-right	duty	disability	liability

a duty *not* to scratch my nose. Having an immunity against being sued (successfully) by my wife for forgetting our anniversary is the opposite of being liable to be sued by her. And so on.

For a complete grasp of Hohfeld's scheme, it is necessary to appreciate the sense in which each of these fundamental concepts is, in addition to being related to the others in the ways the tables set out, relational in yet another sense. A person X may have a claim-right against Y's interfering with X's φ-ing, but no right against interference with ψ-ing, where ψ-ing is something distinct from φ-ing. That seems easy. It is also the case that X's having a claim-right against Y's interference does not assure that X has a claim right against someone else's interference, say, Z's. For example, to help me quit smoking, I might give my roommate permission to confiscate my cigarettes. I still have a claim-right against *your* interfering with my cigarettes, but I have surrendered my claim-right against my roommate. Some Hohfeldian claim-rights hold against "all the world" – all the world, for example, has a legal duty not to assault me unlawfully. Where a Hohfeldian relation holds between a person and all the world, it is sometimes spoken of as holding "*in rem*" (Latin for "in the thing," but we must not think that there has to be any "thing" that is the subject of the relationship in the way that my pack of cigarettes is the subject of my ownership). Many claim-rights hold not *in rem* but only *in personam* – that is, only against certain people (perhaps a very large number, but less than all the world). Contractual rights are mainly of the latter type; my contract of employment creates claim-rights and correlative duties connecting me and my employer but no one else (although others may have legal duties not to interfere knowingly with the performance of the contract). I have a legal duty to my employer to teach Thursday's 6 PM class, but no duty to you, the reader, to teach that class.

Permissions, by their nature, tend to hold against all the world, or *in rem*. Permissions tend to be *in rem* because they consist simply in the absence of a legal duty not to do something, and that absence of legal duty, normally, is an absence of a duty to *anybody* not to do that thing. My permission to scratch my nose is just the absence of any legal duty not to scratch my nose; but, again, by entering a contract I might lose that permission against the person I contract with – suppose I am an actor and scratching my nose detracts from my performances. In this case,

I have no permission to scratch my nose vis-à-vis my employer, although I retain it against the rest of the world (we don't need to grapple with the question whether now to call my permission to scratch my nose *in personam* or *in rem*: the important point is simply the relational nature of each Hohfeldian element).

Another important point about permissions is that, because they are logically independent of claim-rights, they do not entail claim-rights. This means that, for example, I might give you a permission to eat my fortune cookie but no claim-right against my interfering with your eating my fortune cookie. If at the beginning of our Chinese meal I say, "You may have my fortune cookie," you would normally expect that I was not only giving you permission to eat my cookie *if you can* but also giving you a claim-right against my interfering with your eating the cookie by, say, snatching it up and eating it first. Perhaps I ought to have said, "You may have my fortune cookie if I don't eat it first." The distinctness of claim-rights and permissions is not a trivial point, as will become plain later when we return to moral rights and the question whether there can be a moral right to do what is morally wrong.

The bare permission to eat a fortune cookie is of considerably less value unless it is coupled with a claim-right against interference with eating it. Important legal rights, as the fortune-cookie example shows, consist of a "bundle" of Hohfeldian elements. Ownership of property, for example, will turn out to consist of a "bundle" of Hohfeldian "sticks": claim-rights, permissions, powers, and immunities and their correlates. Owning a fortune cookie means having claim-rights against interference with possession of the thing, permissions to use the thing, powers to sell, lend, or give away the thing or particular legal elements of ownership in the thing, and immunities against others' attempts to alter the contents of the "bundle of sticks" that constitutes ownership.

I have said that claim-rights and permissions are logically independent. But doesn't a claim-right entail a permission, in Hohfeld's scheme, even if a permission does not entail a claim-right? In other words, would it be possible for me to convey to you a claim-right against interfering with your eating my fortune cookie, without thereby conveying to you a permission to eat it? Giving you the permission to eat it is simply to relieve you of any duty to me not to eat it. So the question becomes, "Does giving you a claim-right against my interfering with your eating the cookie entail relieving you of the duty not to eat it?" The answer is "No," although it would be an odd circumstance. I might accomplish this by saying, "I promise not to interfere with your eating my fortune cookie, but it is my cookie and I'd rather you let it alone." My promise not to interfere gives you a claim-right against my interfering, but at the same time I hold you to your duty not to eat the cookie, so you have no permission to eat it. You do me a legal wrong by eating it even though I have surrendered any right to resist or seek redress: the claim-right does not entail the permission. I have a "right without a remedy," as a lawyer might put it. Of course, at this point, looking at the duty correlative to the right, one might want to chime in with Bentham and say, "What's a duty without enforcement?" (Or is the question, rather, "What *good* is a duty, without enforcement?" – in the same spirit as our earlier question, "What *good* is a permission without a claim-right against interference?") The logical independence of claim-rights and permissions will be of great significance as we now take up the question of the applicability of Hohfeld's scheme to rights generally – that is, to moral as well as legal rights.

Are Moral Rights "Hohfeldian"?

Can Hohfeld's scheme of distinctions be applied to rights generally? Although Hohfeld was concerned solely with the analysis of legal rights, the opinion of moral philosophers has generally been that his work reveals most, though not all, of the fundamental logical interconnections and relationships of moral rights, as well as of legal rights. Moral claim-rights are distinct from moral permissions, powers, and immunities, and each has corresponding moral correlates and moral opposites. Certain sticky issues arise (or arise more vividly), however, when Hohfeld's analysis is extended in this way, and now we turn to the most important of them.

Duty "Not to" or "Duty that"?

One issue has to do with the question of interpreting the idea of *duty*. Hohfeld considered the idea of legal duty – like the rest of his four fundamental conceptions of "legal advantage" (71) and their opposites – to be *sui generis*, and not usefully definable except by showing its relationship to other of the fundamental conceptions, and by describing concrete examples. Hohfeld's examples of duty turn out to have been of two types: (1) duties *not to interfere* with another's doing something, and (2) duties *that* some state of affairs obtain. The first type of case involved, typically, someone X's ownership of something, and someone Y's correlative duty not to interfere with X's possession and enjoyment of it. The second type of case was one in which X has a right that Y do something or make something happen.

In the second type of case, X's right correlates with something that it would be awkward to describe as Y's duty of noninterference. If, for example, Y has promised to deliver 100 widgets to X by Monday, it would be odd to say that X's right to the delivery of the widgets is equivalent to Y's duty not to interfere with Y's delivery of the widgets. This is a contract example, but the same type of legal duty could arise by common law or by statute – say, a duty that parents support their minor children, or a duty that one not sell misbranded drugs. In these cases, children have a claim-right to support from their parents and consumers have a claim-right to proper labels against merchants, but it would be very odd to say that parents have a correlative duty not to interfere with their support of their children, or that merchants have a duty not to interfere with their offering properly branded drugs for sale to their customers.

On the other hand, it would be quite easy to think of the first type of case as consisting of special instances of the second type. A duty that such-and-such be the case is general enough to encompass a duty that someone not interfere with the right-holder's doing or peacefully enjoying something. A duty of noninterference, in other words, is just a special instance of a duty that such-and-such be the case, as in: "It is Y's duty that it be the case that Y does not interfere with X's φ-ing." This may seem a trivial point, but it isn't. It undermines the view, held by many, that rights are in a fundamental, conceptual, way *rights against interference*, and that their correlatives are *duties of noninterference*. This may be true, but nothing in Hohfeld's analysis requires or supports it. If, as many believe, rights are in some sense fundamentally "negative" – that is, claim-rights against interference or coercion – that has to be shown in some way other than by appeal to Hohfeld.

Legal "Interference" versus Moral

Another issue that arises when we consider generalizing Hohfeld is whether his analysis is helpful in deciding what constitutes a breach of duty. To say that a duty is a duty that such-and-such be the case leaves it wide open as to what the duty requires, but once the "such-and-such" is specified, detecting a breach is as straightforward as determining whether or not such-and-such is in fact the case. If it is, the duty has been complied with: if not, the duty has been breached. With respect to duties of noninterference, the specification of what the duty requires may or may not nail down what will and what will not constitute a breach of duty. For, example, my claim-right to eat my fortune cookie entails your duty not to interfere with my eating it. But what, exactly, counts as interference? Suppose you trick me into not eating my fortune cookie; you tell me that we have to leave the restaurant immediately or we'll miss the start of the movie we've decided to see. In our haste, I forget my fortune cookie. Have you infringed my claim-right? Would it matter if you hadn't meant to make me forget my fortune cookie?

Examples like these could be multiplied, but they seem to be of little consequence as long as we confine ourselves to the issue of *legal* rights. Causing another a loss, even deliberately, does not constitute a legal wrong unless the loss is caused in some way that is legally recognized. If I open a fast-food restaurant next door to yours with the express purpose of driving you out of business, and do so, I have infringed no right of yours. Competition and interference are not the same thing in Anglo-American legal systems. In the fortune-cookie case, nothing I've done even comes close to infringing your legal rights unless I've deliberately misled you; and even if I did deliberately mislead you, a court would have to find that I had interfered with you in a legally cognizable way. The question of legal interference might involve exploring analogies to earlier, decided cases, and there may be some legal controversy lurking here, but I think it is unlikely that my trick would be found to have infringed any legal right of yours; but that would not settle the separate question whether your *moral* right was infringed.

Obviously, one crucial part of understanding moral rights is to understand how to draw the distinction between interference and all other conduct. If the force or "punch" of a moral claim-right is the duty of noninterference it imposes on others, then the measure of that punch will vary, depending in part on how broadly or narrowly "interference" is construed. American law generally allows me, for example, to build a forty-foot "spite" fence for the sole purpose of throwing a shadow across my neighbor's swimming pool. Legally, there's no interference with my neighbor's property. But morally? Courts themselves often imply that moral rights are more extensive than what the law has yet recognized. (In England, the law would be on my neighbor's side.) But clearly the law has sometimes recognized legal rights that have no moral counterpart (think of slavery). Bentham's complaint about the indeterminacy and uncertainty of natural rights, in contrast to legal rights, has to be answered.

Once we step outside a body of settled legal doctrine, the issue of what constitutes and what does not constitute interference with someone's doing something becomes inescapably controversial. One influential view is that moral rights are "negative" rights in the sense that they are claim-rights against "interference" interpreted very narrowly to mean physical force against the person or threats thereof. Beating you up, or threatening to, infringes your right to the "negative" liberty of being free of such treatment. But nothing else counts as interference, even if it is intended to, and does, have disastrous consequences for someone. This very narrow view is usually relaxed a little in order to count fraud and slander as interferences, even though they do not normally involve force or threats of force.

The view that our moral claim-rights are to be understood primarily as curbs on interference by means of force or fraud, and that the point of such claim-rights is to protect a privileged sphere of individual liberty, is often referred to as a *classical liberal* or *libertarian* view, or as a view based on *negative rights* or *negative liberty*. In contrast, any asserted moral right to assistance in distress, or to a minimum level of subsistence, or to respect, for example, would be classified as an assertion of a "positive" right, on this type of view. If you are lying unconscious and face down in a puddle of water, and I walk past you whistling a tune, leaving you to drown, I have not infringed any negative right of yours to be free of interference (on this sort of view), although I will have violated your (asserted) positive right to assistance in an emergency.

Some of those who have argued that "interference" just means "interference with negative liberty" have drawn breathtaking conclusions from that interpretation – such as that *there is no* moral right to positive assistance, and that forcing anyone to give assistance is, almost by definition, an infringement of her moral right to negative liberty. This approach has clear-cut, if rather harsh, consequences. Other approaches are possible as well, which may involve a more complicated story about what interference is. One such approach might view my failure to provide an "easy rescue" to an unconscious person drowning in the puddle at my feet as an interference with his liberty, and an interference of a very grave kind – for by denying him the easy rescue to which he is morally entitled I deprive him of life itself and the enjoyment of all its liberties. But this approach may have its own set of awkward consequences. If not providing an easy rescue is interference, why isn't failure to provide a difficult and risky rescue interference as well? And if the bystander's failure to rescue is interference, why isn't the failure of persons elsewhere likewise an interference? Where does the interference end? Are all of us, right this instant, interfering with the liberty of famine victims around the world, whom we are failing to aid? And are those victims, reciprocally, interfering with our liberty by the very fact of their need? Treating failure to lend "positive" assistance as *interference* seems to require some line-drawing in order to avoid the absurd result that everyone is interfering with everyone all the time.

We will return to the issue of interference in Chapters 10 and 11. The point here is that because the only ambition of Hohfeld's analysis was to account for legal rights, it could simply assume a background body of legal doctrine to fill out the idea of interference. But those (like ourselves) who seek a more general account will not have the benefit of that fall-back assumption as we try to push out beyond the relatively well-marked territory of law. Although, as we have seen, it is logically appealing to treat duties of noninterference as simply a species of duty that such-and-such be the case, there is considerable sentiment in favor of the position that rights have primarily to do with protection against interference rather than with the provision of "positive" benefits. For ease of exposition, I will provisionally accept the "the correlative duty is one of noninterference" reading, until the time comes to revisit the question, "What is interference?"

Do Hohfeldian Duties Entail Rights?

Another issue arises when we try to extend Hohfeld's conceptions beyond law to morality. We know that, for Hohfeld, to say that *the correlative* of a claim-right is a duty is to say that a claim-right *entails* a duty, but is it also to say that a duty entails a claim-right? Does the entailment go both ways between the correlatives, or one way only? Because duty is a relational concept for Hohfeld, asking this question is just to ask whether whenever Y has a duty to X, X has a claim-right with respect to Y. Hohfeld has no place to fit duties that aren't duties *to*, or at least duties *with respect to* some assignable person (natural or legal). So, from a Hohfeldian perspective, the question, "Do duties entail claim-rights?" is the same as the question, "If Y has a duty to (or with respect to) X that p, does it necessarily follow that X has a claim-right against Y that p?"

It is not clear how Hohfeld would have answered this question. Anglo-American legal doctrine is ambiguous about recognizing legal duties with respect to persons who have no remedy against the duty-bearer, but, if Hohfeld had any impulse to take a stand on the issue, there is nothing in his writing that commits him either way. But there is reason to doubt that the answer can be "Yes, all duties entail claim-rights" if we are speaking of moral rather than specifically legal rights. A standard example used to show that moral duties don't logically entail moral claim-rights is the duty of *charity*. Everyone has a duty to be charitable, and in certain circumstances some individuals X might even be said to have duties to be charitable to certain persons Y. Imagine that a starving, badly injured hiker falls unconscious outside the door of your luxurious mountain chalet – surely you have a moral, if not a legal, duty to help her. Even so, many would hesitate to say that such persons Y would have a right to X's charity. Saying Y has a right to X's help even seems inconsistent with characterizing what X does as acting charitably.

We have encountered the term "imperfect" duty used to mark the category of duties that carry no correlative claim-right, and the duty the Good Samaritan discharges is of this type. It doesn't matter to us here whether we think that imperfect duties are imperfect because they are owed to no one in particular, or because they are not duties that must be discharged on each and every occasion, or because they are not enforceable. The important point here is that it seems that, in the case of moral rights anyway, there may be more to Y's having a right against X than X's having a duty with respect to Y.

But many people, when they ponder this example, are inclined to say that the hiker *does* have a moral right to assistance, and that legal systems that do not recognize a coordinate legal right to assistance are to that extent morally defective. Philosopher Joel Feinberg would allow those who want to insist that beneficial duties always generate claim-rights to speak of rights in a "manifesto sense" (67). A "manifesto right" is not really a right but something that some advocate as a candidate for recognition as a right. It is not easy to resolve this disagreement without seeming arbitrary. Although there is a clear sense in which it can be true that there morally ought to be a legal right, where there is none, it is hard to understand how it can be true that there morally ought to be a moral right unless, in fact, that moral right exists. Recognition may be a necessary condition of the existence of a legal right (as legal positivists hold), but it can't be a necessary condition of the existence of a moral right (unless morality itself is, at bottom, conventional).

A parallel question may be asked about the relationship between moral permissions and moral "no-rights" – a moral no-right being simply the absence of a moral right. Applying Hohfeld's table of correlatives to the moral case, if X enjoys a moral permission to φ, with respect to a person Y, then that person Y has no moral claim-right to X's not φ-ing. But does the converse hold? That is, from the fact that Y has no moral claim-right that X not φ, does it follow that X has a moral permission, with respect to Y, to φ? That seems doubtful. Think again of the hiker example: Even those who insist that the hiker has no moral right – except perhaps in the "manifesto" sense – to your help, may want to deny that it follows that you are morally permitted to withhold it from her.

Group Rights versus Individual Rights

Another feature of Hohfeld's analysis is that it is intended to apply equally to both "natural" and "legal" persons. A natural person is an individual. A legal person is not necessarily a human being but may be a legally recognized entity such as a corporation or partnership. Legal persons may simply *be* a certain group of individuals – a two-person partnership, for example – but it needn't be. A corporation, as a legal person, may survive the total replacement, many times over, of the legal persons (individuals or otherwise) who first formed it. All legal persons depend on the existence of individuals in order to act, but a legal person may have interests adverse to those of the individuals who own it or act for it. For Hohfeld, "group" right-holders and "group" rights were perfectly familiar. True, Hohfeld never *denied* that assertions of such group rights are in the end logically equivalent to some set of statements about the legal advantages enjoyed by individuals. The point is that his analysis of rights did not by itself commit him to asserting that equivalence.

In any more-than-rudimentary legal system, there will be rules that govern the scope of legal personhood, and rules governing the creation, continuity, and dissolution of non-natural legal persons. Extending Hohfeld from the realm of legal rights to that of moral rights will mean leaving these limiting legal rules behind. Nothing rules out the possibility that Hohfeldian moral rights might be held by right-holders other than individual human beings. If the gate is to be regulated, nothing in Hohfeld's conceptions is designed to do that job. This leaves open the possibility of asserting group rights held by nations, tribes, local communities, linguistic communities, cultural groups, and "affinity" groups of all sorts, whether or not they are legally recognized or internally organized. This openness means that an account of moral group right-holders is likely to be much messier than an account of legal group right-holders. Moreover, also left open is the possibility of asserting "majority" rights capable of counterbalancing and effectively canceling any and all conflicting individual rights of those in the minority. The value of individual moral rights is diminished if our conception of rights is not more discriminating with respect to purported group rights.

To summarize, Hohfeld's distinctions, developed to analyze rights discourse in the legal domain, promise to be useful as tools in our more general inquiry into the nature of rights. The elementary legal notions – claim-right, permission, power, and immunity; duty, no-right, liability, and disability – each have recognizable analogues in the moral realm. Moreover, exploring the relation of correlativity between elementary notions in the moral domain uncovers a number of issues having an interest that their legal counterparts may lack. In particular, Hohfeld's distinctions allow us to ask what sort of bundle of elements a moral right must, at a minimum, contain. This will be of great help in Chapter 8, where we take up the question whether there can be a right to do wrong. We have also seen that correlativity may be interpreted either as a one-way relation of entailment, or as a two-way relation of mutual entailment. Which interpretation we adopt may be crucially important in deciding whether those to whom duties are owed may properly demand their performance as a matter of right.

PART TWO

The Second
Expansionary Era

6

The Universal Declaration, and a Revolt Against Utilitarianism

The end of the Second World War marked a watershed in the history of rights. In the wake of the massive civilian suffering caused during the war – much of it knowingly and even intentionally inflicted, and on a scale without historical precedent – there was a resurgence of interest in international cooperation to prevent war and, failing that, to mitigate its severity. The United Nations was founded in 1945, and in 1948 its General Assembly unanimously adopted the Universal Declaration of Human Rights (the Soviet bloc, Saudi Arabia, and South Africa abstaining). Its preamble contained the following recitations:

> *Whereas* recognition of the inherent dignity and of the equal and inalienable rights of all members of the human family is the foundation of freedom, justice and peace in the world,
>
> *Whereas* disregard and contempt for human rights have resulted in barbarous acts which have outraged the conscience of mankind. . . .

Now, Therefore,

The General Assembly
proclaims

This universal declaration of human rights as a common standard of achievement for all peoples and nations. . . .

The Universal Declaration contains thirty articles, whose main provisions are as follows:

Article 1 states that "All human beings are born free and equal in dignity and rights. They are endowed with reason and conscience. . . ."

Article 3 declares that "Everyone has the right to life, liberty and security of person" – echoing Locke and Jefferson but substituting "security of person" for Locke's "property" and Jefferson's "happiness" (Article 17 does recognize the right to own property).

Article 7 declares a principle of equality before the law and equal protection against discrimination, which is fleshed out by the recitation in Article 2 of forbidden grounds of discrimination, which include race, color, sex, language, religion, political opinion, property, and "birth or other status."

Articles 4 through 10 forbid slavery, torture, or "cruel, inhuman or degrading" punishment, and arbitrary arrest, and require a public trial and a presumption of innocence against criminal charges, which are only to be based on law existing at the time of the offense.

Articles 13 and 14 declare a right of freedom of movement and residence within a state, a right of exit and return, and a right to seek political asylum (but no right to immigrate).

Articles 18 through 21 guarantee rights to religion, opinion, thought, and expression; to assemble and to associate; to participate in free elections and to stand for office. These articles express what are often referred to as "first generation" rights, or political and civil rights, and most (but not all) have counterparts in the Bill of Rights of the U.S. Constitution.

What have been termed "second generation" rights begin to appear in Article 22, which speaks of a "right to social security" enjoyed by "everyone, as a member of society" and to "the economic, social and cultural rights indispensable for his dignity and free development of his personality." This has no counterpart in the U.S. Constitution, although the "right to work" of Article 23 has – but only in the very limited sense that one may not be dismissed from state employment without "due process of law."

Article 23 further provides, however, a right to "just and favorable" working conditions, "protection against unemployment," "equal pay for equal work," for "just and favorable remuneration," and a right to join a trade union. None of these has a counterpart in U.S. constitutional law, although as a matter of ordinary legislation (which is always subject to repeal), many have statutory counterparts.

Similarly, Article 25's right to an "adequate" standard of living, "including food, clothing, housing and medical and necessary social services" and Article 26's right to free education are guaranteed to U.S. citizens not as matters of constitutional right but (if at all) of legislative grace.

The most ridiculed provision of the Universal Declaration is Article 24, which recognizes a "right to rest and leisure," which requires, in particular, "reasonable limitations of working hours and periodic holidays with pay." What the *Lochner* Court in 1905 found contrary to the fundamental right to liberty is postulated by the 1948 Universal Declaration as a human right. Skeptics about the entire human-rights enterprise have seized upon Article 24 with the same sort of glee with which Bentham recited the French National Assembly's tergiversations between 1789 and 1795.

Article 30 rounds out the list by cautioning that "nothing in this Declaration may be interpreted as implying for any state, group or person any right to engage in any activity . . . aimed at the destruction of any of the rights . . . set forth herein." This caveat may have been intended to disavow any revolutionary frenzy of the sort that the French Declaration had fed.

The language of rights – amplified by the adjective "human" – once again seemed to be the only suitable means of formulating the concerns of the world-historical moment. The second expansionary period had begun.

The Post-War Resurrection of Moral and Political Philosophy

Moral and political philosophy, however, languished during the early post-war period. In Britain, Australasia, and North America, the dominant view was that *metaethics* – inquiry into the metaphysical and epistemological status of the ethical – was the proper concern of philosophy, rather than substantive theorizing "within" ethics. The traditional concerns of moral and political philosophy – inquiry into subjects such as the nature of the good and the just – were not assumed to be meaningful and worthwhile endeavors. Rather, it was questioned whether such concerns were capable of being satisfied within the boundaries set by reason, science, and the nature of language. The metaethical discussions that took place did so under the lingering influence of pre-war emotivism and logical positivism. *Emotivism* held that ethical propositions are not cognitive – not capable of being true or false – but functioned instead to express attitudes. "Murder is wrong" came to mean nothing more than "I disapprove of murder; do so as well." Adherents of *logical positivism* tended to relegate noncognitive discourse to the dustbin of intellectual history, along with myth and superstition. Obviously, in an intellectual atmosphere dominated by such views, skepticism about the possibility of meaningful *talk* about rights would tend to foreclose further thought about their nature.

On the Continent, the Cold War tended to lock the left-leaning intelligentsia into a Marxist line of thinking that continued Marx's suspicion of the bourgeois individualist proclivities of rights discourse – an attitude which the Continental left has shaken off only recently. Although Marxism has had numerous intellectual opponents, few seemed to be inclined to undertake the task of providing a theoretical foundation to support the rights rhetoric that proved so effective against the Soviet bloc's legacy of totalitarianism. The heavy hand of the Soviets in Eastern Europe, coupled with the gradual exposure of the depth of Stalin's terrorism, may have made the anti-Communist case for rights seem too easy to require much in the way of theoretical elaboration. On the other hand, as Michael Ignatieff has suggested, it may be that the Communist states' greater emphasis on the rights of employment and economic equality acted to discourage the thought that a comprehensive theory of rights would decisively favor either side in the Cold War.

In the English-speaking world, the ice that had frozen rights theory had begun to break up by the 1960s. At Oxford, H. L. A. Hart was elaborating a descriptive theory of law, which led him to inquire into the nature of legal rights, and thence into the nature of rights generally.

Also at Oxford, R. M. Hare was moving beyond an investigation of the language of morals toward an account of moral reasoning that took a utilitarian cast. And at Cambridge, Bernard Williams began an attack on the utilitarian tradition that had lain, dormant but undisturbed (since G. E. Moore's attack on naturalism at the turn of the twentieth century) in the snowbank of indifference that had covered substantive moral philosophy. Rights had already begun their ascendancy in the sphere of political rhetoric, and it was only a matter of time before philosophers warmed once again to their traditional task as critics, especially after 1971, the year in which John Rawls's monumental *A Theory of Justice* appeared.

Rawls's theory cannot be faithfully summarized here; for our purposes it will be enough to describe it as a major representative of a *contractualist* approach to moral questions. Contractualism, as the name suggests, continues the social contract idea inherited from Grotius, Hobbes, and Locke. What is distinctive, though, about modern contractualism is its hostility to the utilitarian tradition, and for this reason among others, the name it is quickest to invoke is Kant's. Contractualism represents a confluence of certain themes or – better – certain theoretical suppositions, and that of a social contract is only one of them.

Contractualists reject utilitarian and other consequentialist approaches for a reason Williams articulated: They do not take seriously the distinction between persons. "*Consequentialism*" is the term popularized by Elizabeth Anscombe to describe a genus of moral theory of which utilitarianism had been by far the most prominent species. Consequentialism equates duty with maximizing good consequences, but, unlike utilitarianism, does not insist that the goodness of consequences be evaluated solely in terms of utility or any other mere proxy for Bentham's "sovereign masters," pleasure and pain. Contractualism's concerns echo those of the early critics of utilitarianism, but are more probing. The problem is not merely that an aggregating approach such as utilitarianism seems capable of licensing outrageous behavior in the name of the greater good. Rule utilitarian and other indirect consequentialist devices might suffice to forestall such objections in practical application of theory. The problem is deeper, for even these indirect and rule-focused strategies subordinate the individual in an objectionable way. To put the point differently, even if a consequentialist theory could be subtly crafted so that its demands coincided precisely with those of commonsense morality, that theory would still be objectionable.

For one thing, the congruence between the demands of consequentialist moral theory and those of commonsense morality looks jury-rigged and unstable. An adequate moral theory should not merely echo our pretheoretical moral intuitions, but should also explain what is meritorious about them, and it should organize them for us and be available to guide us when unclear or novel cases arise. Lurking within consequentialist theories is an intrinsic tendency to subordinate the individual to the greater good, to underplay distributive concerns such as fairness and equality, and to treat our individual existences as significant only as repositories of a quantum of good to be aggregated with the good accumulating in the lives of others. Persons are otherwise without significance for consequentialism – their lives are without intrinsic value, and they are valuable only as receptacles of and vehicles for the good.

This line of objection links up with another. A moral theory should explain and justify morality's claim to authority over us. Morality pretends to be able to override our desires and inclinations, and to tell us how we should live our lives regardless of what we might think about the matter. But if my inclination is to do one thing and morality commands me to do another – what reason have I to follow morality's lights rather than my own? Because morality tracks the greater good? Very well, but what reason do I have to prefer the greater good that is not mine, to a lesser good that I will realize and value? Simply to avoid sanctions? But in that case, it would have to be admitted that the sanction provides the reason, not morality itself, and morality collapses into prudence. Consequentialist theories, such as utilitarianism, fail to explain how morality can motivate and guide individual action, except in the rare (or nonexistent) case of those selfless ones whose only motive is to bring about the greatest good.

Contractualism that is of Hobbesian inspiration tries to explain morality as consisting of rules that rational individuals have reason to adopt and follow, even if they happen to care about nothing but what is important to themselves. It is an effort, in other words, to explain morality in a way that relies on no authority, other than that of reason, over our sovereign and intrinsically valuable selves. Morality, on a contractualist view, is enlightened self-interest – or, more accurately, *enlightened interest of the self* – since nothing in contractualism requires the self to be interested only in itself, but merely that it be interested only in its own interests, which will normally extend to include the well-being of others, if not of all others. Contractualism differs from prudence in that the actor has a reason other than avoidance of an external sanction to comply with moral rules. The reason is that the moral rule is one that a rational agent would freely impose upon himself.

Contractualists, just as much as consequentialists, are sensitive to the many invidious comparisons that might be drawn between ethics and science. Contractualists have enlisted a branch of social science – the theory of rational choice – in service of their moral theorizing. By capitalizing on the results of rational choice theory, contractualists have hoped to achieve two things: First, to explain how familiar moral rules might be rationalized by appeal to nothing beyond principles of rational individual choice; second, to avoid relying on either (1) distinctively moral axioms, whose ontological and epistemological status would be questionable, or (2) aggregative principles of social choice, which would introduce undesirable complexity and at the same time threaten to subordinate the individual to the social.

On a contractualist view, moral rights are simply those constraints that we, as rational actors, would place on any aggregative or social-choice principles we might also find rational to adopt. If, for example, we would find it rational to enter into social arrangements for the purpose of increasing our safety and economic well-being, we would also find it rational to insist on certain rights against others and against the public authority in their pursuit of such goals. Yes, it is in my individual interest that there be a legislature, police, and a court system, but, no, it is not in my individual interest that the state so constructed have unlimited authority over me – for I might be unjustly accused, or be targeted by legislation intended to serve the interests of my economic rivals, and so forth.

Moreover, a moral (and even a legal) rule of limited beneficence might be justified on a contractualist basis. It might be me who winds up unconscious, face down in a shallow pool, and thus me who would benefit by being rescued. Therefore it would be rational for me to assent to a rule requiring the easy rescue. The costs it would impose on me are minimal – the rule requires me to rescue another only if it is easy; and the benefits great – my life might be saved by the rule's being complied with. But, notice, it might not be rational for me to adopt a general rule of beneficence that looked anything at all like the "greatest happiness" principle of the utilitarians. The "greatest happiness" principle might subordinate my life utterly to the service of others, and benefit me only negligibly. (I might also find it annoying and infantilizing to have others trying to help me whenever they think that's the best they can do with their time.) So a contractualist approach might be able to resolve a tension at the very basis of our moral thinking – that between doing good and living our own lives. From the impersonal standpoint that even an indirect consequentialism demands, it is hard to see how to secure a principle of limited beneficence, because the limit (as Godwin saw) has no basis other than our knowledge and means, and as those grow, the limit erodes. But from the self-interested standpoint that contractualism makes basic, beneficence makes sense, yet its limit is firmly fixed by a principle of rational choice that centers on the agent and his own values and projects.

Contractualism promises to ground and justify moral rights in a way that properly reflects the primacy of the individual while, at the same time, genuinely restraining the individual without subordinating her to goals she may not share. The idea is to show how the bounds of morality are determined by reason alone, without appealing to controversial ideas of the good, without appealing to a capacity for sympathy, and without appealing to divine ordinances or to "nature" in the manner of natural-rights rhetoric. The derivation of rights proceeds in three stages: At the first stage, a choice situation is characterized in general terms which reflect what we might call "the circumstances of morality" – that is, the circumstance that there exists a number of individual, rational agents, who possess certain needs and capacities, such that those capacities are not infinite and those needs are not constantly satisfied. An important feature of these circumstances is the possibility, even the inevitability, of conflict between persons. Conflicts will be due in part to the differences in information and situation between individuals, but in part also to differences between what individuals value.

At the second stage, principles of rational decision are identified, which are to govern the process by which individuals would choose moral rules governing their interactions in the circumstances of morality.

Idealized decision principles from mathematically rigorous theories of rational choice come into play here. Certain principles will seem almost trivial: rational agents will seek consistency in their beliefs and their preferences will be transitive – that is, rational agents will not at a given time prefer C to A if they prefers A to B and B to C. Rational agents will have to deal with risk and uncertainty, and so principles have to be stipulated to govern their reasoning in this respect. Of particular importance is the rational agent's attitude toward risk. Individuals might be represented as straightforward maximizers of individual net-expected utility – that is, as preferring the choice having the highest payoff after discounting for the chance of the payoff's not being realized. Alternatively, individuals might be represented as minimizers of "worst case" individual disutility – that is, as avoiders of choices that involve catastrophic, even though unlikely, negative outcomes for themselves.

At the third stage, the contractualist derives rules that rational individuals would agree to by applying principles of rational choice in the circumstances of morality. A sample derivation might go this way: There is a moral rule against committing fraud, even where an agent can attain his most highly valued outcome only by employing fraud. Why would anyone agree to such a rule? Answer: Rational agents perceive that in a world in which fraud is practiced, they stand to lose more by being defrauded than they stand to gain by practicing it, and so they agree to foreswear the use of fraud on the condition that others do so as well. Other rational agents, reasoning similarly, agree to foreswear the use of fraud on the same conditions. Further, rational agents agree to institute sanctions against fraud to deter deviations from the norm of "no fraud." A norm of "no fraud" would thus be agreed to, no contrary norm of laissez-faire toward fraud could be agreed to, and the absence of a norm would not be a preferred outcome for rational agents. Therefore the moral rule against fraud is compelled by reason. QED.

As sketched, the contractualist account of the moral rule against fraud is open to an obvious objection: What reason does a self-interested agent have to comply with the rule even when he calculates that he can commit fraud with impunity? This is not the place to trace the efforts contractualists have made to resolve this basic difficulty, often referred to as *the compliance problem.* Nor is this the place to address the difficulty posed by the economist John Harsanyi's (1977) contractualist argument leading to the adoption of utilitarianism – obviously, contractualism fails as an alternative to consequentialism if on its own terms it could justify a version of consequentialism. Instead, for our purposes, it is more important to notice some other deficiencies of any attempt to give a purely contractualist account of rights.

One difficulty arises from the fact that the contractualist structure generates intuitively repugnant outcomes unless the original choice situation is adjusted to guarantee fairness. A second difficulty flows from the first. What account can be given of the fairness conditions that contractualists have to build in to their structure in order to avoid the first difficulty? If those fairness conditions encapsulate independent moral requirements that look anything at all like rights, then (much as Samuel Clarke (1705) argued against Hobbes) the contractualist enterprise will have failed insofar as it aspires to provide a foundation for rights. Rather, it will appear that the contractualist apparatus presupposes, instead of explains, moral rights.

Go back to the first stage, at which the contractualist specifies the initial choice situation facing rational agents. Suppose that some agents are vastly more powerful – cleverer and physically stronger – than others. Hobbes made the contrary assumption, but others (notably Thrasymachus, Socrates's adversary in the *Republic*) would not. A person of average or less-than-average intelligence might benefit from the moral rule against fraud, but why would a supremely clever person agree to such a rule if her decision to agree were based solely on what was in her own interests? The answer has to be that she would not. But this admission would be fatal to the contractualist enterprise; can it be avoided?

One move would be to provide a backing for Hobbes's assumption of the rough equality of people – turning it into a conclusion rather than an assumption. This move seems unpromising in view of the fact that people do in fact possess aptitudes in different degrees, and (as Nietzsche disparagingly observed) moral rules are supposed to bind everybody, not just the unremarkable. A different move would be to admit that people actually possess aptitudes in a variety of degrees, but to stipulate that rational choosers are to be deprived of knowledge of their own particular powers in the initial choice-situation. By the same token, choosers are not to know what their own values are, to foreclose the distorting possibility that choosers might try to rig the moral rules, or veto them, to advance their own personal agendas. This is the idea behind John Rawls's celebrated "veil of ignorance" (1971, 136–42).

The veil of ignorance device seems to be a promising way of dealing with the fact of human variety – Thrasymachus would not have been likely to define justice as the interest of the stronger unless he counted himself among the stronger. But this way of treating the first difficulty leads immediately into the second: What reason would lead a rational agent to agree to choose rules from behind a veil of ignorance? What reason would induce a person to make a choice based on less than the fullest relevant information? Reason itself, evidently, cannot motivate this stipulation – but then, what would? If the answer is that only in this way will the contractualist procedure be *fair*, then the question becomes, Whence this notion of *fairness*? If reason itself does not impose it, we want to know where it came from.

But we want to know another thing too. Is fairness itself a source of rights? If fairness itself is a source of rights, and the contractualist account presupposes fairness, then it seems to follow that contractualism presupposes, and therefore cannot provide a foundation for, rights. Contractualism gets things backward: to paraphrase Judith Thomson's observation (1990) about the contractualist conception of wrongness, we would choose what's fair because it's fair – what's fair isn't fair because we would choose it. If it is acceptable to say that individuals have a right to reject putative moral rules that are derived *unfairly*, then rights are functioning as constraints on a procedure of which they are supposed to be the outcomes.

It is not implausible to think of fairness as a source of rights in and of itself. In fact, H. L. A. Hart (1955) posed the question, *Are There Any Natural Rights?* and suggested that something like a right to fair treatment would be a natural right, if anything were. According to Hart, when one sufficiently benefits from others' having submitted to a rule for mutual benefit, then one has a duty to abide by that rule *whether or not one would be compelled by reason to agree to it.* And this duty would correlate with a right held by others to expect, even to exact, one's compliance. Hart's idea has been the subject of extensive debate, which would lead us far afield were we to follow it. For our purposes, it is enough to observe that this purported right to fair treatment, if it exists, escapes the contractualist net, and may even turn out to be a necessary extracontractualist supplement to any contractualist theory (recall the "compliance problem").

In sum, contractualism has not furnished an adequate foundation for rights. This is, in a way, not surprising. Even Hobbes represented people in a state of nature as already possessing two sorts of Hohfeldian rights: permissions to do what is thought necessary to survive, and powers to surrender these permissions. Modern contractualist efforts – despite their determination and ingenuity – have so far failed to reconstruct morality on a foundation of rational self-interest. Rights are not the whole of morality, and contractualism perhaps need not explain the whole of morality – but it turns out that contractualism cannot explain the part of morality that is the domain of rights. Once a framework of rights is assumed, of course, it is probable that the contractualist style of thinking will illuminate some of the patterns of use that people make of their rights – but that is another inquiry.

None of these criticisms has been unnoticed by contractualists. The preferred way of dealing with them – a way that is said to respond to a Kantian rather than a Hobbesian inspiration – is to introduce the idea of the *reasonable*, as contrasted to the *rational*. The difference between the two concepts is that the reasonable includes a "willingness to propose and honor fair terms of cooperation" (Rawls 1993, 49 n1), whereas the rational need not. Reasonableness in this sense means taking the interests of others into account insofar as it would be unfair not to; but it does not require giving any weight at all to "the general good as such" (Rawls 1993, 50). Being reasonable additionally means being motivated not to cheat or free-ride once fair terms of cooperation have been settled on.

A contractualist theory of rights built on a notion of the reasonable raises new issues. One is this: The reasonable is an "idea with moral content," and contractualists confess that the invocation of it "invites the charge of circularity" (Scanlon 1998, 194). The charge of circularity would appear to be particularly apt with respect to the moral right to fair treatment. Contractualist reasonableness is defined in terms of fairness, and so contractualism seems to presuppose, rather than to generate, the right to fair treatment. This worry is aggravated by the fact that other moral notions, such as the general good, are excluded from contractualist reasonableness. Why is it unreasonable to treat others unfairly but reasonable to ignore the general good, or to ignore anything at all that a consequentialist would take into account?

Another question has to do with the relationship between the rational and the reasonable. Rawls argues that the reasonable is not derivable from the rational but the two are "complementary ideas" (1993, 52). Why, one wonders, does the reasonable not simply replace the rational in the contractualist framework? The answer is that "merely reasonable agents would have no ends of their own" to be furthered by cooperation (Rawls 1993, 52). But this response raises further questions: If agents must have some end suitable for furthering by cooperation, why is that end not simply fairness itself, or fair cooperation itself? And if the promotion of fairness or of fair cooperation, standing alone, is simply not nourishing enough as a motivating end, why then not "the general good as such," especially if the general good can be understood in terms that take not just some account, but full account, of the interests of all? If the answer is that contractualism would then cease to be genuinely opposed to consequentialism, one may begin to wonder whether resistance to consequentialism, rather than some reconciliation with it, is worth the special effort.

Accounting for fairness is a stumbling block not only for contractualism, but also for its opponent, consequentialism. Consequentialism deals with fairness by having it count in the evaluation of outcomes, along with other factors such as well-being. The best outcome, from a consequentialist perspective, will be one that may or may not be fair – that will depend on what other factors are counted, and their relative weights. For a rule-consequentialist, there may or may not be a right to fair treatment: whether there is or not will depend on whether the best rule is one that assures fairness to a great-enough degree for it to be worth calling a *right*. (The degree of protection rights afford is the subject of subsequent chapters.) There is no prior guarantee that the rule that assures the best outcome will be a rule that is fair – unless of course we decide that fairness is the only measure by which to judge outcomes, and that seems unlikely. Given a choice between a smaller fair share and a larger unfair share, most of us will first want to know: How much larger is the unfair share? And we will ask similar kinds of questions when evaluating the whole. This shows that fairness (like equality) is but one value among many.

Kantian contractualism seems to *ensure* fairness because of the way it builds fairness in "up front," so to speak. But does it? That will depend on how the reasonable and the rational are permitted to interact. "Rational me" may be willing to give up some degree of fairness in order to get more of something else I want. If the rational can outweigh the reasonable, then the contractualist rule may very closely resemble the rule-consequentialist rule. If, on the other hand, "Reasonable me" has absolute priority over "Rational me," fair rules are guaranteed, but (as noted before) the right to fair treatment seems to have been presupposed, rather than generated, by the contractualist method.

CHAPTER

7

The Nature of Rights
"Choice" Theory and "Interest" Theory

In our thinking about rights, we have to try to avoid confusing questions of two different kinds, one of which has been called "conceptual," and the other "justificatory." Conceptual questions are questions about what rights *are*, what their makeup is, and what follows from an assertion that *X* has a right of such-and-such a description. Hohfeld's work is an example of conceptual inquiry in its purest form. Justificatory questions, in contrast, focus on the grounds for, and reasons behind, the distribution of rights. Granted that a right is a certain kind of thing, why should we think that any exist? What grounds could there be for assigning rights? What purposes do rights serve, and could we do without them?

The distinction between the conceptual and the justificatory is not razor-sharp, and often the two exert influence on each other. Our conceptual picture of what a right *is* has been shaped by factors that involve judging what a right would have to look like to be worth having. Making this kind of judgment goes beyond simply registering what might or might not sound "odd" to our ears as a matter of ordinary usage. If, for example, a right were a mere Hohfeldian permission to φ, it might seem to be a trivial thing unless it were coupled with a permission *not* to φ. If we want a term, we could call this simple Hohfeldian molecule an *option*, or *bilateral liberty*, though sometimes I may simply call it a permission, with the understanding that it is "bilateral." Take this thought to the next step: What justifies us in thinking that anyone has a permission to do anything? Recall that Godwin denied this, for a permission in this sense is precisely what he disparaged as an "active" right. For Godwin, we have a duty to perform that act which will bring about the greatest good, and a duty to omit all other acts, and thus we never have a permission (in the "bilateral" sense). A dispute with Godwin on this issue will not be a merely conceptual one, because its justificatory aspects will ultimately influence the conceptual positions of the parties. People are rarely satisfied merely to note conceptual subtleties; even Hohfeld was partial to the claim-right as the only right properly so-called.

The conceptual and the justificatory are mixed up to an even greater degree today, when we find ourselves well into what I have termed the second expansionary period. Many people have been alarmed that rights-discourse has been debased by conceptual clumsiness. Too many moral issues are being framed, inappropriately, in terms of rights issues, or so some fear. This could lead to a devaluation of rights and a consequent loss of their distinctive contribution to our moral thinking. Animal rights, fetal rights, group rights, environmental rights, and so on are phrases that are feared to generate more heat than light. Accordingly, more than a few thinkers have called for greater conceptual meticulousness, and have proposed conceptual analyses that would cut down on the proliferation of rights claims.

Interest Theory of Legal Rights

At this point, recall Bentham's definition of a legal right in terms of a beneficial duty. This somewhat vague formula seems compatible with Tom Paine's view that Man "acquires a knowledge of his [natural] rights by attending justly to his interest . . ." (178) or with Burke's, that the "rights of men . . . are their advantages. . . ." The kernel of the idea is that rights are justified by the interest of the right-holder: that is their function and *raison d'être.* I have been calling this idea *Interest Theory*, although the term "Benefit Theory" is sometimes used. On an Interest Theory, rights exist to serve relevant interests of the right-holder, and different, specific types of Interest Theory may vary according to what "interest" is taken to be relevant. This is not to say that the interests of others or of society do not count; it is merely to focus on the function that rights have of protecting the right-holder's interests, rather than interests generally. In this way, Interest Theory marks the medieval distinction between subjective and objective right.

Interest Theory, so stated, has both a conceptual dimension and a justificatory dimension. The conceptual implications of Interest Theory are fairly modest. Only beings capable of having interests are candidate rights-holders, but within the category of beings with interests, Interest Theory per se does not draw any boundaries. If animals have interests – say, in avoiding suffering – then there is no conceptual barrier to our entertaining the question whether animals have moral rights, and what rights those are, if any. So also with fetuses, social groups, inanimate objects, artifacts, and so on. Interest Theory does little conceptual filtering, and authorizes a wide range of debate about interests and their importance. Nor does Interest Theory predetermine how the interests of a putative right-holder are to be taken into account – in particular, it does not exclude either rule utilitarian or contractualist approaches to evaluating interests. It does, however, sit uncomfortably with act-utilitarian or act-consequentialist thinking. Interest Theory accords a modicum of magic to the pronoun "me" when the right-holder is the referent of the pronoun. As we have seen, an act-consequentialist views the right-holder's interests as *nothing but* another input, while a rule-consequentialist can justifiably build rules around the interests of rights-holding individuals. If the best rule turns out to be one that protects certain interests of certain creatures, then that rule has the blessing both of Interest Theory and of rule-consequentialism. But notice, for an act-utilitarian, the fact that a certain act will protect the interests of any *specific* individual can never furnish a *specially significant* reason in favor of it.

Interest Theory does not, by itself, identify or distinguish among interests. It does not tell us what interests are, or whether all are important enough to generate correlative duties. For that matter, Interest Theory does not tell us what must be the contents of the Hohfeldian molecule that constitutes a moral right. Bentham assumed that the minimum content of a legal right was what we would call a Hohfeldian claim-right, with its correlative duty. But if interests are of moral significance, perhaps they are capable of generating more complex and robust molecules. If, for example, my interest in survival is sufficient to generate a claim-right against all others that they not kill or seriously injure me, how could it not be sufficient to impose on others a duty to punish violations of my claim-right? And if my interest is sufficient to do that, might it not also be strong enough to generate a duty to compensate me for any injuries I might suffer by violation of that right? Or a duty to provide financial assistance to those who might otherwise be tempted to rob me in order to support themselves? Where does it end? Interest Theory exhibits a kind of generative power that many find attractive, but others find disturbing.

Choice Theory of Legal Rights

Interest Theory is not the only candidate, however. Recall Austin's departure from Bentham's analysis of a legal right. For Austin, a legal right might or might not be beneficial to the right-holder, but the acid test of right-holding is the availability of a remedy for a breach of the duty correlative to the right. Austin's thought was a precursor of the *Choice Theory* (sometimes called the "Will" Theory) of legal rights, elaborated in the latter half of the twentieth century by H. L. A. Hart in England and Carl Wellman in the United States. Choice Theory (again, note the fact that this is a family of theories, within which differences will be found) presents both conceptual and justificatory aspects. Its conceptual aspect can be put this way: Nothing counts as a right unless it has an assignable right-holder, and no one counts as a right-holder unless she holds the option of enforcing or waiving the duty correlative to the right. Its justificatory aspect can be put this way: The function of rights is to protect and foster individual autonomy. We must now explore what these aspects mean and how they fit together in the realm of legal rights, and then consider their implications as we extrapolate from the legal realm to the moral.

A Choice Theory of legal rights is conceptually fastidious insofar as it insists that assertions of legal rights meet a certain test of validity.

It is important to see that this fastidiousness has a motive that is as much descriptive as prescriptive. The idea is not so much that nothing ought to count as a legal right unless it passes the Choice Theory test, it is rather that in legal systems of particular interest (read: in Anglo-American legal systems), judges and other legal officials do not count a putative right as a legal right unless it passes the Choice Theory test in some form. Choice Theory, in other words, might be offered as the most accurate description of the practices of legal officials in certain well-developed legal systems. An advocate of a Choice Theory of legal rights might stop here, satisfied with having made this descriptive claim, or he might go on to add, "And it's a good thing, too!" – an evaluative claim with obviously justificatory overtones.

What case do Choice Theorists make for the descriptive claim? The evidence is found in Anglo-American legal doctrine. One example is the doctrine of *ius tertii*, or "third-party rights." Generally speaking, parties cannot base their prayers for legal remedies on the rights of others, of third parties. Suppose, for example, that my neighbor has stopped making payments on his car because it will not run, and that he has left the car in his front yard in an unsightly manner that detracts from my enjoyment of my property. I ask that he remove it, and he refuses. I sue in court to have it removed. I cannot assert the finance company's right to have the offending car removed from my neighbor's property; I have to assert some right of my own. I will not be heard to say that I stand to benefit from my neighbor's performance of his duty to the finance company to keep the car in good running order. Nor can I sue the finance company to force it to repossess the car; its right of repossession is one that it may enforce or waive at its option. Thus, the linguistic conventions governing the legal use of the term "rights" do not behave as a crude Benthamite formulation would suggest. The legal conventions tell us that the law recognizes a right in X against Y only where Y has a duty to X, and X may decide whether or not to hold Y to the duty. The legal conventions do not show that the law recognizes a right in X against Y in every case where Y is under a duty whose performance would benefit X. Rather, the existence of X's legal right depends on whether X has a power to enforce and a power to waive enforcement of a legal duty of Y's.

A more straightforward example can be given. Courts make a point of distinguishing between moral duty and legal right in the following way.

Suppose X hits a bad golf shot. The ball carries over the green and strikes Y in the head, injuring Y. There are at least two distinct issues. One is whether X has a moral duty to Y to compensate Y for the injury X has caused. Another is whether Y has a legal right to be compensated by X. Is there a third question, Whether X has a legal duty to compensate Y even though Y has no power to enforce X's legal duty? The language of the courts suggests that X's duty, once divorced from any legal enforcement power on Y's part, is no longer worth calling a legal duty: it is a merely moral one, and, as expressed by the court in the famous English case of *Bolton v. Stone* ([1951] A. C. 850), "With merely moral duties the law does not deal." Although Hohfeld showed (and Bentham knew) that it is logically possible for a claim-right to exist apart from a power, the linguistic conventions of the law seem to reserve the designation "legal right" for the more complex Hohfeldian molecule, which consists of a claim-right in combination with a legal power to enforce that claim-right. In fact, fully spelled out, the molecule will include a power to enforce, a power to waive enforcement, and a bilateral option with respect to each of these powers – that is, a permission to enforce the claim-right and a permission to waive enforcement of the claim-right. And, to be complete, the molecule should include a legal immunity protecting the other components of the molecule from alteration (but liable, perhaps, to legislative amendment and extinction). For simplicity's sake, we will not dwell further upon the precise composition of the Hohfeldian molecule insisted on by a Choice Theory of legal rights. For our purposes, it is enough to observe two things: (1) A legal right, for Choice Theory, is conceptually connected with the rightholder's possession of powers of enforcement and waiver of the legal duty correlative with the right; and (2) a legal right, for Choice Theory, cannot be adequately understood in crude Benthamite terms – namely, as a beneficial duty.

As a descriptive account of Anglo-American legal doctrine, Choice Theory has consequences. Put tersely, a descriptive Choice Theory of legal rights entails that within a system of legal rules, no one has a legal right, properly so-called, unless she has a legal power, within that system of rules, to seek or to waive enforcement of another's legal duty. This seems to mean that infants and incompetent adults, because they cannot exercise the relevant legal powers, have no legal rights. This seemingly absurd consequence can be finessed by an adjustment that allows infants and the incompetent to hold powers through proxies, such as parents and legal guardians.

Another odd, if not absurd, consequence of Choice Theory: Y has a legal right against X that X not commit civil battery against Y, but Y has no legal right that X not commit criminal battery against Y. Choice Theory has these consequences because Y possesses a power to seek civil redress but possesses no parallel power over criminal prosecution. While Y may initiate, or forgo, a civil suit in battery for damages against X, Y normally may not initiate a criminal prosecution for battery, and Y may not block the state's prosecution of X even if Y has decided to forgive X. The strangeness of this consequence cannot be finessed by casting the state prosecutor as exercising a proxy power on behalf of Y, for two reasons. The first is that Y will in many cases not be incapacitated in any developmental or psychological sense, so Y is not really in need of a proxy, in the way that an infant is. Second, the state prosecutor, in deciding whether to prosecute X for battering Y, need not make her decision based on what she deems to be in Y's interests; rather, she will decide on the basis of what she deems to be the most efficient use of her office's resources in advancing the goal of maintaining public order.

In this case, Choice Theory has to confess that, strictly speaking, citizens hold no legal right not to be criminally battered even though they hold legal rights not to be subjected to tortious battery. The sting of this conclusion is palliated by the fact that a civil remedy exists for many, though not all, criminal wrongs. Where there is no civil remedy for a criminal wrong, Choice Theory will insist that, properly speaking, the victim holds no legal right not to be wronged. Think of this example: Suppose there is a statute making "reckless endangerment" a crime, but there is no possibility of a civil recovery in tort for merely having been recklessly, though harmlessly, exposed by another to even a serious risk. Now suppose that X violates the statute by acting in a way that exposes Y to danger – say, X drives at high speed on the wrong side of the freeway, endangering but not harming Y. Choice Theory will insist that there is nothing odd here about saying that, although X has violated a legal duty, X has violated no legal right held by Y. If we are still uncomfortable, Choice Theory will insist that we disentangle the descriptive reality – that Y has no legal right – from our evaluation of that reality – namely, that Y perhaps *ought* to have such a legal right.

Most of the legal rights we enjoy may be waived, surrendered, or forfeited, and Choice Theory, as a descriptive account of legal doctrine, is tailored to this phenomenon. But not all legal rights are waivable, for some are "inalienable." The right to be represented by counsel in defending against a criminal charge, and to a trial by jury, are rights that are waivable; but the right not to be punished by torture is not. We are in fact legally disabled from giving valid consent to being executed by torture. How can Choice Theory account for the fact that we have no power to waive certain of our legal rights? On this point, Choice Theory might simply emphasize that such legal disabilities are rare indeed, and caution that what might be referred to as a legal "right" not to be tortured is in fact a Hohfeldian molecule whose core consists of a legal duty of officials not to torture and a legal disability of all to consent to torture.

To summarize, as a descriptive account of the concept of a legal right, Choice Theory has both advantages and disadvantages vis-à-vis Interest Theory. The advantages consist in Choice Theory's ability to explain certain aspects of legal doctrine, such as the *ius tertii* rule and the asymmetry between civil and criminal law. Insofar as our concern is to sharpen our understanding of legal rights, Choice Theory supplements Hohfeld's account, and corrects and extends it by showing how a legal right, properly speaking, does not consist of a bare claim-right, but rather is a molecule composed of a claim-right (and its correlative duty) combined with further elements including, at the very least, a power of enforcing or waiving the claim-right element. Choice Theory thus requires a more definite conceptual shape of legal rights than Interest Theory. The generative nature of Interest Theory seems unbounded, whereas that of Choice Theory is limited to the minimum needed to serve the function of legal rights – namely, not the service of interests generally, but the interest persons have in exercising autonomous choice. Because of its sharper boundaries, the Choice Theory conceptualization of legal rights bars admission to candidates that would ordinarily seem to count as legal rights (the legal right not to be murdered, or executed by torture, for example). Choice Theory can be adjusted to account for these rulings, in order to lessen the offense to our ordinary patterns of speech.

So what? The stakes in this debate are increased considerably once we move from its conceptual dimension to its justificatory dimension and, as we do so, begin to appreciate its implications for our understanding of moral rights rather than specifically legal ones. In the justificatory dimension, Choice Theory can be viewed as a species of Interest Theory. Interest Theory simply tells us that rights are justified by their serving to protect and further the interests of individuals (or of groups smaller than the whole universe of interest-bearing individuals). Choice Theory can be viewed as a specification of the interest rights serve – namely, the interest in exercising autonomous choice. At this justificatory level, Choice Theory and Interest Theory are competitors only if Choice Theory is understood to deny that any interest *other than* that in exercising autonomy is capable of justifying the assignment of rights. Once Choice Theory is taken this way, it appears to have some rather striking consequences.

From Legal to Moral Rights

Once Choice Theory is taken to be committed to the thesis that the sole *raison d'etre* of rights is to foster the exercise of autonomous choice, it seems to follow that the only beings eligible for right-holding are beings capable of autonomy. In particular, none of the following will count as possible moral right-holders: infants, the mentally incompetent, the dead, the unborn, animals, the ecosystem, and artifacts and natural objects generally. Or, more precisely, no members of these categories can qualify as right-holders unless the case is made that they (and not some proxy) possess, in some sense, a capacity for autonomous choice.

This teaching has a harsh aspect, one that advocates of Choice Theory may wish to mollify. To say of creature X that X cannot possibly possess moral rights is not to say that there are no moral duties governing the treatment of X. Let $X =$ babies. Babies cannot make autonomous choices because they lack sufficient powers of comprehension to appreciate the significance of what they do. Their conduct is better viewed as instinctive than as autonomous. Choice Theory denies the strict propriety of attributing moral or legal rights to babies, but it is fully consistent with insisting that babies are the beneficiaries of a stringent set of moral duties borne by all members of the community of autonomous agents. But, *pace* Interest Theory, there is more to a moral right than merely being the beneficiary of another's moral duty. Choice Theory is fastidious about how we characterize the moral protections that babies enjoy, but it need not be in the least stingy in the amount of moral protection they enjoy.

Critics of Choice Theory may point out that babies are in fact denied a crucial degree of moral protection if they are deemed incapable of being rights-holders. Moral rights, after all, are supposed to function as constraints on the pursuit of goals, and particularly on any pursuit of goals that treats interests as mere inputs into an aggregative decision procedure. It is simply false to say that babies without moral rights are nonetheless beneficiaries of moral duties that accord them just as much moral protection as rights could give them. It is false because it overlooks the fact that a moral duty to X, which does not amount to a *right* held by X, might be balanced away by interests competing with X's interests, and this possibility looks even more formidable if those competing interests are the interests of right-holders. To recall Jonathan Swift's *Modest Proposal*, in conditions of famine, non-right-holding babies might be the first candidates to be fed to right-holding adults, whereas *right-holding* babies would not.

Choice Theory is not without resources to avoid the charge that it arbitrarily legislates an invidious distinction between what it considers proper right-holders and all others. One tack is to point out that Choice Theory is not committed to the position that rights have absolute priority over other goals. Obviously, rights have to be able to resist the general balance of interests to some extent, but that extent need not be absolute. We can call this the *threshold problem*: At what point (if any) must rights yield to other moral considerations? This is a general problem for any account of rights, whether a Choice Theory account or otherwise. It may be that the interests of babies are sufficient to surmount this threshold while, for example, the interests of zygotes, blastulas, and first-trimester fetuses are not.

Another tack that Choice Theory might take, to avoid the charge that it arbitrarily and invidiously stipulates a necessary qualification for right-holding, is to challenge us to work out a connection between babies and autonomy. An adult human normally holds rights while sleeping or otherwise unconscious, despite her incapability of exercising autonomy during those periods. The rights endure despite the temporary lapse of autonomous capacity, presumably because the right-holder will normally recover the capacity within a reasonably short interval. The relationship between the capacity and the right-holding is thus a complex one, and it is open to the advocate of moral rights for babies (or fetuses, or higher mammals) to delineate this relationship in a way that includes the advocate's candidate for right-holdership on the same terms as the standard case of the normal human adult.

To summarize, Choice Theory began modestly as a descriptive account of specifically legal rights. Once it presents a justificatory aspect, Choice Theory has implications for moral rights as well, whether or not they have been legally recognized. In its justificatory aspect, Choice Theory fixes on the protection of the exercise of autonomous choice as the characteristic purpose and value of rights. So viewed, no purpose would be served, and the independent goal of conceptual clarity would be disserved, by even so much as discussing the question whether a being utterly incapable of autonomous choice holds rights of any description. *Pace* Bentham, a capacity to feel is not enough – a moral right-holder must have a capacity to choose autonomously – that is, to choose in more than the Pickwickian sense in which a mollusc "chooses" to close its shell to avoid intruders and to open it to admit nourishment. What autonomy is, and what a true right-holder's relationship to it must be, are subjects for further analysis and reflection – but these are the terms in which the discussion of rights must be conducted unless it is to degenerate into empty sloganeering.

What, then, of inalienable moral rights, from the Choice Theory perspective? Interest Theory can readily account for the existence of inalienable rights – they are simply those rights supported by interests of the right-holder that are so profound that the right-holder himself has no power to surrender them on any account. In contrast, Choice Theory has a problem, because rights properly so-called are supposed to include a power to waive the associated moral claim-right. On a Choice Theory of moral rights, in other words, there are no inalienable rights in the strict sense. This result may seem shockingly counterintuitive but, again, Choice Theory has resources at its disposal to restore its credibility. As in the case of the babies, an advocate of Choice Theory may in perfect consistency say that all agents are subject to certain inviolable, unalterable moral duties not occurring in the combinations properly denominated moral rights. Thus, for example, one might say that we all have a duty not to treat others as slaves no matter how willing those others may be to enter into slavery. It is not correct to say that we have a moral right not to be enslaved – it is not correct to say that because we possess no power to submit to slavery, precisely as Locke argued. It is better to say that all are subject to a moral duty not to enslave.

Again, as in the case of the babies, a critic of Choice Theory may object that this tack devalues the stricture against slavery and, for analogous reasons, any other of the absolute strictures that we have come to think of as the core of the idea of human rights – the stricture against torture, for example. To say that there is a duty not to torture, but no right not to be tortured, suggests that the distinctive anti-aggregative constraint that rights represent does not apply to slavery and torture. But, as before in the case of the babies, it is open to the Choice Theory advocate to say that this alleged consequence assumes that Choice Theory is committed to a particular treatment of a general problem, what we have called the threshold problem. (We will turn to the threshold problem in Chapter 9.) Until the threshold problem is addressed, it is unfair to Choice Theory to assume that it devalues the strictures against slavery and torture, just as it is unfair to assume that it devalues the constraints on the treatment of babies and animals.

Yet another tack is open to Choice Theory here. We have distinguished the conceptual and the justificatory dimensions of Choice Theory and Interest Theory. In the realm of legal rights, advocates of Choice Theory have had two reasons to insist on a narrow conception of a legal right as including powers of enforcement and waiver. One reason was tied to the justification or function of legal rights, as seen from a Choice Theory perspective, but there was another. Advocates of Choice Theory have also been interested in giving a descriptive account of the conceptual machinery of law, and have been persuaded that a Choice Theory molecule best answers to the actual patterns of official legal usage. But when Choice Theory is extended beyond the legal to the realm of moral rights, descriptive adequacy counts for relatively less, and justificatory persuasiveness for more. Put succinctly, outside the legal community there is a wider and less technical vernacular of rights, and a greater importance placed on rights as expressions of moral values. Accordingly, an advocate of Choice Theory may decide that the importance of autonomous choice is so great that, in the moral realm, there are not one but two concepts of rights at work: the first is captured by a molecular picture including a power of enforcement and waiver; but the second need not – the second may therefore be an inalienable right. In this fashion, Choice Theory may be reconciled with the existence of inalienable rights.

The reconciliation is not arbitrary because there is no compelling reason to think that moral and legal rights are conceptual isomorphs in every detail. In fact, if we are attracted to legal positivism – the theory that law can be identified as law by empirical methods not involving any moral evaluation – we should not be surprised to find some conceptual dissimilarities between moral rights and legal rights. Even if we are drawn to natural law theory – the view traditionally cast as the foil to legal positivism – we may not be surprised to find a divergence between the conceptual makeup of legal rights and moral rights. In other words, even if, as "natural lawyers," we impose a test of moral adequacy before admitting any putative legal right as legally valid, we may freely concede that legal rights, so validated, exhibit additional conceptual complexity after being "promulgated" in an actual human legal system.

To summarize once again, and to elaborate, the Choice Theory and the Interest Theory are not straightforward, across-the-board combatants, and it would be misleading to suggest otherwise. Interest Theory – as a category – tends less to emphasize conceptual concerns than justificatory ones, and even its justificatory aspect is rather sketchy pending some more detailed filling-out. Interest Theory per se is so sketchy a justificatory theory that Choice Theory, in its justificatory aspect, could be regarded as a specific type of Interest Theory. Roughly speaking, individual interests justify rights, according to Interest Theory; and, Choice Theory adds, the individual interests that justify rights are interests in exercising autonomous choice. Because of its more specific focus on the interest in autonomy, Choice Theory tends to determine a more specific conceptual composition for the molecules of Hohfeldian elements that make up rights. In the realm of specifically legal rights, a good, but far from conclusive, case has been made for the proposition that legal rights, "properly so-called," are molecules containing a power of waiver and enforcement (and, as we noted earlier, perhaps also immunities and permissions to fill out these powers). The case is not conclusive because Choice Theory has to stretch somewhat to deal with certain apparent legal rights: those held by infants and the incompetent; those protected by the criminal law; and those which are not waivable. In contrast, Interest

Theory in the realm of legal rights is – many have felt – annoyingly fecund; it leads us to expect to find legal rights where none have in fact been recognized, and in some instances have been authoritatively denied (as in the case of *ius tertii*). An Interest Theory of legal rights can be modified in ways intended to tame or palliate this apparent fecundity (Kramer 2001); but, measuring by descriptive adequacy, the contest between a Choice Theory account and an Interest Theory account of legal rights in Anglo-American jurisprudence may be too close to call.

Going beyond the legal realm to the moral, the fecundity of Interest Theory may seem less annoying – the fact that a moral right has yet to be recognized is not a good reason to deny its existence (consider the case of women's rights under fundamentalist theocracies, or the rights of African-Americans in the antebellum American South). Moreover, Interest Theory reinforces the commonsense view that some of our moral rights – in fact, the most important ones – are inalienable. We could not give them up even if we wanted to. Choice Theory, on the other hand, enters the moral realm with, so to speak, an axe or two to grind. Beings lacking autonomy do not seem eligible as rights-holders, and so Choice Theory seems to stipulate the terms of some heated moral debates in ways that appear to be tendentious, arch, and unfair. In particular, fetuses and animals are denied rights, and on grounds that will strike partisans of those rights as either aridly fastidious or disingenuously biased. Inalienable moral rights also come under close scrutiny from a Choice Theory perspective. Choice Theory can be adjusted to accommodate inalienable moral rights, but it need not be, and so it can be invoked in defense of a stringent conceptual thesis that would declare that moral rights, by their very nature, may be surrendered. As we cast our eyes back to the early history of the idea of rights, and recall the role that rights played in the apologetics of slavery, we may be uneasy about transposing Choice Theory from the legal domain to the moral.

8

A Right to Do Wrong?

Two Conceptions of Moral Rights

Beginning with the set of Hohfeldian elements, it is possible to design any number of molecular combinations that may come closer to approximating what we mean by a moral right than any of those elements in isolation. In the last chapter, we looked at the particular molecule favored by Choice Theory of legal rights, and considered the question whether that molecule was also distinctive of moral rights. Another common suggestion about moral rights (and moral, rather than legal, rights will be the focus of this chapter) is that a person X's moral right to φ is a precise bundle of Hohfeldian elements consisting of a moral claim-right against interference by Y with X's φ-ing, a moral claim-right against interference by Y with X's not φ-ing, coupled with X's moral permissions both to φ and not to φ – that is, with the absence of a moral duty either to φ or not to φ. This is to be taken as a proposed stipulation of what is to be understood by talk of a moral right. The force of such rights will be brought out (in part) by unpacking what is meant by interference. The scope of the right will be brought out by specifying the range of persons and entities Y who are duty-bound not to interfere. And the substance of the right will be the action, φ-ing, that the right-holder has a moral option to do or omit. Further, we can pose the question of the alienability or prescriptability of a moral right as a question about what powers and liabilities exist with respect to the core bundle.

The "Protected-*Permission*" Conception

We can call this the *protected-permission* conception of rights. "Permission" because a moral option – that is, a moral permission to φ and a moral permission not to φ – is at the core of the idea. "Protected" because others are duty-bound not to interfere with the right-holder's exercise of the option. To the extent that the protected-permission conception of rights captures what is distinctive and useful about speaking of moral rights, it deserves to be thought of not as a mere stipulative definition but a reasoned reconstruction of what a moral right is.

To illustrate: To say that I have a moral right to thumb my nose at you is, on the protected-permission conception, to say that others are duty-bound not to interfere with my thumbing or not thumbing my nose, and that I have no duty either to thumb it or not to thumb it at you. Of course, the protected-permission conception is not committed to my having this *particular* right: it is simply an account of what it *means* to say that I have a moral right. The protected-permission conception has an important implication; it implies that there is no such thing as a moral right to do what is morally wrong. This follows immediately from the fact that a moral right, on the protected-permission conception, includes a morally permitted option. To say that I have a morally permitted option to do something is to say that I have no moral duty to do it and no moral duty not to do it; but it follows that if I violate no moral duty in doing something, I do no wrong by doing it. Therefore, if I have a moral right to do something, I do no wrong by exercising that right: there can be no such thing as a right to do wrong. This analysis is consistent with Godwin's line on what he called "active" rights: an active right is a right to do "as one lists," but – because there are practically no moral options in life, on Godwin's view – to have an active right would be to have a right to do wrong.

To some, it seems intuitively clear, as it did to Godwin, that there can be no right to do wrong, and absurd to suggest the contrary. But, to others, the intuition is not so clear, and in fact must be rejected after careful reflection on the distinctive role of rights in moral thinking. But admitting the possibility of a right to do wrong means rejecting the protected-permission conception of moral rights. The most direct way of doing so is to deny that having a moral right entails having a moral permission, and to assert that moral rights are moral claim-rights, pure and simple. Can a moral claim-right stand alone and apart from a moral permission? Hohfeld can be invoked here as having shown the way to recognizing the logical independence of a legal claim-right and a legal permission. So also, moral claim-rights are logically independent of moral permissions. Those who reject the protected-permission conception of moral rights adopt, instead, the view that moral claim-rights are moral rights, "strictly speaking," in much the same spirit as Hohfeld's position that only legal claim-rights are legal rights, properly so-called. This is not to say that moral permissions do not come bundled with moral claim-rights; it may be that many moral rights do consist of such bundles. The point is, that they need not, and, for moral rights to perform their distinctive role in moral thinking, in an important range of cases they do not come bundled – the moral claim-right stands alone. Call this the *protected-choice* view – where what is protected is sometimes a choice between right and wrong.

The "Protected-*Choice*" Conception

The protected-choice view seems to offer a better account of the following kinds of case: a lottery winner ignores a charitable appeal for financial assistance to disaster victims; a voter casts a ballot for a racist candidate; an athlete ridicules an obese person struggling to board a bus. In each of these cases, we would want to be able to say that the actor acted wrongly even though others had no moral right (that is, permission, or Hohfedlian moral "liberty") to interfere with the actor's doing what he did. We can admit that the lottery winner has a right to her winnings, the voter has a right to vote for any candidate she chooses, and the athlete has a right to free speech, without *condoning* what each did. On the protected-choice view, we can still condemn what each did as morally *wrong*. On the protected-permission view, on the other hand, we are unable to say what we want to say. We have to choose between denying that the actor had a moral right to do what he did, and denying that what the actor did with his right was wrong. Neither denial seems appealing, and the protected-choice conception looks attractive as a way to escape the dilemma.

The protected-choice view can be supported by an explanation of what tempts us to deny that there can be a right to do wrong. The explanation appeals to the distinctiveness of rights with respect to other terms of moral assessment, and points out the misleading homophony between "right" as opposed to "wrong," and "a right," as opposed to "no right." There is a difference between *having a right to do something* and that something's *being the right thing to do*. Having a right to do something does not mean that it is the right thing to do; it does not even mean that there is a reason to do it. In contrast, to say that something is the right thing to do is to say that there is a very good, yea even compelling, decisive, mandatory reason to do it. At some level, of course, reasons support the existence of rights, but sometimes there is simply no good reason to do what one has a right, nonetheless, to do. And sometimes there is every reason not to do it. The protected-choice conception of rights avoids confusing what have to be recognized as two different dimensions of morality. Because the protected-permission view does confuse them, it has to be rejected despite its initial intuitive appeal.

Notice that the protected-permission view need not deny the logical independence of moral claim-rights and moral permissions. The protected-permission view could be explained by the following analogy. Hydrogen and oxygen are distinct elements, just as claim-rights and permissions are distinct elements. Each may exist apart from the other. Nonetheless, nothing can be a molecule of water unless it combines hydrogen and oxygen in the right proportion. Similarly, nothing counts as a moral right unless it combines a claim-right with a permission in the right way. Although there may be a point to distinguishing the claim-right and the permission for certain purposes, it is important to understand that there is no moral right, properly speaking, except where the elements are properly combined. Just as water is useful for putting out fires, as hydrogen and oxygen separately are not, so also a moral right has its distinctive properties only where the two elements exist in combination. Although this analogy cannot by itself establish that the protected-permission view is superior, it does show that an appeal to Hohfeld will not decide the issue between the protected-permission and the protected-choice conceptions.

The protected-choice conception must, however, confront the following difficulty. If the "bite" or *force* of a moral right consists in the moral prohibition of interference with the exercise of choice, what does the bite of moral wrongness consist in, if not in the moral permissibility of interference with choice? The protected-choice conception is incoherent unless it denies that the moral wrongness of an act entails the moral permissibility of interfering with it. Otherwise, the protected-choice view would countenance the possibility of actions that it was both morally wrong to interfere with (because the act was the exercise of a moral right) and morally permissible to interfere with (because the act was morally wrongful).

Among the possibilities open to the protected-choice conception, two seem most prominent. One is simply to deny that anything pertaining to enforcement follows from the moral wrongness of an act. To put the point more dramatically, although the moral wrongness of interference follows from the fact that a moral right is being exercised, nothing of interest follows from the fact that an act is morally wrongful. But this line of thinking seems not to be evenhanded: rights have a definite bite, but wrongness has no definite bite. Surely some account of the relationship between wrongness and enforcement has to be offered. The second possibility does offer such an account: the wrongness of an act entails the moral permissibility of social sanctions short of interference, but not interference.

This possibility maintains the coherence of the protected-choice conception; a "right to do wrong" now comes to this: It is morally forbidden to interfere with the exercise of the protected choice, but it is morally permissible to sanction the wrong choice by social measures not amounting to interference. But, now, the protected-choice conception owes us an account of the distinction between interference and those other sanctions, and, on the borderline, the difference may seem ephemeral. In many cases, the manifest disapproval of society may be as crippling as physical compulsion; and yet we will have to say that the former is compatible with recognition of a right to do wrong, while the latter is not. This will seem unsatisfactory from the perspective of the protected-permission view, which will hold that recognition of a moral right must include the recognition of the moral permissibility of either choice on the part of the right-holder.

Another line of argument is available for the protected-choice conception. This line emphasizes the function and point of moral rights, which is to protect *important* choices from interference. The domain of human conduct and choice can be divided into three mutually exclusive, jointly exhaustive compartments: the morally forbidden, the morally required, and the morally indifferent. On both the protected-permission and the protected-choice conceptions, decisions to do what morality requires are protected from interference. Moral rights are not really needed here, since what morality requires morality itself will protect from interference. In other words, normally it is morally forbidden to interfere with the doing of what morality requires, so moral rights are not doing any work in this compartment.

The practical difference between the two conceptions therefore comes to this: The protected-choice conception protects decisions both in the morally indifferent compartment and the morally wrongful compartment, but the protected-permission conception only protects decisions in the morally indifferent compartment. So, on the protected-permission conception, rights provide protection against interference with morally indifferent choices – as between chocolate and vanilla ice cream – or choices that morality otherwise protects from interference anyway. This seems to trivialize rights. The protected-choice conception, on the other hand, protects some choices to do what is morally forbidden. This is something that morality need not otherwise do, and which gives moral rights a distinctive role. The protected-permission view, in contrast, has moral rights protecting morally indifferent choices or choices that morality requires one to make anyway. This would give us an impoverished conception of the function and point of rights. Therefore, the protected-choice conception must be preferred as respecting the importance of the choices moral rights are called on to protect.

This argument is not conclusive, however. A defender of the protected-permission conception will want to point out that the compartment of the "morally indifferent" – defined simply as that which is neither forbidden nor required – is not one wholly lacking in moral significance. Think of our earlier examples: the stingy lottery winner, the racist voter, the sneering athlete. Are we really to think of each as doing what is morally *wrongful* – that is, as failing to do what morality *requires*? Another way of looking at what these actors do is available: we might say that what they do is morally permissible but blameworthy – not wrong but merely bad. The lottery winner merits praise if she gives to an agency providing disaster relief, and she may deserve to be thought ill of if she does not, but this is not to say that what she does is wrongful. There is a subcompartment of things that are neither morally required nor forbidden but which are not morally insignificant nonetheless. Undertaking a risky rescue, for example, is often heroic, beyond the call of duty, not morally required. Moral rights have a role here in protecting us against interference with our decisions not to be heroic, not to be charitable, not to be kind, and so forth. These choices have moral importance, and moral rights, on both the protected-permission and the protected-choice views, have an indispensable function in protecting them from interference. But because moral rights are at work on both conceptions, there is, so far, no good reason to prefer one over the other.

The Function of Rights: Recognitional, or Reaction-Constraining?

One function that the protected-permission conception serves is what we could refer to as a *recognitional* function of rights. Attributions of rights often serve as a way of recognizing the worth of individuals or groups. For example, homosexuals campaign for gay rights as a way of persuading society generally to recognize that the lives they lead are not despicable or inferior. In other words, gay rights are not meant to be understood as a "right to do wrong," but as a right to do what a majority has traditionally, but mistakenly, *thought* to be wrong. By the same token, those who resist recognition of gay rights often do so on the ground that recognition would implicitly carry with it a removal of the stigma attached to morally wrongful conduct. The protected-permission conception captures this feature of the debate about gay rights; on both sides of the issue, it tends to be assumed that recognizing a moral right involves withdrawing the stigma of wrongfulness from the exercise of the right.

On the protected-choice conception, in contrast, recognition of a moral right to engage in homosexual acts does not entail the moral permissibility of doing so. Doing so may be condemned as wrong, consistently with affirming the moral right. But the assignment of moral rights may have a function other than a recognitional one. Sometimes, the language of rights is used in a way that seems intended to withhold approval of the exercise of the right. Think again of the cases of the stingy lottery winner or the hectoring athlete. We may be uncertain whether to condemn their conduct as wrongful even though we are convinced that interference with it *would* be wrongful. Often it is more important to reach a conclusion about the moral permissibility of interference than it is to decide finally about the moral value of the conduct that would be interfered with. This is how many people view abortion: abortion may or may not be wrong, on this view, but interfering with a woman's right to elect an abortion is certainly wrong. Invoking a woman's moral right to choose to abort is intended here to forestall or "bracket" discussion of the issue of the wrongness of abortion, and to isolate and focus on the issue of the wrongness of interference. Here, invoking a moral right is intended to serve a *reaction-constraining* function.

The reaction-constraining function of moral rights may have a superficial appeal for those who view morality skeptically. Since we can never hope to sort out essentially subjective matters of right and wrong, why not set those aside and focus instead on the rightness and wrongness of interference? The problem with this is how to disentangle the issue of the rightness and wrongness of interference from the (supposedly subjective) issue of the rightness and wrongness of the conduct that is the candidate for being interfered with. This is not to say that the recognitional function is any better off, for, of course, any attempt to establish moral rights that recognize the worth of a conduct of a certain type will also have to confront the epistemological difficulties we have already noted that cast doubt on the possibility of moral objectivity and truth.

Choosing between the protected-permission conception of moral rights and the protected-choice conception seems to come down, then, to a choice between a conception that serves a recognitional purpose and one that, instead, serves a reaction-constraining purpose. To the extent that moral rights are thought important because they vindicate certain ways of living, the recognitional function will be valued. But to the extent that moral rights are thought important as ways of creating "breathing space" for choice in a world of moral uncertainty and controversy, the reaction-constraining function will be valued. It is of course logically possible to maintain that both functions are important, and to divide the world of moral rights according to which of the two functions predominates. Where the recognitional function is more important, the protected-permission conception will apply, and the issue of the rightness, innocence, or wrongness of a category of conduct will be in play. And where the reaction-constraining function is more important, the protected-choice conception will apply, and the issue of the rightness, innocence, or wrongness of the underlying category of conduct will be bracketed – "off the table," so to speak.

Unfortunately, perhaps, no such division is likely to be agreed to by parties who are at loggerheads about the wrongness of the underlying conduct. Some within the "pro-choice" camp on the abortion issue will argue that the right of a woman to choose to abort does not have a recognitional point, but a reaction-constraining one. Others within that camp will disagree and will, in that respect only, agree with the "pro-life" camp that a recognitional point is inseparable from a moral right to abort. Many gay-rights advocates are unsatisfied with any right to intimacy that is merely reaction-constraining; what they demand is recognition of the moral innocence – more, the positive moral worth – of a way of life. Their opponents agree with them on this, if little else, but many of their sympathizers may feel that a moral right that constrains reaction is all that they should claim.

The two conceptions, and the divergent functions they serve, come up in disputes about "positive" rights as well. My right to an easy rescue seems to serve the recognitional function of vindicating the value of my life. The reaction-constraining function does not seem applicable here since it is not a question of my doing anything, but of receiving: the idea of bracketing the question of the value of my doing, or of receiving, seems odd and out of place. Does this tend to show that the recognitional function is more general, and that therefore the protected-permission conception is more fundamental? That would be too quick. Controversy about positive rights essentially involves conflict between an asserted positive right and a negative right against interference asserted defensively by someone who has been called on to satisfy that positive right. In rescue situations, *my* positive right can come into conflict with *your* right to autonomy. Your right to autonomy – stated with this generality – seems likelier suited to be serving a reaction-constraining rather than a recognitional function. This is so because the exercise of your autonomy may take any number of morally dubious forms. (As to negative rights as a class, the more general their form, the less likely they are to have a recognitional point, simply because the more general their form, the more likely they are to encompass morally suspect subclasses of conduct.) To say, "The bystander had a right not to take even a slight risk to save the baby," is unlikely to constitute an endorsement of what the bystander did.

The Pressure of Consequentialism

We have examined Hohfeld's classification of "legal advantages" and transposed his work from the realm of legal to that of moral rights. We have seen that Hohfeldian elements can be combined in various ways, yielding various conceptions of a moral right. In particular, we distinguished the protected-choice and protected-permission conceptions. A moral right, according to the protected-choice model, is simply a moral claim-right against interference by others with the right-holder's performing (or failing to perform) some type of act. That type of act may or may not be one that it would be wrongful for the actor to perform; in other words, the protected-choice model depicts a right to do (what may be) wrong. In contrast, the protected-permission model combines the basic claim-right against interference with a moral option to perform the specified act – a moral option being a combination of a Hohfeldian moral permission to perform the act and a Hohfeldian moral permission not to perform the act. There is no right to do wrong, on the protected-permission model; what is protected on this model is the actor's moral right to choose whether to do or not to do something that is neither morally required nor morally forbidden for him to do.

We have also considered Choice Theories of rights. As a theory about the conceptual makeup of moral rights, Choice Theory insists that any molecule of Hohfeldian elements purporting to constitute a moral right must include an additional element – namely, a bilateral moral power to waive or enforce the core claim-right against interference. Choice Theory could be incorporated into the protected-choice model by simply adding the bilateral power of waiver and enforcement to the basic claim-right against interference. The protected-permission model could similarly incorporate Choice Theory by adding a bilateral power of waiver and enforcement to its combination of claim-right and moral option. The conceptual possibilities are obviously endless, but to explore them would add complication without interest. What makes the Choice Theory's addition of a bilateral power of waiver of enforcement interesting is the question of alienability. As we have seen, some human interests, and the rights they generate, are of such great importance that it may be denied that the right-holder can possess the moral power to waive or alienate the right's protection.

Yet, in each of the various conceptions of rights that we have considered, the core of a moral right is a Hohfeldian claim-right, and its correlative duty of noninterference. Although some have doubted that a moral claim-right is part of every moral right, properly so-called, what cannot be doubted is that the moral rights that we most value involve, at a minimum, a claim-right against interference. I want now to focus on the idea of a moral claim-right and return to a question postponed from earlier on: What is interference? Or, more precisely, where and how is the line to be drawn between interference and other kinds of unwelcome activity (or inactivity)? In this chapter, we will also pursue a separate but related question: When is interfering with a right a violation of it? Or, in other words, when is it permissible for others to interfere with a right-holder's enjoyment of her rights, if ever? This second question can also be put this way: Are rights absolute, or are there circumstances in which they may be overridden by competing moral considerations? The two questions – (1) what is interference? and (2), are rights absolute? – are closely related, as we shall see, even though they are different questions. It will be helpful to address the second question first.

Are Rights "Trumps"? Thresholds and Defeasibility

Are rights absolute? One possible response is to say, in the phrase of philosopher Ronald Dworkin, that *rights are trumps*. Rights have absolute priority over all other considerations, just as any card in the trump suit takes the trick over every card in the other suits. If clubs are trumps and aces high, the two of clubs beats the ace of hearts. If rights are trumps, then rights prevail over all other competing moral considerations, whatever their strength. In particular, rights trump moral considerations of aggregate welfare. Unless rights have this preemptive power over considerations of aggregate welfare, it is thought, rights amount to no more than just another consideration to be fed into the hopper to be weighed and balanced against other reasons. The "rights are trumps" account of the force of moral rights places rights on a different plane from any aggregative calculus of interests, and so – the story goes – properly reflects the distinctive contribution of rights to morality.

The "rights are trumps" account invites the objection that it would unrealistically forbid imposing sacrifices to avoid massive catastrophe. To illustrate the objection, consider the "Trolley Problem," first posed by Phillipa Foot. You find yourself in the following situation: a trolley car is running out of control and is hurtling toward six people, who will be crushed unless the trolley is diverted. You are able to divert the trolley onto a siding by pulling a switch, but there is a person on the siding who will be killed if you do. You must act quickly: Your only options are (a) do nothing, with the result that six die, and (b) pull the switch, with the result that only one dies. Assume that no one is at fault for the situation's arising. What ought you to do?

Many people respond to the Trolley Problem by saying that it is permissible to pull the switch, and some go further and say that it would be morally wrongful not to pull it. Others disagree, and insist that it would be morally wrongful to sacrifice the one to save the six – it would be a rights violation of the most serious kind, and properly prosecutable as murder. The Trolley Problem has stimulated, and continues to stimulate, intense discussion, but this is not the place to recapitulate the arguments that have been made or the positions taken. For our purposes, it is sufficient to note that the rights-are-trumps view is not committed to any particular response to the Trolley Problem. This is because the right held by the one on the siding has yet to be *specified*. There are innumerable ways of specifying her rights in this situation, and some of them will not impose on others a duty not to throw the switch to save the six. Her right to life, for example, might be specified as a *right to be free of life-threatening risks absent the need to avoid the overwhelming loss of innocent life*. So described, the right would not be violated by throwing the switch. But this description will strike many as gutting the idea of having a right: if rights are specified in a way that makes them overridable by an aggregation of other interests, then they are rendered incapable of standing up to and resisting the very thing that gives them their point. Notice that, by (re)describing the right in the way suggested, the rights of the victim of your switch-throwing haven't even been interfered with!

Specifying the rights that individuals possess is an important task. Because rights are grounded in regard for individuals and their interests, and because individuals and their interests often conflict, there is the possibility that their rights will conflict also. Where rights conflict, the rights involved are devalued to some degree: we look to rights to guide our behavior, and where rights conflict, they fail to guide us. By carefully and not too expansively specifying the rights individuals have, we can minimize the occurrence of rights conflicts. But there is no reason to be confident that rights conflicts are altogether avoidable; and, where they occur, we will have to resolve them. But how? Two possibilities come to mind: One is to arrange rights in a hierarchy, so that conflicts between rights at different levels in the hierarchy can be resolved in favor of the holder of the "higher" right. The other possibility is to assign each right a weight and to judge between the conflicting rights by considering the aggregate balance of all reasons. On reflection, it appears that these two strategies come to the same thing. A hierarchy of rights makes sense only if there is some property that rights possess in unequal measure, and what property could be relevant to such a decision if it did not fairly reflect the balance of all morally relevant reasons? So, whether or not we suppose that rights fall into a hierarchical arrangement, it seems impossible to avoid the conclusion that rights – however specified – must be subject to being overridden by a sufficiently weighty balance of other reasons.

Moreover, these overbalancing moral reasons need not themselves be tied to rights. Consider the Trolley Problem again. Suppose that in this scenario, it were possible for you to save the six without sacrificing anybody.

It would then be wrong of you not to save the six. We noted earlier on that there will be disagreement as to whether the wrongness of failing to save the six can be translated into the language of rights in terms of a right, held by the six, to be saved. To put the point differently, what you ought morally to do in this variation of the Trolley scenario is clear whether or not a right to be rescued is attributed to the six. Now, put the one person back on the side track. You must decide whether to let the trolley kill the six, or to pull the switch, which will divert the trolley, save the six, but kill the one. Does it matter whether we think the six, as a general matter, have a right to an easy rescue? In other words, does it matter whether we construe the Trolley situation as involving a rights conflict – that is, between the six's right to be rescued and the one's right not to be killed? It is easy to specify the rights held, respectively, by the one and the six, in such a way that the apparent rights conflict disappears. We have already seen how the one's right not to be killed might be respecified, and obviously the six's right to be rescued could be given a narrow construction in addition or instead – in particular, it doesn't seem that the rescue is so easy in a case in which you, the actor, will cause the death of an innocent one in order to make the rescue. The Trolley Problem cannot be solved by simply invoking rights. Rights have to be specified, and even after we are confident that we've correctly specified a particular right, we seem to have to admit that for every right there are possible countervailing considerations that, once they reach a certain threshold, overcome the right.

It is possible to deny that rights have thresholds. There is no self-contradiction involved in saying that, in Trolley situations, the one's right not to be killed, even to benefit a greater number of others, simply trumps. But now put six hundred people in place of the six. Is it plausible to say that the right of the one prevails over the lives of the six hundred? What about six hundred thousand? What about six billion? At some point, what has been called the "no threshold" view begins to seem implausible. Imagine that aliens from outer space have forced you to choose between the following two outcomes: (a) one innocent person (of your gender) and yourself survive, the remainder of the human race perishes, and (b) that one innocent person dies, the remainder of the human race survives. You are to indicate your choice by manipulating a switch, which is in position (a). If you do not flip the switch from (a) to (b), six billion people die; if you do flip the switch, one person dies. It is implausible to say that it would be wrong to save the human race at the cost of a single human life. The right of the one not to be killed is not violated but, to borrow an expression, "infringed" by sacrificing him. This is more sensible than the "no threshold" view, which holds that the right not to be killed is trumps, come what may, "though the heavens fall." And it is more sensible than the view that would allow us simply to redescribe the right of the one in such terms that would, in effect, make it inapplicable.

What is the practical difference between the "threshold view" that subordinates rights to countervailing considerations, and the "redescription approach," which simply redescribes rights in a more limited way while maintaining that they are trumps within a narrower domain? An analogy drawn from American constitutional law may help. The bundle of Hohfeldian "advantages" that make up private property rights includes an immunity against the extinguishment of one's option to refuse to sell one's property against one's will. The "takings" clause of the Fifth Amendment (to the U.S. Constitution), however, states that private property is not to be appropriated for public use except upon payment of "just compensation." How does the takings clause affect the bundle of rights that property consists in? A "redescription" account would represent the takings clause as removing one of the sticks – namely, the immunity against forced sale, vis-à-vis the state. A "threshold" account, in contrast, could represent the bundle as intact, but the immunity as "defeasible," where the public interest so demanded. Under the redescription account, the requirement of "public purpose" and "just compensation" appears merely to specify the circumstances defining the immunity against forced sale to the state. Under the threshold account, in contrast, "public purpose" marks the fact that normally the immunity is absolute, and "just compensation" signifies that a departure from the norm has occurred and that the property holder is therefore entitled to payment as a matter of right to compensate for the infringement (not "violation") of her right to refuse to sell. Although either account is capable of describing what is going on, the threshold account makes it plainer that in all but extraordinary circumstances, private property is not subject to forced sale, and that when the state deems that the threshold of the extraordinary has been surmounted, the property owner is to be compensated.

The concept of a rights infringement, which the threshold account alone can incorporate, reflects what has been called the "defeasible" characteristic of rights. "Defeasible" means "important enough to be conclusive in normal circumstances, but subject to being overridden in extraordinary ones." When overridden, rights do not simply vanish, however. The right-holder will normally be owed residual consideration, which may take various forms, such as apology, compensation, and so forth. If, on the other hand, a redescription account were adopted, it is not as easy to see why such residual consideration would be owed. Conceiving rights as defeasible rather than absolute also makes better sense of the role they have in moral and legal discourse. American constitutional law offers another illustration here: the First Amendment to the Constitution states that there shall be "no law" abridging the freedom of speech. Does this mean that there can be no law penalizing, say, those who declaim poetry over bullhorns in the wee hours of the morning? The U.S. Supreme Court has interpreted the First Amendment in a way that allows the states to regulate speech to assure that it occurs in a reasonable "time, place, and manner." A strict redescription approach would send us in search of a specification of these reasonable times, places, and manners, in order to discover the precise content of the right to free speech. The threshold approach would, more sensibly, have us understand "time, place, and manner" as specifying a range of possibly countervailing considerations that, when sufficiently weighty, may overbalance the interests supporting a particular exercise of the right to free speech.

The Neo-Godwinian, Consequentialist Challenge to the Protected-Permission Model

Suppose we conclude that rights have thresholds, and are in that sense defeasible rather than absolute. Suppose also that we agree that in some cases the needs of others would be wrong for us to ignore. In so supposing, have we stepped onto a "slippery slope" that leads to an act-consequentialism of Godwinian proportions? Recall that Godwin rejected the very idea of a "right to do wrong" (what he idiosyncratically termed an "active" right). For Godwin, there could be no such thing as a permission to do anything other than that act which would bring about the most good in the

world, impersonally considered. Godwin believed that there are no genuine moral options. It is not clear whether Godwin believed that there are
any genuine moral *constraints* – that is, duties not to perform certain acts
that promise to bring about the greatest balance of good. Godwin wrote
that it is forbidden to compel another to do what is best, if the other is sincere but mistaken in his judgment. But Godwin also refused to constrain
the use of relentless social pressure, amounting to ostracism, upon those
who were mistaken. On Godwin's view, then, the protected-permission
conception of moral rights is empty, for the simple reason that there are
no genuine moral options – we are morally required at all times to act
to bring about the best. The protected-choice conception is grudgingly
accepted by Godwin despite its implicit, though limited, endorsement of
a right to do wrong. For Godwin, others have a duty not to "interfere"
with our acting upon our sincere though mistaken reckoning of what
will bring about the best consequences – but interference here means
only what amounts to physical compulsion and threats thereof. The only
right we have on Godwin's account is the right to make sincere mistakes
about how best to serve the good, and even that right is a defeasible one
that must yield in emergencies.

If we grant Godwin that rights are defeasible and that we are required
to help others in great need when we can do so at little cost, is it possible
that we are drawn into a series of further concessions that leads us into a
Godwinian world in which we have no moral options and there are only
the mildest constraints against using others – and our own being used –
to further the greater good? There are powerful neo-Godwinian lines of
argument leading to just that conclusion. Suppose I do have a right to
"do as I list" (in Godwin's phrase), subject only to my duties correlated
with the rights of others (including their right to do as they list). This
supposed right is however subject to a threshold, as is evident in easy
rescue cases. Where I can, at little cost to myself, rescue another person
from mortal danger, it would be morally wrong for me not to do so. We
need not say that the person in danger has a right to be rescued; nor need
we even say that the rights of others not to be harmed may be infringed in
order to carry out the rescue. The only concession demanded here is that
it would be wrong not to perform an easy rescue – and this is a concession
that is very difficult to resist. Notice that making this concession does not
necessarily commit us to approving of criminal or civil sanctions against

those who fail to perform the easy rescue – the question whether such "Good Samaritan" laws would be proper is a further question.

It is a principle of moral reasoning that if it is wrong to perform (or omit) a certain act in certain circumstances then it is wrong to perform (or omit) that act under any circumstances unless there is some morally relevant difference between the two sets of circumstances. Call this the "Principle of Morally Relevant Differences." This principle has been called other things, but this name fixes our attention on what is important for our purpose: Anyone who admits that an act of φ-ing is wrong in circumstances C but wants to deny that φ-ing is wrong in circumstances C' is bound by logic to point to some morally relevant difference between C and C'. It won't do to say, for example, that speeding is wrong on residential streets but not wrong on freeways, unless one is prepared to say what is the morally relevant difference between residential streets and freeways. Not all differences between residential streets and freeways will count as morally relevant. The fact that freeways are off-limits to pedestrians, and residential streets are not, is a morally relevant difference, but the fact that freeways have big green signs and residential streets don't, is not (at least not in any obvious way).

It is a fact that there are millions of people in the world, many of them children, now at risk of death, whose deaths could easily be prevented, but who will die soon because the steps required to prevent their deaths will not be taken. It would be very wrong to fail to perform the easy rescue of a child drowning in a shallow pool right in front of us, so – by the Principle of Morally Relevant Differences – it would be very wrong not to perform the easy rescue of a child in Africa who will soon die of malnutrition, unless there is some morally relevant difference between the two cases. There *are* obvious differences: the hypothesized shallow pool is at our feet, Africa is far away; the hypothesized infant in the pool can be saved by no one else, the African child can be saved by many others; the identity of the hypothesized child would be determinate in an actual case, the identity of the needy child in Africa is not known to me; I would save the hypothesized child directly, by an easy physical action, but to save the African child I would have to take a long trip or rely on a series of intermediary helpers; I am almost certain to be successful in my efforts to save the hypothesized child, but my saving an actual African child is chancy – and so on.

Given the inexhaustible number of differences between the nearby drowning child case and the starving African child case, it may seem certain that there are some, and probably many, morally relevant differences between them. But what, exactly, are they? Clearly, the difference between starving and drowning is not relevant, but the drowning child is hypothesized to be nearby, and to be present to the potential rescuer's mind, and to be savable by no one else, and to be savable by the potential rescuer's direct action. All of these differences seem, at first anyway, to be morally relevant. But are they, either individually or taken together?

What about direct action? Suppose that you happen to be confined to a wheelchair, and depend on a nurse to get you from place to place. Your nurse is an excellent swimmer, but has poor eyesight. As your nurse is pushing you along the boundary of a shallow pool, you notice the drowning child. You can do nothing, directly, to save the child. But surely it would be wrong not to draw your nurse's attention to the child and to see to it that the nurse performed the easy rescue. The fact that in this case you cannot directly save the child is morally irrelevant. Suppose that the nurse is not a good swimmer, however, but there is someone close by who is. Surely it would be wrong of you not to see to it that your nurse told the good swimmer that her help was needed. The fact that you would be effecting the child's rescue only at two removes is in itself morally irrelevant. In fact, it is irrelevant whether one, two, or many intermediaries stand between you and the child. Directness is a difference, but not a morally relevant difference.

Now that we have imagined that others are involved, suppose that you are not wheelchair bound, but that there is a crowd of good swimmers around the pool. Everyone present is perfectly capable of rescuing the child, and everyone is aware of the child's distress. Surely, now, it isn't up to you to put yourself out to rescue the child, is it? Of course not, if someone is in fact in the process of rescuing the child. But suppose no one is, and all the others in fact appear to be totally unresponsive to the child's predicament. Is it open to you to say that it isn't wrong for you likewise to ignore the child because others are doing so? Surely not. The fact that others act wrongly by doing nothing does not excuse you from doing what you can. The fact that others might help but aren't helping is not a morally relevant difference between our initial two cases. Wouldn't it matter, though, if some of the bystanders were close relatives of the drowning child, and were fully capable of the rescue? Suppose the child's father were right at hand, doing nothing. The father's failure to act is terribly wrong, but how does that alter your moral situation? Your duty to act is the same, isn't it, whether the father is absent or present but doing nothing? His omission is worse, but yours nonetheless would be very wrong.

Does it matter that the distress of the hypothesized drowning child is supposed to be evident to you, while that of the African child is known only by reading the paper and watching the news on television? Alter the drowning child example: You are seated at a poolside table browsing the web on your laptop computer, which has a wireless connection to the internet. An e-mail message pops up, from a friend who has been trying out a telescope at a camera shop some distance away. Your friend's e-mail informs you that there is a child in the process of drowning in the pool. Surely it would be wrong of you not to act to save the child, despite the fact that the child and the child's distress aren't directly evident to you. And surely it doesn't matter whether the report came to you via your friend's e-mail or by a news broadcast that you heard on your transistor radio. You know of the child's distress; how you came to know of it is of no moral relevance.

Does distance matter? Distance may affect the reliability of our perception that there is in fact someone in distress, and it may affect the cost to us of helping and the chances of our help being effective. But there is no doubt that there are millions of children who will die easily preventable deaths during our lifetimes, and there is no doubt that our discretionary incomes could prevent some of those deaths. The probabilities are not relevantly different between our two initial cases, the drowning child case and the starving African child case. But does distance still matter, even after it has been accounted for in the reckoning of costs and probabilities? It is difficult to understand why it should, although some have insisted that it does. Suppose you can walk five times faster than I and can see five times farther. We are on opposite sides of the pool, and are unaware of each other's presence. I am nearer the pool, and let's suppose you are five times farther away. With respect to what happens in the pool, you can see and do from where you are precisely what I can from where I am. Assume now that circumstances are such that it would be wrong for me not to rescue a child I see drowning in the pool, and that you see it too. Is it plausible to say that it would be permissible for you to do nothing *just because* you are farther away? I am unaware of any reason why it should. Distance, standing alone, has no moral relevance.

Maybe the discussion of the preceding paragraph overlooks something of significance. You have greater powers than I have, we supposed. But it wasn't stated where we stood, respectively, in relation to normal powers of sight and movement. Let's make this explicit. Suppose that I am enfeebled, with respect to the norm, and you are normal. In other words, my sight is only one-fifth what it should be for a person of my age, and so also my speed of movement. In this case, it seems very obvious that if I, so handicapped, have a duty to help, then you, possessed of normal capacities, have a duty too. Distance doesn't matter. But now suppose that I am the normal one, and you happen to be gifted with extraordinary eyesight and speed afoot. Perhaps in this instance it is less clear that, if I have a duty, so do you, distance notwithstanding. Why, you might ask, should your happening to be able to see and move better subject you to burdensome obligations that you wouldn't have if you were merely normal? Let's assume that from your distance, if you were normally endowed, you would be too far away to know what was happening and to do anything about it if you did. Why should you be penalized, so to speak, for happening to be abler than normal? To put the point in a positive way, you might say that distance matters because normal human capacities matter. To impose on us duties to help distant others is to ignore normal human capacities, and that's why distance matters.

This defense of the moral relevance of distance fails, however. Suppose you are normally endowed, but have worked very hard to earn enough money to buy a pair of binoculars, and have worked very hard to build an all-purpose, all-weather, go-anywhere robot, which you are able to operate by remote control. You are seated at a cafe table five times farther away from the pool than I am. You are putting your robot through its paces in the pool, watching through your binoculars, when you happen to spy the drowning child. You can easily have your robot rescue the child. Surely it would be wrong for you not to do so. Your distance from the pool is irrelevant; the fact that you will have to rely on greater than normal powers of vision and movement is irrelevant. Suppose the robot were not already in the pool, would that matter? Surely not, if we suppose that the robot can get to the child as quickly as I can, with my normal endowment of human powers, from poolside. But if you grant that in this case you, though distant, have a duty to aid, how can you deny that you would have a duty in case you possessed extraordinary but unassisted powers of sight and locomotion? After all, it would seem that your working hard to get your binoculars and build your robot would make you *more* entitled to reap the rewards without having to take on additional burdens than if you had been born with extraordinary natural advantages. How can having done less to earn special powers entitle you to do less, for others, with those powers? Normal human capacities matter, all right, but not in a way that makes distance per se morally relevant.

If this neo-Godwinian line of argument has been successful and can be generalized, it shows that – given the unmet needs in the world and the means at our disposal – there are few, if any, genuine moral options facing us at any given moment. Can it be extended to show that there are no moral constraints operating upon us either? A moral constraint is a moral requirement that forbids us to perform a certain action (such as murdering a wealthy man) even though that action would have the best consequences, of those actions available to us at the time (it would allow us to distribute his wealth to the needy). Moral constraints are the obverse of moral options: moral options exist when we are morally permitted to do something other than what would have the best consequences, moral constraints forbid our doing something despite the fact that it would have the best overall consequences. Rights on the protected-permission model depend on the possibility of moral options, but rights on the protected-choice model do not.

Rights on the protected-permission model offered us rights that combined moral permissions to do and not do with a claim-right against others' interference with that moral option. The neo-Godwinian argument knocked out that model, but seemed to leave the claim-right untouched. We are, so far anyway, still able to understand moral rights as moral claim-rights against interference – as "rights to do wrong" – and so rights are still able to perform a reaction-constraining function: if others disapprove of how we exercise our rights, they are nonetheless forbidden to interfere with our exercise. Although, as we have seen, rights as constraints against interference have thresholds, if those thresholds are set high enough rights normally protect us against interference with how we live our lives even if how we live is far from the best way to live.

The recognitional function of rights also survives the neo-Godwinian assault, but in a limited way. For an act-consequentialist, an action such as having an abortion or engaging in sodomy is never optional: it is either forbidden or required, and it is forbidden or required only because it either brings about or fails to bring about the best consequences. Nothing else about the act counts. So, in this sense, act-consequentialism achieves what rights on the protected-permission model sought to achieve – it furnishes support for the view that there is nothing per se wrong with abortion or homosexuality or not wearing a chador or whatever. But that is only because, for the act-consequentialist, there is nothing per se wrong with anything, except failing to bring about the best consequences. To put the point differently, from the neo-Godwinian perspective all the recognition any type of action or way of life is due is to be determined by considering its consequences. The discussion shifts to that subject, and of course there will be disputes about which consequences are to count and how they are to count, but the idea that any particular action or "lifestyle" is wrong, per se, has already been dismissed once this shift has been made.

True, there are reasons to adopt a rule-consequentialist rather than a strictly act-consequentialist perspective, as we have already seen. It may be, for example, that act-consequentialism fails to achieve its own goal as well as the indirect strategy endorsed by rule-consequentialism. It is easy to understand how rule-consequentialism's indirect strategy might operate to constrain actions in pursuit of the best consequences. An analogy to what has been called "the tragedy of the commons" should be helpful here. If no one owns a certain area of land, those who live in the vicinity will tend to overuse it. If, for example, there are fruit trees on the land and the fruit belongs to the first comer, then each has an incentive to take as much fruit as he can, as quickly as he can, and no one has an incentive to let the fruit ripen or to cultivate the trees. The trees get picked clean and everyone suffers. It would be better for everyone if permission to take fruit were restricted somehow, either by making the land subject to communal control or by parceling it out to individuals as private property. Unless use is restricted, tragedy – in the form of overuse and spoilation – is inevitable. But notice that tragedy also results if we assume that individuals seek to maximize not their own consumption but the supply of fruit for all. Unless individual efforts are coordinated in some way, the effort of each to maximize the common yield is liable to be frustrated by the efforts of others. If, for example, you insist on fertilizing what I have already fertilized, the result is overfertilization, scorched roots and, eventually, dead trees. So also with human conduct generally. Unless certain restrictions are imposed to limit our presupposed permission to pursue the good, individual *or* common, we all may find ourselves worse off. What is needed is a set of rules preventing interference (*interference*, in the sense of undesirable interaction).

So it is fairly easy to see why there is reason to move from a world of unrestricted permission to pursue the good to a world of restricted permission to pursue the good. But what is not easy to see is why there is reason to move from a world of restricted permission to pursue the good to a world including a permission *not* to pursue the good within the limits set by the needed restrictions. To put the point differently, the argument for constraints is not an argument for options. Is there some other argument that can be suggested for options? If there is not, then there seems to be no place for options from a consequentialist perspective (act- or rule-consequentialist). A rule-consequentialist account of rights will provide for constraints and thresholds, but not – so far as appears – for options. Rule consequentialism would support the recognitional function of rights in this sense: some traditionally forbidden types of action would not be forbidden by any rule supportable on consequentialist grounds. Rule consequentialism would support the reaction-constraining function of rights in the more straightforward sense that consequentialist rules would forbid certain types of interference with persons, even to bring about the greater good, at least so long as a certain threshold is not met (as in Trolley cases). But consequentialism offers no support for options unless there is some consequentialist basis for a rule that permits actors to ignore – within the range of rule-consequentialist constraints – the action that will have the best consequences. What basis could there be?

One thought might be that actors do best if they have some moral "time off." Unrelenting moral demands might, as a matter of empirical fact, lead to moral burnout. But in that case, as we noticed in connection with Godwin, what seems to emerge is a rule *demanding* that we take time off, not a rule permitting us to take time off or not, as the whim might take us. Again, we see that moral options are not easy to construct on a consequentialist basis, even on a rule-consequentialist one.

Separate Lives and "Agent-Relative" Reasons

A consequentialist account of rights seems inhospitable to the idea that rights not only protect us from the interference of others, but also from the demands of morality. But we aren't forced to accept a consequentialist account of rights: consequentialism has been criticized for a number of other alleged failings, as we noticed earlier. One failing is said to be its failure to respect the distinction between persons. This criticism is directed toward consequentialism's method of aggregating consequences, which tends to have two different undesirable effects on how the individual's moral situation is assessed. First, the individual actor is required to take into account effects that she is not particularly interested in, from the perspective of her own life and how she wishes to lead it. Second, the individual is exposed to treatment by others that will similarly ignore the special place her interests, values, and pursuits have for her. Another failing of consequentialism is said to be its failure to recognize a distinction between two different kinds of reason. One kind of reason has been called "agent-neutral," anything that is an agent-neutral reason for action is a universal reason, which every rational agent has reason to weigh in deciding how to act. Another kind of reason has been called "agent-relative," so-called because such reasons are reasons only for the actor; they need not be reasons for anyone else. Consequentialism would have us think that all reasons are agent-neutral reasons, ignoring agent-relative reasons and giving them no place in morality. But agent-relative reasons count for quite a lot in our ordinary moral thinking. If (recalling Godwin's example) my father and Archbishop Fénelon are both drowning in my presence, and I cannot save both, I have a reason to save my father that perhaps no one else (outside our family) has – namely, that he is my father and Fénelon is not.

These two alleged failings – the failure to take seriously the difference between persons and the failure to recognize two importantly different types of reason – are related. The difference between persons that the consequentialist's aggregative method of moral reasoning obliterates goes deeper than the fact that people normally assign a greater importance, or weight, to their own desires, aversions, friends, relatives, projects, and goals. The difference is one not merely of degree but of kind, and the difference of kind is reflected in the difference between types of reasons distinguished as agent-neutral and agent-relative. Taking the difference between persons seriously means more than allowing people to add a few points to the value of their own and their loved ones' lives and interests in a process of general weighing and balancing of everything against everything. The contractualist attempts to take this difference into account by giving agent-relative reasons a foundational role in the explanation of morality. The contractualist may not be successful, but the effort suggests the possibility of an alternative account of how rights fit into morality that might give options a more secure place.

How is a distinction in kind between agent-neutral and agent-relative reasons supposed to make room for moral options? A full answer to this question would lead beyond the scope of this book, but two possible ways of depicting options have suggested themselves. One way is to say that agent-neutral and agent-relative reasons are incommensurable vis-à-vis each other. Agent-neutral reasons may be comparable one to another, and ranked and possibly even weighed against each other. So also, agent-relative reasons may be comparable one to another, ranked, and weighed. But comparisons across the two categories cannot be made, at least not reliably. Options exist, on this line, because for a given actor the cumulative weight of agent-neutral reasons is not always possible to compare with the cumulative weight of her agent-relative reasons. Sometimes it is possible – as, for example, in the case of the easy rescue – but it isn't generally so. Moral options exist within the shelter of these incommensurabilities. Where agent-neutral and agent-relative reasons are comparable, options vanish because (we may assume) the actor is morally required to perform that act which she has the most moral reason to perform. But when there is incommensurability, there is no such action, and so no moral requirement that she either perform it or omit it – there is an option.

"Exclusionary" Reasons

Another way of explaining options is to appeal to the idea of *exclusionary reasons*, which are a kind of "second-order" reason that has this defining characteristic: Exclusionary reasons are reasons not to act on the balance of first-order reasons within their scope. For example, if I adopt a rule against trading stocks after 5 PM, that rule serves as an exclusionary reason with respect to the first-order reasons for and against trading in a certain hot stock after 5 PM. My conduct is not to be based on the balance of reasons for and against making the trade: those reasons are excluded by my practical rule. This "exclusionary reasons" account gives a particular substance to the intuitive idea of incommensurability, but without suggesting that there is anything particularly mysterious going on that makes two reasons incommensurable. Two first-order reasons may be capable of being measured against each other, but when one of them falls within the range of an exclusionary reason, the actor is not to act on the balance of those reasons. A moral option, then, can be understood as a permission to do or to omit a certain act that arises where and because there is a moral exclusionary reason that enjoins the actor not to act on the balance of moral reasons. Agent-relative reasons could be understood in terms of these option-creating exclusionary reasons. Suppose, for example, that I am in a position to help Fénelon or help my cousin, but I can't help both. The fact that one of two is my cousin is an agent-relative reason that both gives me a reason to help my cousin and acts as an exclusionary reason against acting on the balance of all reasons, which would favor my helping Fénelon instead.

These two ideas – incommensurability and exclusionary reasons – suggest at best a sketch of how moral options might be included in a wider account of morality, such as consequentialism. But the hard questions remain. How can morality tolerate reasons *against* doing what the balance of moral reasons favors? How can something be a reason for you and you only? Why would we want to say, of two reasons relevant to the same decision about what to do, that they were neither of equal weight nor of different weights, but "incommensurable"? There may be perfectly satisfactory answers, but until they have been worked out, the belief that there are moral options will remain badly in need of a defense.

10

What Is *Interference?*

Our concept of rights, properly speaking, first showed itself in history only when people began to distinguish between what is right in a general sense and what is right with respect to a certain person. This distinction is the one we marked by the unfortunately misleading terms "objective right" and "subjective right." There is dispute about when in history this distinction began to be made, and whether in fact that moment has arrived at all in at least some non-Western cultures. This possible historical and cultural variability feeds the worry about relativism – that is, the worry that rights may not be universal after all, at least not unless they are imposed on all the globe (a means that may raise a related worry about imperialism).

But the conception of subjective right, although necessary, does not exhaust what many believe to be the essential nature and contribution of the concept of rights. Practically everyone agrees that the vigor and interest of rights rests in the correlative duties they entail. As we noted in Chapter 5, Hohfeld's analysis of rights and their logical relationships does not make anything of the distinction between *duties of non-interference* and *duties that such-and-such be the case*. Hohfeld's framework thus does not build-in what many have felt to be *the* essential function of rights – that is, to protect a sphere of individual liberty from *interference*, particularly by the state and its agents. If it all comes down to some duty that such-and-such be the case, then the distinctive contribution of the concept of rights has been lost, at least on this view.

There is another dissatisfaction with letting moral rights have as their correlates duties that such-and-such be the case, rather than duties of noninterference. This dissatisfaction could aptly be described as an *expansionary worry*. The worry is that the currency of the language of rights to express moral assertions of all kinds will lead to a tendency to make inflated and unjustifiable – even nonsensical – claims unless the precise conceptual content of rights is insisted upon. Assertions of the right to noninterference (what Sidgwick also called the right to freedom, and what Brandeis invoked by "the right to be let alone") seem far less liable to be abused and to cause confusion, disappointment, and unwarranted resentment than assertions of a right that such-and-such be the case.

Are Rights of Noninterference Primary?
General and Special Rights

Is there a way to show that rights of noninterference are primary over rights that such-and-such be the case? One way that primacy might be grounded is by an appeal to the difference between *general rights* and *special rights*. General rights are rights that persons hold simply in virtue of being persons or having certain characteristics. For example, my right to free speech is a general right because I possess that right simply in virtue of being a person – I don't have to do anything to earn the right and to cast upon others a correlative duty of noninterference. In contrast, a creditor's right to repayment is a special right: it arises from the creditor's action of making a loan to the debtor. True, the creditor's special right is derivable from the conjunction of a general right to the repayment of debts and the special fact that this particular creditor and this particular debtor have conducted themselves in the relevant way. A right is a special right not because it is divorced from a background of general rights, but because it cannot be derived from general rights alone. From the fact that I have a right to free speech it follows that I have a right to sing in the shower – but this doesn't make my right to sing in the shower a special right in the sense under discussion. A special right is not a mere specification of some more particular act already within the scope of a general right; rather, it depends on the right-holder or the correlative duty-bearer having acted in some way.

Given the distinction between general and special rights, the following thesis may be formulated: General claim-rights are rights against interference; their correlates are never duties that such-and-such be the case, but are always duties of noninterference. Certain special rights are the only moral claim-rights that correlate with duties that such-and-such be the case. Call this the "*positive duties are voluntary*" thesis. It tells us that all duties are either (a) duties of noninterference, or (b) duties incurred in virtue of some voluntary act. The "positive duties are voluntary" thesis is an appealing one to those who think that the world of rights includes both a general right to be free of interference by others as we live our lives as we choose and such special rights that come into being in virtue of voluntary conduct – but does not include any general right that anything be the case.

The "positive duties are voluntary" thesis rules out the possibility of any general right to welfare, subsistence, or any other kind of assistance. It also rules out the possibility of status-based duties – such as parental or filial duties – except to the extent that they can be linked in some way to voluntary conduct. General claim-rights have correlative duties of noninterference, but failure to provide necessities is not intended to be understood as interference. Failure to provide necessities might be a breach of a duty correlative to some special right, but special rights presuppose some voluntary action on the part of either the right-holder or the duty-bearer. If, for example, I have made no promise to save you from drowning, you have no right that I rescue you from drowning, no matter how safe and easy it might be to do so. Of course, I have a duty not to interfere with your rescue, but that is a general duty incumbent upon me apart from any voluntary undertaking. Again, failure to act and interference are to be contrasted.

What kinds of actions trigger special rights? Three candidates are prominent: actions by the duty-bearer, actions by the right-holder, and combinations of the first two kinds. Actions by the duty-bearer that trigger special rights are easiest to understand. Let us say I promise to put your laundry in the dryer. My promising is a voluntary action that creates a special right whose correlative duty is a duty that such-and-such be the case – that is, that your laundry be put in the dryer. You, the beneficiary of the duty, need do nothing for the right to come into being. But I, the duty-bearer, have to do more than refrain from interfering with your laundry's being conveyed from the washing machine to the dryer; I have to make it the case that it is conveyed there.

The second type of case – involving voluntary conduct on the part of the right-holder alone – is more problematic. How can the right-holder's unilateral voluntary act cast upon another a burdensome duty? Even where the duty-bearer benefits by the right-holder's conduct, and the burden of the duty is less than the benefit, there is something in us that makes us doubt. If I, unbidden, wash your windshield, do I thereby acquire a right that you make something nice happen for me? Although for some cultures (Mauss 1990), the answer would be Yes, most of us (who are not Trobriand Islanders or members of the Tlingit or Kwakiutl tribes) would say, No. What we need is a compelling example of a right-holder's unilateral conduct placing others under burdensome duties.

John Locke's theory of property rights is the type of explanation that we are in search of. Locke's theory rests on the idea that by "mixing" my labor with an unowned piece of the world, I may thereby acquire property rights in it. All the world then has a duty not to interfere with my dominion over the thing so acquired. The property right is special, not general, because having whatever traits are necessary to be a general right-holder isn't sufficient to create *my* right to *this* thing. If merely being a person, for example, were sufficient to create property rights they would have to be shared with all other persons; but what Locke was after was a justification of *private* property – that is, rights in property that give one person dominion over a *thing to the exclusion of* all other persons.

My acquiring private property rights imposes correlative duties of noninterference upon all others. What have they done to incur such duties? Nothing. Here is a case of special rights arising from the activity of the right-holder alone or, if you prefer, from the activity of the right-holder combined with the inactivity or untimely activity of those who failed to mix their labor with the thing before I did. But those who are drawn to the idea that special rights presuppose some voluntary action *on the part of the duty-bearer* will find Locke's justification of private property unsatisfactory. What have later-mixers *done* to deserve being interfered with in their use of the thing to which the earlier-comer claims an exclusive right, a right that disregards the element of chance that may have favored the earlier-comer, as well as the possibility that the later-comer may have the greater need and greater capacity to cultivate the thing from which she is excluded? Locke's theory is subject to the famous provisos that the earlier-comer leave "enough and as good" for the later-comers to acquire by mixing their labor, and that the first-comer not leave what he appropriates to spoil. But even with the provisos, Locke's theory fails to address one crucial point: Why should anyone be burdened by a duty that is neither a general duty of noninterference (as the right of private property is not, since the owner is allowed to interfere with me but not I with the owner, with respect to the thing owned), nor a duty incurred by the duty-bearer's voluntary act? To put the point another way: If your acting to benefit me, unbidden, is generally insufficient to impose a duty upon me, how can your acting, unbidden, to *benefit yourself at my expense* be sufficient?

It seems that if rights are in some sense fundamentally "negative" – that is, claim-rights against interference or coercion – that fact has to be shown in some way other than by invoking the distinction between general and special rights. Just as an appeal to Hohfeld does not establish that the duties that correlate to claim-rights are fundamentally duties of noninterference rather than duties that such-and-such be the case, so also an appeal to the general rights/special rights distinction fails to establish the primacy of duties of noninterference.

Does the Primacy of Autonomy Assure the Primacy of Rights of Noninterference?

There are other possible grounds for the view that duties of noninterference are primary. These grounds might be found by turning our attention back toward rights and what they add to the correlative idea of duty. Many have argued that it is because the value of individual autonomy is so central to the concept of rights that what must exist at the core of a moral right is a claim-right against interference rather than a claim-right that such-and-such be the case. Let us assume that this argument is sound and see where it leads. Making this assumption, we can explain what moral rights are in the following general way. Rights constrain what others are permitted to do: even if the best outcome could be brought about by interfering with the right-holder in a certain way, the existence of the right means that that sort of interference is morally forbidden – that is, forbidden unless a threshold is surmounted, and even in case it is, the right does not vanish but generates residual duties of repair for the injury done by the infringement. This constraining potency of rights protects individuals against interference with their choices about how to live and extends that protection on a basis not dependent upon the correctness or worthiness of the particular course of action the rightholder chooses. Rather, the basis of the protection rights afford is the importance of autonomous choice itself, judged apart from the merits or demerits of the ends to which that autonomy is directed. This sketch of the basis of rights is consistent with both Choice and Interest Theories as justificatory theories, and it has an obvious affinity with the protected-choice conception of moral rights.

Because autonomous choice normally presupposes an ability to act according to the choice one has made, respecting autonomy means forbidding interference with action. The clearest cases of interference are those in which the actor is rendered physically incapable of acting as she would choose to act were she capable. Persons who have been killed or maimed, imprisoned, exiled, or confined by the actions of others have been interfered with in obvious ways. But persons who have been bullied, intimidated, or threatened have also suffered interference as well. But now we have to consider two kinds of borderline situation. One, in which the actions of others make a certain choice costlier to the right-holder than she is willing or able to pay in order to do as she chooses. Another, in which the right-holder lacks the means necessary to act as she would choose. Both situations involve costs, but in the first situation others impose or threaten to impose costs upon the right-holder, while in the second the costs are not imposed by others prospectively, but already attach to the right-holder's choice in such a way that her choice is prevented. The two situations present, respectively, the question whether costs can ever properly be imposed upon a right-holder's choice of action, and the question whether a full accounting of rights allows such costs to lie where they fall. We will look at the first question in the remainder of this chapter, and at the second question in the next chapter.

Is Imposing Costs Always Interference?

We are proceeding on the hypothesis that a moral right to perform an action φ entails a duty others have not to interfere with the right-holder's choice whether or not to φ. But, as we have seen, a moral claim-right to φ, standing alone, does not entail that the right-holder has a moral option with respect to φ-ing. The protected-permission model of moral rights would add that option to form a new molecule of Hohfeldian elements, but in Chapter 9 we found reason to doubt that moral options exist. The question therefore arises: If the right-holder has a claim-right against interference with his choice whether to φ, does that leave him protected or not against others who would impose costs upon his choosing wrongly? To put the point more bluntly: If rights are rights to do wrong, what, if any, costs may others impose upon the right-holder's acting wrongly but within his rights? To put the question into context, consider the example of motorcycle goggles.

Suppose that in a state of nature without traffic laws, failing to wear goggles while operating a motorcycle creates sufficient risk of injury to self and others that it is wrongful not to wear them. Suppose also that the importance of individual autonomy is sufficiently great that motorcyclists have a moral right to choose whether or not to wear goggles. Motorcyclists might for any number of reasons prefer not to wear them: goggles may impair or distort vision to some extent, they may be expensive, they may be a nuisance to wear, and they may subtract from the sense of freedom that makes motorcycling enjoyable in the first place. Some motorcyclists might go so far as to claim that it is safer for them to drive without goggles than with them – but we are supposing that they are wrong about this. Goggles keep matter from blowing into the eyes, and so prevent the sudden impairment of vision that can cause collisions and other accidents. It is wrong, we are supposing, not to wear goggles, but motorcyclists have a right to do this wrong.

What would constitute interference with the right not to wear motorcycle goggles? Hiding, stealing, or destroying the motorcycles of goggle non-wearers would clearly constitute interference. Letting the air out of the tires of non-wearers would be interference. Surgically attaching goggles to the faces of motorcyclists would be another kind of interference. So would throwing rocks at nonwearers. So would making credible threats to do any of these things. Godwin would surely agree, at least with respect to the conscientious motorcyclist: Even if both generally and on every particular occasion wearing goggles would be best, respecting the individual's autonomy to make and act upon his own judgment as to what is best requires the rest of us not to interfere. But Godwin, we recall, would allow us to exhort the non-wearers to change their ways, and even to hector them into leaving the vicinity if they will not. To say that it is wrong for one not to wear goggles while operating a motorcycle is to say that others are morally permitted to make unwelcome, even hurtful, comment upon one's wrong action. This is not interference, nor is it infringement. Infringement occurs when what would otherwise be a rights violation is permitted due to a threshold of countervailing reasons having been met – but that is not what we are imagining here. Permitting this kind of social pressure is what it means to take wrongs seriously.

In between the polar extremes of permissible criticism, on the one end, and violent compulsion, on the other, we can discern a variety of other types of reaction to (or anticipation of) the conduct in question, many of which can be said to attach costs to the right-holder's choice to act wrongfully. One type has to do with assigning responsibility for bad outcomes of the right-holder's choosing to do wrong. If a bit of grit blows into the cyclist's eye, causing him not to see a pedestrian in time to avoid colliding with her, then we might hold him responsible for the accident and find that he has a duty to compensate the pedestrian for any injury she suffers. The basis for holding him responsible would be that his wrongful failure to wear goggles caused the accident. Had he worn the goggles and the bit of grit somehow gotten into his eye anyway, we would not find him at fault, and might not expect him to compensate the pedestrian.

Another type of reaction – in the anticipatory sense – to such conduct consists of measures to influence motorcyclists to wear goggles by way of fostering a goggle-wearing culture. This could involve incentives and indoctrination. Would it be permissible to require motorcyclists to contribute financially or otherwise to these measures? The right not to wear motorcycle goggles does not obviously entail a right to refuse to contribute to pro-goggle education. In other words, being required to contribute to the eradication of φ-ing isn't automatically an interference with one's right to φ. (Government measures to discourage smoking, to take another example, aren't thought to interfere with the right to smoke, although measures that restrict indoor smoking to private dwellings come closer to the line.)

As we leave a state of nature and imagine a legal regime to be in operation, still other possible reactions come into view. Is respecting the right to φ consistent with forbidding φ-ing without a license? Is it consistent with charging φ-ers for a license to φ? If licensing and license fees are permissible, why not modest fines for each act of φ-ing? The distinction between interference and noninterference becomes fuzzy at the boundaries. If there is nothing wrong with φ-ing, then we are inclined to say that it is wrong even so much as to criticize or poke unwanted fun at those who choose to φ. But once we suppose that φ-ing is wrongful, we seem to experience a reversal of this inclination even as we also suppose that there is a right to φ. The existence of a right to φ logically demands that certain reactions to φ-ing be morally forbidden. But the wrongness of φ-ing similarly demands that certain other reactions to φ-ing be morally permitted. The moral landscape in the vicinity of any supposed right to do wrong will be shaped by these two opposite, contending, moral forces.

What can be said, then, about the nature of interference? Compare the goggle-wearing case with a case of a wrong which there is *no* right to do – stealing, for example. There are limits to the morally permissible reactions to stealing. Surely it is not morally forbidden to impose costs upon those who steal, but just as surely there is no moral "open season" on thieves. Just as there are moral norms that loosely define what is and is not interference with not wearing motorcycle goggles, so also there are moral norms that define what is and is not "interference" with stealing. What may strike us as odd is the suggestion that there might be anything even prima facie wrongful about a measure taken in response to a wrong-without-a-right, such as stealing. But that suggestion is what talk about "interference with stealing" seems to convey!

A bold thought may strike us: Talk about a claim-right against interference with φ-ing simply boils down to talk about the range and contours of morally permissible reactions to engaging in actions of the φ-ing type. This range is subject to limitations whether or not the act-type φ-ing is one the actor has a right to engage in. When we juxtapose two wrongful types of action, one which there is a right to do and another which there is no right to do – for example, not wearing motorcycle goggles, on the one hand, and stealing, on the other – we discover that as to both types there are burdens that it is morally permissible to impose upon actors in virtue of the wrongness of actions of the type. At the same time, we discover that there are moral limits to the range of burdens permissible to impose upon actions of either type. We are no more permitted to boil thieves in oil than we are ungoggled motorcyclists. What, then, does a right on the protected-choice model come to, other than perhaps a narrower and milder range of morally permissible sanctions to which the right-holder is subject? The conclusion we are led to is that this difference in the range and severity of morally permissible sanctions is the *only* difference between having a protected-choice right to φ and not having one. Godwin might be pleased.

Noninterference Rights as Standing and Proportionality Norms

So, reflection shows that the protections rights offer us are limited in two different ways. One, our rights do not exempt us from social pressures and consequences that fall short of interference. Two, our rights may not in every case (and perhaps in no case) exempt us from interference when there is an extraordinary balance of reasons going in favor of interference. Rights are distinctive and valuable despite these limitations. If rights are best understood according to the protected-choice conception, the protection rights afford is best understood in terms of what I will call *standing* and *proportionality* norms. Proportionality norms are simply duties that specify, within a range, the degree of pressure that may permissibly be brought to bear on an individual to ensure that her conduct conforms to what morality demands. Not all moral wrongs are permissibly corrigible by the same expedients – imprisonment may be a permissible corrective for theft, but not for overtime parking, for example. Similarly, not everyone has the proper standing to apply pressure to correct moral wrongs – it may be perfectly appropriate for a parent to correct a child's boisterousness, for example, but wrongfully officious for a stranger to interfere. *Interference*, then, can be understood as whatever violates relevant standing and proportionality norms. This means that interference is a moral concept rather than a merely physical one, but that implication is exactly right. The soprano's aria and the humming of the gentleman seated next to me in the opera house are both acoustic vibrations, but only one of the two is an interference with my right to enjoy the performance of the orchestra.

Once rights are understood in terms of the protected-choice conception, we can better appreciate their value to us in terms of standing and proportionality norms. On the protected-choice conception, at least some of our rights are "rights to do wrong." The wrongness of our choice must expose us to some permissible social pressure, but not to disproportionate or officious pressure. In contrast, when a right is conceived in line with the protected-permission model, I do no wrong whichever choice I make, so there is no occasion for social sanctions, much less for interference, with my choosing. We can understand the reaction-constraining function of moral rights, as embodied in the protected-choice model, as protecting us against *undue* social pressures and *unwarranted* interferences – while recognizing that we remain vulnerable to a due degree of social pressure, via suitable agents, and subject to interference warranted by extraordinary circumstances.

We can extend this understanding of the protection rights afford to the case of positive rights as well. The right of X to Y's assistance, for example, cashes out in terms of Y's duty to assist X. The sting of X's positive right resides, in other words, in the coordinate retreat of Y's negative right of noninterference. But – just as in the case of Y's stealing from X – standing and proportionality norms apply that limit what may permissibly be done to Y to secure that assistance or punish Y's failure to provide it. These norms apply generally to all actions, whether they are forbidden, permissible, or required. Permissible or morally required actions are actions that do not warrant adverse reactions by others, and so the actor needs no further moral protection from such reactions (given the general duty not to react unwarrantably toward the actions of others). Forbidden actions do require protection from the reactions of others, for reactions of some kind *are* warranted. But the wrongdoer's rights protect her against disproportionately severe and officious reactions – this is the value of rights as constraints on reactions, and this is what must be meant by a right against interference.

11

The Future of Rights

We have been exploring the twentieth-century effort to understand the nature of rights and to locate their moral footing. But this intellectual enterprise is at best only a part of the story. As we noted in Chapter 6, the 1948 Universal Declaration of Human Rights inaugurated a second expansionary period of rights discourse. The expansionary tendency of rights discourse was held in check for at least a decade and a half, however, by the global standoff between the West and the Soviet bloc – the Cold War. Owing, in part, to the expanse of the rights set forth in the 1948 Universal Declaration, both sides in the Cold War could draw on the Universal Declaration for propaganda purposes. The West emphasized the denial of political rights in the Communist world, while the Communists pointed to the economic insecurity and inequality tolerated in the West, as well as the residual injustices of colonialism – including apartheid in Africa and racial segregation in the southern United States. Given the tension and hostility between the parties, there was more than ample incentive to propagandize. A seeming stalemate between propaganda and counter-propaganda was broken, however, by a series of developments, which included decolonization by the Western powers, the dismantling of official racial segregation in the United States, and the diplomatic isolation of apartheid South Africa. The turning point may have been the Helsinki Final Act of 1975, a set of accords between the West and the Soviet bloc which had the effect of enabling non-governmental organizations (NGOs) based in the West to monitor Soviet and Eastern European compliance with agreements to respect their citizens' political rights. The dissolution of the Soviet bloc in 1989 and of the Soviet Union itself in 1991 ended the Cold War. The movement for human rights could rightly claim to have catalyzed all of these events, on both sides of the "iron curtain" dividing East and West; and these events seemed to signal the approach, if not the arrival, of a global consensus about the priority, as well as the universal existence, of a set of political and civil rights.

But the end of the Cold War has not marked the end of the history of rights, nor the end of the second expansionary period. For one thing, a preponderance of the nations of the Earth, and of its people, do not yet enjoy the effective protection of what have been termed the "first generation" human rights – the civil and political rights that citizens of economically developed Western democracies generally take for granted. In much of the world, political dissent is not tolerated, political participation is nonexistent or meaningless, arbitrary arrest and detention are commonplace, and caste and gender discrimination are institutionally enforced. Those governments and societies that deny these first-generation human rights do so in a manner unlike that in which they were denied in the former Soviet bloc. The Communist governments of the Soviet era did not repudiate, but shared, a common intellectual heritage of Enlightenment thought about the importance of individual well-being. Differences with the Western democracies centered around issues of priority and implementation. Moreover, the constitutions of the Soviet states at least facially honored the first-generation rights, and Soviet bloc women enjoyed certain limited possibilities of advancement somewhat before they were realized in the West.

At the threshold of the twenty-first century, resistance to first-generation rights came to be expressed and defended by appeal to what have been called *second-generation rights*: a motley grouping of economic, social, and cultural rights. Two main strands of argument can be identified. The first – which was also prominent during the Cold War period – rests on an appeal to the priority of economic rights, in opposition to the West's priority for first-generation political and civil rights. The second – which is contrary to the internationalism of the Communist ideal – is an appeal to rights held, not by individuals but by collectivities, to determine and pursue their own cultural values. These two, distinct, strands of argument deserve further discussion.

Second-Generation Rights, and Third-...?

Among nations, there are wide disparities in economic development and, consequently, individual well-being. According to the World Bank's statistics for the year 2000, the nation with highest average per-capita income in the world is Luxembourg ($45,100 US); the nation with the lowest is Ethiopia ($100 US). This difference is huge. Poverty almost as extreme as Ethiopia's persists in much of the world despite the existence of global markets. Without a decent standard of living, rights of any kind are worth little; furthermore, a second-generation right to a decent standard of living is recognized in Articles 22 and 25 of the 1948 Universal Declaration. As former Prime Minister Lee of Singapore has argued, there is not a unique path to successful economic development (Singapore's per-capita GNP is among the world's highest). The economic success of different nations requires different means, and for some nations a more authoritarian mode of governance may be needed in order to establish a decent standard of living. Accepting the autonomy and well-being of individuals as the proper end of state policy does not necessarily entail the priority of first-generation civil and political rights. The contrary may be true, as the success of "Eastern Tiger" economies such as Singapore's suggests. Therefore, the argument goes, honoring the human right to a decent standard of living requires that it have priority over certain of the first-generation civil and political rights.

Amartya Sen (1999) and others have responded by arguing that as a matter of empirical fact nations that violate first-generation rights invite economic disaster. Sen's work shows that famine is often not a matter of food shortage but of misallocation brought on by an authoritarian government's denial of free speech and press. Moreover, according to what has been termed the "*democratic peace*" hypothesis, authoritarian governments are likelier to engage in aggressive war than democracies. Therefore, authoritarian government is likelier to lead a nation into the disasters of famine and war than into a condition of prosperous peace. Whether or not first-generation rights deserve any theoretical priority, they are a necessary means to – rather than an obstacle to – the fulfilment of second-generation economic rights.

Two sorts of reply to these points are possible. One will emphasize the empirical nature of the question of what best serves economic and cultural development in a particular country, and the incompleteness of Sen's analysis of modern famines and of the democratic peace hypothesis. Not all underdevelopment is the same, and not all of it is the consequence of war or famine. Nor have all authoritarian regimes landed their countries in famine or war. Because local conditions vary, and needs and remedies are best known to local officials, this reply concludes, it should be up to each nation to determine for itself what relative priority to assign first- and second-generation rights.

The second sort of reply also appeals to self-determination, but as a human right belonging to peoples rather than as a merely prudential rule of thumb. Not only do the people of each nation know better what is best for them, they have a collective moral right to determine their own priorities. Any attempt by Western governments or NGOs to force developing nations to give absolute priority to first-generation rights – or even worse, to give absolute priority to *Western conceptions* of first-generation rights – is a species of neo-colonialist imperialism. This twist is a manifestation of the imperialism worry mentioned in Chapter 1, but here it takes a subtler form. This reply need not express skepticism about the very idea of human rights, or dispute their universal applicability. Rather, it introduces an appeal to a right of self-determination, held by entire peoples rather than individuals, standing in opposition to international efforts to guarantee a universal regime of first-generation rights. Although some second-generation rights – the right to at least a minimal subsistence, for example – can be taken as straightforwardly individual rights, other second-generation rights – such as a right to cultural integrity, or to national self-determination – cannot. These latter examples can only be construed as *group* rights – that is, as rights held not by individuals singly but by groups collectively.

A group-rights construction of second-generation rights has been supported from what has been called the *communitarian* perspective. Communitarians emphasize the importance of belonging to a distinctive community as an essential component of, as well as a means to, individual well-being, or "flourishing," as it is often termed (with appropriately gestural connotations). Communitarians have defended (usually with qualifications) the importance of patriotism and nationalism, which tend to be disparaged from the cosmopolitan viewpoint connoted by the idea of universal human rights, as well as from the individualistic perspective sometimes said to be fostered by the "culture" of rights.

A group-rights construction of what have been termed "third-generation" rights seems even more apt. *Third-generation rights* are rights that the environment be of a certain quality, or that the economy be developed to a sufficient degree. Rights of future generations most naturally fall within the third-generation category. Third-generation rights are not communitarian, but neither are they individual rights; they have to be understood as somehow belonging to humankind without being held by anyone or any group in particular. Although third-generation rights will seem to some to be "manifesto" rights, at best, the fact that the classification exists at all serves to emphasize the degree to which "rights talk" has become an international language in which all manner of moral arguments and claims are now framed. (From a radical perspective, Roberto Unger (1987) proposes that the disempowered and underprivileged be given "destabilization rights" to disrupt concentrations of economic and political power.)

As we have seen, the concept of rights is sufficiently flexible to admit many – if not all – of these expansive conceptions. To speak of a right held by future generations, or a right that the environment be unpolluted, seems to be to speak of *what is right*, rather than of *a right held by* any determinate individual or group – to speak, in other words, of objective rather than subjective right. But, rather than try to legislate against certain third-generation rights claims on the ground that they confuse what we have termed subjective and objective right, it may be better to note the ambiguity and then to assess each moral claim as most charitably construed.

Although, as we saw in Chapter 5, there is no absurdity in attributing a ("subjective") right to a group, the dispute about the relative priority of

first- and second-generation rights can easily be muddled if it is miscon-
strued as equivalent to a dispute about the relative priority of individual
and of group rights. This confusion is conspicuously irrelevant in the case
of the second-generation right to at least minimal subsistence. Each and
every Sudanese individual possesses this right, if it exists, and possesses it
whether or not it would make sense to say that each and every Sudanese
individual has, say, a right that there be a Sudanese state. By taking sufficient care, it is possible to isolate treatable and intelligible moral issues
within the admittedly crowded bandwidth of human rights claims.

Minimalism About Human Rights

There is another approach, however, which instead deals with the problem of dissension surrounding the issues of human rights definition and
priority by insisting that human rights claims be restricted to a minimum.
So-called "minimalist" approaches are perhaps motivated by the worry
that human rights discourse seems to be on its way to becoming "a club
too heavy to lift." As rights claims proliferate, the language of human
rights takes on unnecessary and unwieldy baggage of both normative
and metaethical kinds. Added normative baggage consists in the fact that
with each additional generation of rights consensus is left farther and
farther behind. Contrast a paradigm first-generation right, the right not
to be tortured, and the second-generation right to a decent standard of
living (a fairer example than the right to two weeks paid vacation stated
in Article 24 of the Universal Declaration.)

   Torture is nearly universally condemned, even if still too often practiced, but talk of a right to a decent standard of living will seem to many to
confuse what is a worthy goal with a yet-to-be-recognized, amorphous,
and unenforceable claim of individual right. If there were a right to a decent standard of living, who would owe the correlative duty? Immediate
neighbors? Immediate wealthy neighbors? The state? The international
community? You and me? If there were such a right, by what means might
it be enforced? Self-help? Appeal to government? Appeal to the conscience
of those able to assist? If there were such a right, would it be forfeitable
by indolence or improvident risk taking? Many, if not all, of the kinds of
skeptical worry that Bentham raised against the French Declaration arise

again here: "Hunger," after all, "is not bread," and many, not automatically callous, people will add that a need for bread is not a right to it. When human rights claims are expanded beyond the reach of consensus, not only is the expansion likely to fail to win any effective advantage for the putative right-holders, but the very language of rights is debased in a way that enfeebles protections even for consensus first-generation rights.

The feared enfeeblement of rights discourse can come about because the inescapable difficulty of settling controversial rights claims raises doubts about the metaphysical basis of all rights discourse, whether controversial or not. The minimalist approach adopts what Rawls calls a "method of avoidance" toward metaethical and metaphysical issues. Minimalism is concerned lest the rights revolution overplay its hand. The moral progress represented by the universal adoption of human rights discourse must not obscure the fact that it has not been supported or accompanied by any parallel metaethical progress. The intellectual basis of moral assertions of all kinds is far more dubious now than it was during the first expansionary period of rights discourse. To ignore this fact is to encourage dogmatism about rights and to ignore the hard lesson of the first expansionary period: Dogmatism about rights (human, moral, or natural) can be as destructive as any other variety of moral dogmatism. The better approach respects the difficulty of moral questions and the irreducible variety of values that different people and peoples employ in answering them. Consensus is to be cherished and guarded, and if this means restricting valid and internationally enforceable human rights claims to a minimal list, including not even all among the first generation – so be it. The alternative is tantamount to a declaration of (quasi-)religious war.

Although minimalism does not logically require the rejection of a human right to an enforceable, decent, economic minimum – whether as a claim by an individual against the state in which she resides, or as a wider-reaching claim against other nations and even individuals everywhere – its spirit is decidedly reluctant. As a tactical matter, setting aside the second-generation right to a decent economic minimum as at best a "manifesto" right may appear to be a necessary and reasonable price to pay to hold together an international consensus in opposition to the most flagrant violations of first-generation rights. Minimalists such as John Rawls not only decline to apply the distributive principles that justice requires domestically to the international arena, they also soft-pedal international enforcement of certain first-generation rights, particularly those having to do with nondiscrimination and political participation (2001).

Is Minimalism About Human Rights Justified?

At this point, it would be worthwhile to recapitulate briefly what is at stake when an assertion is made about the existence of a human right. At the very least, a human-rights claim is a claim that certain human interests are of sufficient importance to generate a duty on the part of others to perform or to avoid a certain type of action that would, if performed, consist in or have the effect of setting back – "interfering with" – the interest of the right-holder, or with actions of the right-holder related to that interest. The right to free speech, for instance, is grounded in a universal human interest in expressing one's thoughts and sentiments, which is of sufficient importance to impose upon others at least a prima facie duty not to silence one by compulsion or threats or to take certain other actions that would deny one's interest in expression. My right to free speech leaves others free to contradict, criticize, ridicule, or ignore me, but others are not free to muzzle me, cane me, or drown me out with sirens. My free-speech right is subject to a range of conditions, and is defeasible in case massive catastrophe would result. This is the core notion we derive when we back a Hohfeldian claim-right with a justification following the general pattern of justificatory Choice or Interest Theory. This simplest molecule serves a "reaction constraining" function in the most literal sense. My free-speech right means that others are in certain ways duty-bound not to react to (or to anticipate) what I might say.

To say that one prefers to be sparing, or "minimalist," in one's approach to rights might mean any one of a number of things. It might mean, for example, that one preferred the lean, protected-choice conception of right, which was just outlined, rather than the protected-permission model, which would build into the right itself a moral option on the part of the right-holder. Or it might mean that one preferred not to build into the conception of a human right the right-holder's bilateral power of enforcement and waiver that is distinctive of the conceptual Choice Theory. Or it might mean that one was prepared to insist that the range of human interests sufficient to generate a claim-right and its correlative duty is a much narrower range than might be supposed. Or it might mean that one preferred some selection of these, or perhaps even other restrictions. (Some find the idea of group rights unappealing, for example.)

But those who counsel a minimalistic attitude toward human rights seem to be motivated not so much by conceptual scruples as by the practical worries mentioned earlier: that the very shortage of logically compelled conceptual boundaries makes it inviting to couch any and every sort of normative assertion in terms of rights, and that this inherently inflationary susceptibility of rights-discourse is capable of undoing much of the moral progress that has been made internationally since the Second World War. The prospect of demands for armed humanitarian intervention to protect human rights in such places as Kosovo and Rwanda puts a finer edge on these worries. If human rights are, in Michael Ignatieff's phrase, "a fighting creed" (1999), then it is only prudent to insist that it be a moderate or even a minimal one.

There is, however, at least one respect in which the minimalist attitude goes well beyond the counsel of prudence in enforcing rights, and that is the aforementioned question of the existence of a human right to a decent economic minimum. The underlying thought here may be that such a right is so inherently destabilizing that its mere recognition – even its being heard as a "manifesto" right – would tend to bring disastrous consequences. A human right may represent a demand of justice in two different senses: it may be a demand on the state (if any) in which the right-holder resides, but it may also be a demand on other states, the international system of states, and on individuals everywhere. Insofar as respecting human rights is insisted upon as a condition for membership among the family of nations, recognizing a human right, in the first sense, to a decent minimum might require states to take domestic redistributive measures, on pain of suffering international sanctions. The second sense in which a human right expresses a demand of justice is even farther reaching. If there is in fact a human right to a decent minimum standard of living, then all states in the international community, and all persons everywhere, are brought within its scope. The worrisome fault line here is not so much between West and non-West as between North and South, Haves and Have-Nots.

Here, minimalism ironically makes common cause with certain strains of the second-generation-rights-based resistance to international guarantees of first-generation rights. This strain is the one that emphasizes not economic rights but rights to national or cultural self-determination. The group right of a people to organize itself politically in a way that reflects and perpetuates its unique cultural traditions is also one that is reflected in basic human rights documents, particularly the 1966 International Covenant on Economic, Social, and Cultural Rights (Brownlie 1992). A minimalist whose concern was solely to minimize both normative and metaethical assumptions might look askance at the idea of such group rights. But a minimalist concerned chiefly to promote consensus would be solicitous of the very widespread allegiance that nationalist ideologies command today. In fact, international law in its "positive" or descriptive sense rests on the assumption that states possess such rights as a right to territorial integrity and a right to exclude immigrants. As moral rights, such expansive group rights should be troubling to a minimalist. For how are they to be reconciled with the "methodological individualism" of empirical social science? How are they to be defended on the model of justificatory Interest Theory? But minimalism in the prudential sense will, on the other hand, suppress these corrosive questions in the hope of maintaining a wide consensus about human rights in a world that remains wedded to nationalist ideologies.

Is Allowing Costs Ever Interference?

The imprecision, difficulty, and potential explosiveness of issues of distributive justice are often cited as reasons to assign priority to first-generation civil and political rights over second-generation economic rights within a theory of justice for a state. These factors are compounded when the question of distributive justice is transposed to an international context, especially given the vexed history and dramatic inequalities that characterize relations between the industrialized nations north of the equator and the developing nations to the south. It might be better if issues of distributive justice were taken off of the international human rights agenda. But it is important not to confuse the issue of the prudence of insisting on a right with the separate issue of that right's existence. A minimalist attitude toward human rights to distributive justice should not trade upon this kind of confusion. Is there any special reason to be skeptical of the very existence of a right to distributive justice (including a right to a decent minimum)?

In Chapter 10, we distinguished two types of case in which an individual lacks the means necessary to act as she would choose and must shoulder the costs of acquiring those means. In the first type of case, these costs are imposed or threatened by others, whereas in the second type, the costs are not imposed by others, but otherwise already attach to the right-holder's choice in such a way that her choice is prevented. The question now is whether it is defensible to maintain that one has a right not to have costs imposed upon one (namely, a right not to be interfered with) but no right to have others help one bear them. If we look at this question in Interest Theory terms, we must find that there is an interest of the right-holder of sufficient importance to justify imposing upon others a duty not to impose costs on his acting, but which interest is nonetheless insufficient to justify imposing upon others a duty to help shoulder the costs of his acting. And what could that interest be? One might insist that an autonomy interest fills the bill – that, in other words, an individual's interest in self-government *is* important enough to deny others a permission to interfere with his actions within a certain range, but *is irrelevant* to their having a moral permission to fail to support or facilitate his actions within that range. Why? Because in the latter case, their support would render his action no longer one of *self*-government? If *helping-to-do* were tantamount to *doing-for*, the argument from autonomy against recognizing a right to assistance might work. But it simply is not generally true that when others help, one fails to do for oneself. Sometimes that is true, but generally not. Granting financial aid to a student is not the same as taking her exams for her. If it were the case that we never truly do anything but what we do all by ourselves, then it would turn out that we truly do very little indeed.

The appeal to autonomy fails to answer the following challenge: If autonomy is so important an interest, why can't it generate duties of assistance as well as of noninterference and, correlatively, rights to assistance as well as rights of noninterference? Or, put in terms of rights, the question becomes: If autonomy is so important an interest, why do humans not possess a right to at least minimal means necessary for the exercise of their autonomy? It is no answer here to say that it is permissible to allow others to lack sufficient means to exercise their autonomy even though it is impermissible to cause them to lack those means. This answer is really only a roundabout appeal to the idea that "negative" rights enjoy some kind of priority over "positive" rights. As we saw in Chapter 10, there are no good conceptual grounds for this priority claim. The grounds for any such priority claim must instead be normative, that is, they must consist of moral reasons, and it is precisely this kind of reason that is conspicuously lacking when we cast about looking for grounds for denying that human beings have a right to a level of subsistence at least minimally sufficient to enable them to act autonomously.

In a world of gross inequality, it is not easy to reconcile minimalism about individual economic rights with "*supra*minimalism" about group rights to exclude individuals from national territories. Millions of productive people are currently present illegally in the United States, for example. Most of these illegal aliens are economic rather than political refugees. They are present in the United States because that is where they can find employers willing to pay them the best wages. By what right might anyone exclude them from this territory, if their presence does not violate anyone's rights – as it does not? There is a gross maldistribution of wealth in the world, and immigrants such as these are acting peacefully and constructively to correct it. They need not assert any right to positive assistance because all they require is the "negative" liberty to be free of interference as they work and reside where work and residence are voluntarily offered to them in the market for such things. They pose no puzzles about how much they are due, for the market itself makes that determination: They are due what their employers freely contract to pay them for their labor. Those who object that immigrants take jobs away from natives ignore the simple fact that such jobs are not anybody's property. True, to the extent that borders are open, natives are deprived of the right to determine the character of their territory by exclusionary means. But do the credentials of that putative (group) right measure up to those of the individual right to move freely about and engage in productive labor? (If Locke's theory of property is invoked to support a group's claim to territory, how can his "nonspoilage" proviso be satisfied, where labor shortages leave jobs unfilled?) This is not to suggest that there is no way at all to defend the practice of restricted immigration, but it is to emphasize that the combination of individualism and cosmopolitanism inherent in the idea of human rights is corrosive of the creed of nationalism. In a way, this is not surprising, because it was as a reaction to the horrific excesses of German and Japanese nationalism that the second expansionary period of rights began, just as the first expansionary period began as a reaction to the wasteful religious controversy that fueled wars in England and Europe.

What's So Special About Humans?

There is another dimension of expansion that the second expansionary period has been witnessing. One way of understanding moral progress is in terms of an "expanding circle" metaphor. Rights in the eighteenth century were largely reserved to white male property owners, but they have gradually come to be extended to persons without regard to race, sex, or resources. Few seriously doubt that this expansion of the circle of rights-protection was moral progress. But the "expanding circle" metaphor is ambiguous in that it fails to define whether the expansion has an inherent limit at the extremity of the human circle (or of the circle of sane adult noncriminal humanity), or whether, instead, the expansion should be understood as capable of carrying beyond the circle of humanity altogether, to encompass, say, higher animals, or all animals, or even all life, or the terrestrial biosphere itself? Is it "expansion *of* the circle" or merely "expansion *to the limit of* the circle"?

An analysis of the concept of human rights does not resolve the ambiguity. Human rights, one would think, are rights possessed by all (and only) humans, who possess these rights simply in virtue of their humanity, that is, in virtue of their being human. Although the point may sound trivial, it is not, and in fact it is controversial and likely to remain so. Controversy is possible, and inevitable, because the phrase "human rights" is as ambiguous as the expanding circle metaphor. The phrase "human rights" may mean "those rights belonging to human beings as such" or it may mean "those rights paradigmatically attributed to human beings in virtue of their possessing important characteristics and capacities." In the first sense, it is trivially true that nonhuman animals can have no human rights (and also trivially true that human fetuses and permanently co-matose humans can have human rights). But in the second sense, it is not trivially true that human fetuses or permanently comatose humans can have human rights (nor trivially true that nonhuman animals necessarily lack them). Obviously it would sound odd to attribute a human right to a right-holder that was neither human nor a group of humans. But is this oddity anything more than an artifact of anachronistic "speciesist" patterns of thought? We have to face the question squarely: What (if any-thing) of significance is added when we speak of "human rights" rather than of rights, simpliciter? (If a term connotes an illegitimate restriction, it should perhaps be avoided, which explains why the phrase "the rights of man," which is capable of connoting that women are not right-holders, is no longer heard.)

One thought is that speaking of *human* rights is simply a way of em-phasizing the universality and noncontingency of certain rights which are distributed equally among humans, in contrast to rights that are contin-gent on some qualification or the satisfaction of some condition. A young warrior's right to sit with the tribal council would not be a *human* right, on this account, because the tribal council is a local institution and partic-ipation in it may be contingent on one's satisfying whatever qualifications the council prescribes. Contrast this with the young warrior's right not to be tortured by the tribal council. This is a human right because it ex-tends at least to all humans, and extends to them unconditionally. Does it makes sense to ask whether a goat has a human right not to be tortured by the tribal council? No, if only humans have human rights. Yes, if the goat might possess the characteristics that give all humans a right not to be tortured.

Another interpretation of the phrase "human rights" would empha-size the status of human rights as legal rights. It could be objected that human rights cannot be construed as positive legal rights because there is no global legal system in which they are promulgated. This objection would be misinformed, however. The world system of independent and sovereign territorial states (sometimes called the "Westphalian system," after the Peace of Westphalia that ended the Thirty Years War) has been in a process of flux. International institutions such as the European Union, the International Criminal Court, and the World Monetary Fund have begun to exercise some of the prerogatives formerly thought to belong exclusively to sovereign states. The Universal Declaration of Human Rights itself is regarded as a source of law if (as some would insist) not law itself. Even for those who take a narrow view of what counts as law, there is a discernible trend among nations, transnational organizations, and NGOs to regard human rights as legal rights.

Despite this trend toward general legal recognition, human rights are preeminently moral rights, whose existence and validity do not depend on their being recognized or instituted. It is tempting to say that human rights are simply what the eighteenth century called natural rights, and leave it at that. Conflating the two would emphasize the continuity over the centuries of core concerns about the relationship between people and their governments and between people and each other. The phrase "human" rights draws attention to the fact that these important moral rights are now nearly universally understood to be distributed among people without regard to race, skin color, religious confession, nationality, property qualification, marital status, or gender. And sexual orientation is on its way to joining these other forbidden grounds of discrimination. In contrast, the term "natural" rights seems to open the possibility of arguing that certain natural differences among human beings are good grounds for distributing rights selectively. It is undeniable that the first expansionary period of rights discourse was one in which many otherwise pioneering thinkers assumed that such natural differences between humans existed and were relevant to the distribution of rights. Refusing to treat the terms "natural rights" and "human rights" interchangeably is a way of acknowledging this profound difference.

The adjectives "natural" and "human" mark a difference that goes even deeper, insofar as they indicate different grounds for assigning rights. It is tempting to think that the "nature" referred to by the eighteenth-century phrase "natural rights" was simply the self-same human nature that we understand to be invoked by the word "human" in our phrase "human rights." But that ignores the fact that the eighteenth century generally viewed nature as a creation intentionally ordered in an ascending hierarchy culminating in the Creator Himself. Although vast numbers of people living today still hold this or similar views, the term "nature" no longer conveys it with any distinctness. Rather, nature has come increasingly to be viewed as the subject of secular science, and any hierarchy discovered in nature to be viewed as the unintended result of blind forces. In the eighteenth century, the idea that men were "endowed by their Creator" with certain rights was the kernel of the notion that such rights were natural rather than artificial. But our contemporary idea of human rights has had to thrive in a wider world in which more various accounts of "the Creator" have to be reckoned with, and in which science rather than religion is looked to for answers to questions about human nature.

The suggestion that the idea of human rights is "ineliminably religious" – as Michael Perry has argued (1998, 11) – is correct in the sense that a physicist's ideally complete description of nature will not include any rights. But it will not employ any other morally significant categories either, such as persons, harms, duties, or values. Rights are no better or worse off than any other moral notion: all could be said to be "ineliminably religious" if "religious" is operating as a residual category for whatever is important to us but not to the natural scientist *qua* natural scientist. On the other hand, we have found no reason to think that the idea of human rights cannot be grasped in terms of other moral notions. If this means that the reductive worry is realized, perhaps we should conclude that that was a valetudinarian worry all along: to say that *A* is best understood in terms of *B*, *C*, and *D* is not to say that *A* is useless baggage. But the most unsettling way to take the suggestion that human rights are "ineliminably religious" is to take it as carrying the implication that religious doctrines must be consulted to determine what human rights there are.

Because eighteenth-century natural rights presupposed a morally ordered world and a morally significant natural hierarchy, it was relatively easy to understand why "natural kinds," such as races, sexes, and species, might have moral significance, and might even be adequate grounds for discriminatory distributions of natural rights. Whether they did have such significance or not was disputable, but the burden of persuasion could more readily seem to lie upon those who would deny the moral relevance of any natural difference. Why would God bother to make both sheep and goats if He did not mean to separate them? Almost two centuries of effort and argumentation were necessary to subdue the position that race and sex might be good natural grounds for differentially assigning rights. During that interval, race and sex as natural kinds underwent a radical transformation. From being conceived as divinely ordained categories whose moral significance resided in ultimately inscrutable divine purposes, natural kinds became, after Darwin, artifacts of a blind natural process of mutation and selection. (The continuing dispute over the very existence of race and gender as natural kinds, rather than as mere "social constructs," represents the residual momentum still residing in the idea that there is a moral order to nature, and that to locate a natural boundary is prima facie at least to locate a morally relevant difference.) The 1948 Universal Declaration of Human Rights, and subsequent human rights achievements, might have represented the conclusion that the human species as a species (and not merely the white, male, property-owning part of it) occupies a special position in a morally ordered cosmos, and that intraspecies boundaries are therefore prima facie morally irrelevant. But that would be to ignore the fact that between 1789 and 1948 the supposition that natural kinds – even species – reflect an underlying moral order had lost its secure hold upon educated minds.

The 1948 Declaration marked a realization that human insight into the processes of nature had brought with it the acquisition of such terrible destructive power that, in the interest of its own survival, humanity had no choice but to accept strict constraints on the behavior of nations, the preeminent wielders and abusers of that power. The representatives of the nations of humanity recognized that humanity no longer enjoyed an assured position in nature, and could in fact, by pursuing its own follies, extinguish itself. It would have seemed ironic, at best, for humanity's representatives to have made a universal declaration of *natural* rights, for their motivation was not so much to reassert a natural moral order as to remedy the lack of one. The force that bound the atom was all-too-evidently not sufficient to bind humankind.

Whose Human Rights?

Claims on behalf of fetuses, children, animals, androids, future generations, and ecosystems as rights-holders present a different aspect when examined from the perspective of human – in contrast to natural – rights. Human rights locate value in being human, which if taken in a biological sense seems to strengthen the claims on behalf of fetuses, children, and future generations of humans, while weakening those of animals, androids, and ecosystems. But being human need not be taken in a biological sense. "Being human" might be a compendious way of referring to certain actualized capacities for awareness, forethought, and autonomy of action. (Interest Theory might put the question in terms of "what it means to be capable of having interests.") This way of taking "being human" weakens the claims on behalf of fetuses and future generations of humans, and of animals, young children, and severely handicapped humans. Dropping the requirement that the capacities be already actualized would tend to elevate claims on behalf of fetuses, young children, future generations, and (perhaps) of androids and the severely handicapped – while leaving those of animals and ecosystems behind.

Rights mark the special importance of certain interests, and so we might conclude our pursuit of the question "What's so special about humans?" by asking what are the interests that humans, as a species, possess that set them apart from nonhuman candidate right-holders, such as animals, androids, and ecosystems. With respect to human beings, developmental qualifications for right-holding are uncontroversially applied to certain rights such as rights of political participation and rights to engage in gainful employment. Children may not vote and may be denied eligibility to contract for employment; but children nonetheless have a right not to be tortured or experimented upon, and so do the profoundly handicapped and the permanently comatose. But then, does a goat not have a right not to be tortured? Do we give the goat his full due by saying that all have a duty not to torture him but he has no right not to be tortured? (Keep in mind that the goat's sentience may exceed that of a profoundly retarded or comatose human being.) Do we give the profoundly handicapped person his full due by saying that all have a duty not to experiment upon him but he has no right not to be experimented upon?

Talk of rights, as we have seen, often serves a recognitional function. Sometimes a right to live a certain way is asserted simply as a manner of saying that there is nothing wrong with living that way. Talk of rights may also serve a recognitional function by indicating that certain interests of the right-holder have a special importance, which is great enough to impose duties of noninterference upon others even where a better outcome or an outcome more satisfactory to others would be served by allowing that interference. Perhaps the best way of understanding the emphasis given to being human in the phrase "human rights" is this: Human rights recognize *extraordinarily* special, basic interests, and this sets them apart from rights, even moral rights, generally. We have a moral right to expect others to keep their promises. We have that right because we have an important interest in being able to plan and structure our lives. But one would hesitate to call this a human right, or to call the breaking of a promise a human rights violation per se. This is because talk of human rights serves the recognitional function of singling out extraordinarily important interests. Once it appears that some such particularly important interest is shared by nonhuman creatures – such as the interest in not being made to suffer gratuitous pain – it in no way derogates from the recognitional point to attribute the right to the nonhuman creature as well. "Even a goat has a right not to be tortured" may be just as emphatic a way of condemning the torture of a human being as it would be to say instead, "Torture violates a human right."

As long as we are clear about what interests are at stake, and what duties are at issue, there seems to be no further reason not to allow discourse about the rights of any putative right-holder – from ecosystem to zygote. To the extent that the expression "*human* rights" tends to obfuscate rather than to reveal what is really going on, perhaps its usefulness has been exhausted – much in the way that the usefulness of the phrase "*natural* rights" expired with the belief in a divinely ordained moral order. To the extent that the expression "*human* rights" suggests that there is some deep conceptual connection between belonging to the human species and having rights, perhaps it should be retired – just as the phrase "the rights of *man*" has given way to gender-neutral equivalents.

The eighteenth century was as alive as we are today to the possibility that there are nonhuman rational beings in existence. (Stray balloonists in France were occasionally mistaken as extraterrestrials.) Immanuel Kant, the greatest philosopher of that century, took care to establish his ethics upon reason alone in abstraction from those qualities of human beings that might set them apart from other reasoning beings in the cosmos. Our era, however, has an additional reason not to restrict ethics to the circle of humanity. That is because our understanding of the basic molecular processes of biology, and our ability to manipulate, alter, and augment them, is becoming so great that the very idea that there exists a biologically given human nature is now in question. The increasing rate of technological change further augments our powers – so much so that it is no longer possible to say to what degree our progeny will resemble us, or in what respect. These are disturbing facts. One response is to insist that controls be set on the application of techniques that might alter what we regard as human nature: The human interests that generate rights are important enough to require us to assure that our basic humanity does not transform itself into something else. Another response is laissez-faire: We have no right (one might say) to insist on a posterity that shares our nature, nor do the eugenic or cybernetic techniques chosen by the living necessarily violate any individual's rights; therefore let come what (or who) may. The concept of rights is unlikely to decide this issue; indeed, it seems not to be easily amenable to any of the tools of moral analysis.

12

Conclusion

Moral rights, I have argued, are best understood as protected choices. The protection may be against interference by others or by the state, but may also be against deprivation by natural circumstances, by bad luck, or by the right-holder's own bad decisions. The protection moral rights afford comes in degrees. I introduced the idea of proportionality and standing norms to explain how it can be that one can have a right to do wrong. No one, I argued, has a right to do wrong with impunity; the question is, what sort of punishment is licensed by the bare fact that a right-holder has made a morally wrong choice? The answer, schematic though it may be, is: Something. Some social sanction, administered by some authorized actor. It may be as dire as capital punishment, or it may be as slight (is it slight?) as scorn, ridicule, and ostracism. But moral wrongness has its bite, just as having a moral right has its.

Those who think that rights have grown all out of proportion to responsibilities are in an obscure way trying to draw attention to this fact. Having a right (understood according to the protected-choice model) does not entail having a moral permission to do what one has a right to do, nor does it entail that others are duty-bound not to apply sanctions (short of interference) in response to one's exercise of one's right. But having a right, per se, entails no duty whatever on the part of the right-holder. The right-holder will normally have duties, but these are not logically derivable from the rights she has. Although many of her duties *are* derivable from reciprocal rights others may have, the concept of rights, standing alone, does not logically entail this reciprocity.

Understood in this way, moral rights serve both reaction-constraining and recognitional purposes. Rights serve a recognitional function not by awarding permissions but by protecting the interests individuals have in making certain choices: rights accomplish this by constraining the reactions of others to those choices. A moral right, as we have seen, may or may not involve a power to waive and a power to enforce the correlative duty that is the core of the right. The conceptual version of Choice Theory makes a strong case for the inclusion of such powers in the case of legal rights in a mature legal system. But in the realm of moral rights, there are some correlative duties protecting some interests so central to our common notions of decency that their protections cannot be waived. This is the realm of inalienable rights. Not all moral rights are inalienable, but some are, particularly those whose special importance has been marked by their recognition as human rights. Some moral rights are forfeitable as well as alienable, but some are neither.

If this is all there is to moral rights, do they represent any sort of conceptual breakthrough, or do they enable substantive moral advances that were not possible at earlier stages of human development? The answer is, No. But neither is it true that rights represent a corruption of moral thinking, or a redoubt in which vicious selfishness has found refuge and a base of operations. As we have seen, rights do not, by themselves, insulate us from the demands of morality. If there is any such insulation, it is not derivable from the bare concept of rights. Nor is there any necessary basis in the concept of rights for the substantive moral claim that negative rights enjoy some sort of primacy over positive rights. That may be true, but substantive moral argument is needed to establish it. One of the reactions that rights can constrain is a reaction of indifference to the needs of others.

The historical career of the idea of rights has been a complicated one. The picture I have offered, of two expansionary periods, is crude and approximate at best. What to make of this (arguably) late appearance of rights on the world-historical stage, and of their ups and downs? Rights are not a confirming instance of the thesis of moral relativism, but neither do they herald a Copernican Revolution in moral thinking. Discontinuity over time always has a Janus face: in one aspect, it manifests inconsistency, but in another, it can represent progress. From one side, it shows us irreconcilable diversity; but from another, progressive approximation to reality. The Copernican Revolution in science showed how we could discover massive error in our old ways of thinking, yet still have some assurance that we had not been totally deceived and were not condemned forever to exchange one illusion for another. This showing emerged not all at once, but by the unfolding of further discoveries that were valuable.

The Rights Revolution has yet to prove itself in a similar way. Rights, like moral ideas generally, and unlike scientific ones, are of small value in predicting events. What is wrong is as likely to occur as what is not and (it is a sad fact) perhaps likelier. Scientific ideas "deliver the goods" in that they enable us to predict and control what experience will show us. Moral ideas have to show that they have a capacity to "deliver the goods" in some other way than by being confirmed by experiment. Yet moral ideas are capable of figuring in experimentation in a looser sense; Mill's talk of "experiments of living" (1859, 68) was not entirely figurative. We know that there are better and worse ways of living, even if we cannot always agree on what is the better way. To the extent that rights make it possible for people to experiment with their lives without making mere experiments of others, they are to be cherished.

Bibliographical Notes

These notes cover only a part of the vast and growing literature on the subject. I indicate the readings that most influenced the writing of this book and other sources the curious reader might next consult.

Chapter 1   The Prehistory of Rights

Although MacIntyre (1981) and Dover (1974) find ancient Greece not to have been receptive to our notions of rights, Fred D. Miller (1995) argues a contrary result. My discussion of the mediaeval disputes is heavily indebted to Tuck's account (1979). Schneewind (1998) and Skinner (1978) are also extremely helpful, and on the "peculiar institution" of slavery, Davis (1966) is indispensable. The differences between Lee Kuan Yew and Amartya Sen are set out by Sen (1999). Glendon (1991) cautions against the contemporary obsession with rights, and Wellman (1998) and others warn of the expansionary tendency of loose rights-talk. The "endowment effect" has been confirmed experimentally by Thaler (1990).

Chapter 2   The Rights of Man: The Enlightenment

The works of Kant, Hobbes, and Locke are widely available; of Paley and
Pufendorf, less so; and those of Grotius are hard to come by. Bishop Butler's
"A Dissertation on the Nature of Virtue" is included among his *Five Sermons*
(1950). The sanction theory of duty is the subject of an excellent essay by Peter
Hacker (1973). Rossiter (1999) reprints The American Declaration of Independen-
dence, and Waldron (1987) reprints the French Declaration of the Rights of
Man and of the Citizen. Schama's book (1990) is a more recent, readable, but
somewhat scornful account of the French Revolution.

Chapter 3   "Mischievous Nonsense"?

Mark Philp (1986) contests the usual classification of Godwin as an act utilitarian.
Godwin's *Enquiry Concerning Political Justice* is currently out of print, but
various editions of Burke's *Reflections* are available. Waldron's wonderful but
out-of-print book (1987) offers excerpts from Bentham (1843), Burke, and
Marx, along with astute commentary and excellent bibliographical essays.

Chapter 4   The Nineteenth Century: Consolidation
and Retrenchment

Ryan (1974) and Hamburger (1999) offer radically divergent pictures of Mill, but
space limitations have made it impossible to explore the many controversies
surrounding the interpretation of this pivotal figure, particularly those arising from the relationship between *On Liberty* and *Utilitarianism*. On U. S.
constitutional law, one good casebook is by Stone et al. (2002); it includes the
text of the Constitution and the Bill of Rights, as does Rossiter (1999). Lacey
and Haakonssen (1991) collect valuable essays on the philosophical underpin-
nings of the U.S. Bill of Rights, and White (1978) particularly emphasizes the
influence of Jean-Jacques Burlamaqui, whom I was unable to discuss in this
short book.

Chapter 5   The Conceptual Neighborhood of Rights:
Wesley Newcombe Hohfeld

Hohfeld's expositors are generally more accessible than Hohfeld: particularly
good are Arthur Corbin's introduction to Hohfeld (1964), Feinberg (1973),

and the more elaborate account by Thomson (1990). H. L. A. Hart (1982) shows in detail that Bentham had anticipated many of Hohfeld's elements and relations. The interpretation and application of Hohfeld's analysis has been further explored by Martin and Nickel (1980), Lyons (1970), Rainbolt (1993), and Kramer, Simmonds, and Steiner (1998).

Chapter 6 The Universal Declaration, and a Revolt Against Utilitarianism

The full text of the Universal Declaration of Human Rights is included in Brownlie's compilation of human rights documents (1992). Nickel (1987) explores the philosophical issues underlying the new emphasis on human rights. Issues between utilitarians and their opponents are ventilated in collections by Smart and Williams (1973) and Sen and Williams (1982). Three major contributors to the contractualist effort to account for rights are Rawls (1971), Scanlon (1982, 1998), and Gauthier (1986). Important papers by Harsanyi (1977) and by Scanlon (1982) can be found in the Sen and Williams collection (1982), along with a number of other (sometimes technical) papers. H. L. A. Hart's "Are There Any Natural Rights" (Hart 1955) is collected in various places, including Waldron's anthology on rights theories (1984).

Chapter 7 The Nature of Rights: "Choice" Theory and "Interest" Theory

Wellman (1995) and Steiner (1994) offer vigorous defenses and propose aggressive applications of Choice Theory. In the early 1970s, Joseph Raz introduced the concept of an "exclusionary reason" (1999), and he has elaborated an influential version of Interest Theory (1986). Kramer (2001) and MacCormick (1977) advance conceptual versions of Interest Theory of legal rights. The exchange between Kramer, Simmonds, and Steiner (1998) is the most thorough and up-to-date treatment of the Choice Theory/Interest Theory dispute. Other notable systematic treatments of the subject of rights include those by Finnis (1980), Ingram (1994), Jacobs (1993), Martin (1993), Rainbolt (1993), Sumner (1989), and Spector (1992).

Chapter 8 A Right to Do Wrong? Two Conceptions of Moral Rights

Jeremy Waldron's essay, "A Right to Do Wrong?" (Waldron 1981) is collected with other papers of his (Waldron 1993). Kramer's contribution to a somewhat technical debate about rights (Kramer, Simmonds, and Steiner 1998) and Waldron's part of an exchange with neo-Godwinian Shelly Kagan (Waldron 1994) are also pertinent. Sandel (1989) examines the idea of rights "bracketing" certain moral disputes.

Chapter 9   The Pressure of Consequentialism

The arguments advanced in this chapter draw on those of the leading neo-Godwinian consequentialists: Singer (1972), Kagan (1989), and Unger (1996). Ronald Dworkin (1981) characterizes rights as "trumps" over the pursuit of goals, and Nozick (1974) coins the term "side-constraint." The 1967 paper in which Phillipa Foot posed the Trolley Problem has been collected with other papers of hers (1978). Frances Kamm (1992–94) has mounted a sustained, case-centered critique of consequentialism. A connection between the thesis of Garrett Hardin's influential paper "The Tragedy of the Commons" (Hardin 1968) and the general need for constraints is drawn by Schmidtz (1991).

Chapter 10   What Is Interference?

Hart (1955) distinguished general and special rights, and Waldron (1988, chapter 4) carefully explores the difference in the context of the theory of property rights. Berlin (1969) emphasized the distinction between positive and negative liberty, which has been criticized by Oppenheim (1961), MacCallum (1972), Shue (1996), and others. Mauss (1990) described the folkways of the Trobriand Islanders, the Tlingit, and the Kwakiutl. Waldron (1994) and Kagan (1994) present opposing accounts of the relationship between duty and sanction. Elsewhere, I discuss standing and proportionality norms in greater detail (Edmundson 1998).

Chapter 11   The Future of Rights

Martin Golding (1984) argues for the primacy of welfare rights, and immigration rights are the subject of the essays collected by Schwartz (1995). For differing views of the human future, compare Moravec (1990) and Kurzweil (1999) with Kass (2002), Fukuyama (2002), and John Paul II (1995). Ronald Dworkin warns that developments in biotechnology threaten to throw us into a "state of moral free-fall" (2000, 448). Two of the pioneering philosophical advocates of the interests of animals divide over the centrality of rights: compare Singer (1975) with Regan (1983). Kramer (2001) defends the potential of animals as legal rights-holders from an Interest Theory perspective. Distributive justice as a human right is advocated by Shue (1996), Beitz (1999), and Buchanan (2003); a contrasting, minimalist approach to international human rights is advanced by Rawls (2001) and Ignatieff (2001). Ignatieff also takes issue with Perry (1998) on the question whether moral rights can only be founded upon a religious basis. Raymond Geuss (2001) suggests that rights are an inherently conservative but ultimately senseless concept, while Derek Parfit (1984) expresses the hope that secular moral theory can reconcile consequentialism with our increasingly rights-centered moral thinking.

References

Austin, John. [1832] 1995. *The Province of Jurisprudence Determined.* Ed. Wilfred E. Rumble. Cambridge: Cambridge University Press.

Beitz, Charles R. 1999. *Political Theory and International Relations.* Rev. ed. Princeton: Princeton University Press.

Bentham, Jeremy. 1843. *Anarchical Fallacies.* In vol. II, *The Works of Jeremy Bentham.* Ed. John Bowring. Edinburgh: William Tait.

―――― 1970. *Of Laws in General.* Ed. H. L. A. Hart. London: Athlone Press.

―――― [1789] 1996. *An Introduction to the Principles of Morals and Legislation.* Eds. J. H. Burns and H. L. A. Hart. Oxford: Clarendon Press.

Berlin, Isaiah. 1969. *Four Essays on Liberty.* Oxford: Oxford University Press.

Brownlie, Ian, ed. 1992. *Basic Documents of Human Rights.* 3d. ed. Oxford: Clarendon Press.

Buchanan, Allen. 2003. *Justice, Legitimacy, and Self-Determination: Moral Foundations for International Law.* Oxford: Oxford University Press.

Burke, Edmund. [1790] 1971. *Reflections on the Revolution in France*. London: Dent.

Butler, Joseph. [1736] 1950. *Five Sermons*. New York: Liberal Arts Press.

Clarke, Samuel. 1705. *A Discourse Concerning the Unchangeable Obligations of Natural Religion*. Excerpted in D. D Raphael, ed. 1991. *British Moralists 1650–1800*. Vol. 1. Indianapolis: Hackett.

Constant, Benjamin. 1820. The Liberty of the Ancients Compared with that of the Moderns. In Benjamin Constant, *Political Writings*. Trans. Bianamaria Fontana. Cambridge: Cambridge University Press (1988).

Davis, David Brion. 1966. *The Problem of Slavery in Western Culture*. New York: Oxford University Press.

Dewey, John. 1927. *The Public and Its Problems*. Denver: Swallow.

Dover, Kenneth. 1974. *Greek Popular Morality in the Time of Plato and Aristotle*. Berkeley: University of California Press.

Dworkin, Ronald. 1981. Is There a Right to Pornography? *Oxford Journal of Legal Studies* 1: 177–212 (adapted and collected in Waldron 1984).

———— 2000. *Sovereign Virtue*. Cambridge, MA: Harvard University Press.

Edmundson, William A. 1998. *Three Anarchical Fallacies*. Cambridge: Cambridge University Press.

Feinberg, Joel. 1973. *Social Philosophy*. Englewood Cliffs, N.J.: Prentice Hall.

Finnis, John. 1980. *Natural Law and Natural Rights*. Oxford: Oxford University Press.

Foot, Phillipa. 1978. The Problem of Abortion and the Doctrine of Double Effect. In Phillipa Foot, *Virtues and Vices*. Oxford: Basil Blackwell.

Fukuyama, Francis. 2002. *Our Posthuman Future: Consequences of the Biotechnology Revolution*. New York: Farrar, Straus & Giroux.

Gauthier, David. 1986. *Morals By Agreement*. New York: Oxford University Press.

Geuss, Raymond. 2001. *History and Illusion in Politics*. Cambridge: Cambridge University Press.

Glendon, Mary Ann. 1991. *Rights Talk: The Impoverishment of Political Discourse*. New York: Free Press.

Godwin, William. [1793] 1976. *Enquiry Concerning Political Justice*. Ed. Isaac Kranmick. Harmondsworth, U.K.: Penguin.

Golding, Martin. 1984. The Primacy of Welfare Rights. *Social Philosophy & Policy* 1: 119–36.

Grotius, Hugo. [1646] 1925. *De Jure Belli Ac Pacis Libri Tres.* Vol. 2. Trans. Francis W. Kelsey. Oxford: Clarendon Press. [Vol. 2: English translation. Vol. 1: Latin original].

Hacker, P. M. S. 1973. Sanction Theories of Duty. In *Oxford Essays in Jurisprudence (Second Series).* Ed. A. W. B. Simpson. 131–70. Oxford: Clarendon Press.

Hamburger, Joseph. 1999. *John Stuart Mill on Liberty and Control.* Princeton: Princeton University Press.

Hardin, Russell. 1968. The Tragedy of the Commons. *Science* 162: 1243–48.

Harsanyi, John. 1977. Morality and the Theory of Rational Behaviour. Reprinted in Sen and William 1982.

Hart, H. L. A. 1955. Are There any Natural Rights? *Philosophical Review* 44: 175–91.

_____ 1982. *Essays on Bentham: Studies in Jurisprudence and Political Theory.* Oxford: Clarendon Press.

Hazlitt, William. [1825] 1964. *The Spirit of the Age.* London: Everyman.

Hohfeld, Wesley Newcomb. [1919] 1964. *Fundamental Legal Conceptions as Applied in Judicial Reasoning.* Ed. Walter Wheeler Cook. Westport, CT: Greenwood Press.

Hobbes, Thomas. [1651] 1996. *Leviathan.* Ed. Richard Tuck. Cambridge: Cambridge University Press.

Hume David. [1789] 1967. *A Treatise of Human Nature.* Ed. L. A. Selby-Bigge. Oxford: Clarendon Press.

Ignatieff, Michael. 1999. Human Rights: The Midlife Crisis. The *New York Review of Books.* May 20, 1999.

_____ 2001. *Human Rights as Politics and Idolatry.* Princeton: Princeton University Press.

Ingram, Attracta. 1994. *A Political Theory of Rights.* Oxford: Clarendon Press.

Jacobs, Lesley A. 1993. *Rights and Deprivation.* Oxford: Clarendon Press.

John Paul II, Pope. 1995. *Crossing the Threshold of Hope.* New York: Knopf.

Kagan, Shelly. 1989. *The Limits of Morality.* Oxford: Clarendon Press.

_____ 1994. Defending Options. *Ethics* 104: 333–51.

Kamm, Frances M. 1992–94. *Morality, Morality.* 2 vols. Oxford: Oxford University Press.

Kant, Immanuel. [1785] 2002. *Groundwork for the Metaphysics of Morals.* [*Grundlegung zur Metaphysik der Sitten*]. Trans. Allen W. Wood. New Haven: Yale University Press. Citations in the text are to *Immanuel Kants Schriften.*

Ausgabe der königlichen preussichen Akademie der Wissenschaften [AK]. 1902-. Berlin: de Gruyter. The translations are my own.

Kass, Leon R. 2002. *Life, Liberty, and the Defense of Dignity*. New York: Encounter.

Kramer, Matthew H., N. E. Simmonds, and Hillel Steiner. 1998. *A Debate Over Rights*. Oxford: Clarendon Press.

Kramer, Matthew H., ed. 2001. *Rights, Wrongs and Responsibilities*. Basingstoke, Hampshire, U.K.: Palgrave Macmillan.

Kuehn, Manfred. 2001. *Kant: A Biography*. Cambridge: Cambridge University Press.

Kurzweil, Ray. 1999. *The Age of Spiritual Machines*. New York: Penguin.

Lacey, Michael J. and Knud Haakonssen, eds. 1991. *A Culture of Rights*. Washington, DC: Woodrow Wilson Center and Cambridge University Press.

Locke, John. [1690] 1952. *The Second Treatise of Government*. Ed. Thomas P. Peardon. Indianapolis: Bobbs-Merrill.

Lyons, David. 1970. The Correlativity of Rights and Duties. *Nôus* 4: 45–57.

MacCallum, Gerald., Jr. 1972. Negative and Positive Freedom. In Peter Laslett W, G. Runciman, and Quentin Skinner, eds. *Philosophy, Politics, and Society: Fourth Series*. pp. 174–93. Oxford: Basil Blackwell.

MacCormick, D. N. 1977. Rights in Legislation. In P. M. S. Hacker and J. Raz, eds. *Law, Morality, and Society: Essays in Honor of H. L. A. Hart*. Oxford: Clarendon Press.

MacIntyre, Alasdair. 1981. *After Virtue*. Notre Dame, IN: Notre Dame University Press.

Martin, Rex. 1993. *A System of Rights*. Oxford: Clarendon Press.

Martin, Rex, and James W. Nickel. 1980. Recent Work on the Concept of Rights. *American Philosophical Quarterly* 17: 165–180.

Mauss, Marcel. 1990. *The Gift: The Form and Reason for Exchange in Archaic Societies*. Trans. W. D. Hall. New York: W. W. Norton.

Marx, Karl. 1844. On the Jewish Question. Excerpted in Waldron 1987.

Mill, John Stuart. [1838] 1962. *Essay on Bentham*. In Mary Warnock, ed. *John Stuart Mill: Utilitarianism*. Glasgow: William Collins.

——— [1859] 1956. *On Liberty*. Ed. Currin V. Shields. New York: Liberal Arts.

——— [1861] 1957. *Utilitarianism*. Ed. Oskar Piest. Indianapolis: Bobbs-Merrill.

Miller, Fred D., Jr. 1995. *Nature, Justice, and Rights in Aristotle's Politics*. Oxford: Clarendon Press.

Moravec, Hans. 1990. *Mind Children: The Future of Robot and Human Intelligence.* New York: Oxford University Press.

Nickel, James W. 1987. *Making Sense of Human Rights: Philosophical Reflections on the Universal Declaration of Human Rights.* Berkeley: University of California Press.

Nozick, Robert, 1974. *Anarchy, State and Utopia.* New York: Basic Books.

Oppenheim, Felix. 1961. *Dimensions of Freedom.* New York: St. Martin's Press.

Paine, Thomas. [1791] 1994. *The Rights of Man.* New York: Random House.

Paley, William. [1786] 1811. *The Principles of Moral and Political Philosophy.* Vol 1. London: J. Faulder et al.

Parfit, Derek. 1984. *Reasons and Persons.* Oxford: Clarendon Press.

Perry, Michael J. 1998. *The Idea of Human Rights: Four Inquiries.* New York: Oxford University Press.

Philp, Mark. 1986. *Godwin's Political Justice.* Ithaca: Cornell University Press.

Pufendorf, Samuel. [1673] 1991. *On the Duty of Man and Citizen.* [*De Officio Hominis et Civis*]. Ed. James Tully; Trans. Michael Silverthorne. Cambridge: Cambridge University Press.

—— [1672] 1934. *De Jure Naturae et Gentium.* Trans. C. H. Oldfather and W. A. Oldfather. Oxford: Clarendon Press.

Rainbolt, George. 1993. Rights as Normative Constraints on Others. *Philosophy and Phenomenological Research* 53: 93–112.

Rawls, John. 1971. *A Theory of Justice.* Cambridge, MA: Harvard University Press.

—— 1993. *Political Liberalism.* New York: Columbia University Press.

—— 2001. *The Law of Peoples.* Cambridge, MA: Harvard University Press.

Raz, Joseph. 1986. *The Morality of Freedom.* Oxford: Oxford University Press.

—— 1999. *Practical Reason and Norms.* 2d. ed. Oxford: Oxford University Press.

Regan, Tom. 1983. *The Case for Animal Rights.* Berkeley: University of California Press.

Rossiter, Clinton, ed. [1788] 1999. *The Federalist Papers.* New York: Mentor.

Ryan, Alan. 1974. *J. S. Mill.* London: Routledge & Kegan Paul.

Sandel, Michael. 1989. Moral Argument and Liberal Toleration: Abortion and Homosexuality. *California Law Review* 77: 521.

Scanlon, T. M. 1982. Contractualism and Utilitarianism. In Sen and Williams 1982.

―――― 1998. *What We Owe to Each Other*. Cambridge, MA: Harvard University Press.

Schama, Simon. 1990. *Citizens*. New York: Random House.

Schmidtz, David. 1991. *The Limits of Government: An Essay on the Public Goods Argument*. Boulder, CO: Westview Press.

Schneewind, J. B. 1998. *The Invention of Autonomy: A History of Modern Moral Philosophy*. Cambridge: Cambridge University Press.

Schwartz, Warren F., ed. 1995. *Justice in Immigration*. Cambridge: Cambridge University Press.

Sen, Amartya. 1999. *Development as Freedom*. New York: Knopf.

Sen, Amartya and Bernard Williams, eds. 1982. *Utilitarianism and Beyond*. Cambridge: Cambridge University Press and Editions de la Maison des Sciences de l'Homme.

Shue, Henry. 1996. *Basic Rights: Subsistence, Affluence, and U.S. Foreign Policy*. 2d ed. Princeton: Princeton University Press.

Sidgwick, Henry. [1874] 1981. *The Methods of Ethics*. Indianapolis: Hackett.

Singer, Peter. 1972. Famine, Affluence and Morality. *Philosophy and Public Affairs* 1: 229–43.

―――― 1975. *Animal Liberation*. New York: Random House.

Skinner, Quentin. 1978. *The Foundations of Modern Political Thought*. 2 vols. Cambridge: Cambridge University Press.

Smart, J. J. C. and Bernard Williams. 1973. *Utilitarianism: For and Against*. Cambridge: Cambridge University Press.

Spector, Horatio. 1992. *Autonomy and Rights: The Moral Foundations of Liberalism*. Oxford: Clarendon Press.

Steiner, Hillel. 1994. *An Essay on Rights*. Oxford: Basil Blackwell.

Stone, Geoffrey R., Louis M. Seidman, Cass R. Sunstein, and Mark V. Tushnet, eds. 2002. *Constitutional Law*. Gaithersburg, MD: Aspen.

Sumner, L. W. 1989. *The Moral Foundation of Rights*. Oxford: Clarendon Press.

Thaler, Richard H., Daniel Kahneman, and Jack L. Knetsch. 1990. Experimental Tests of the Endowment Effect and the Coase Theorem. *Journal of Political Economy*. December. 1325–48.

Thomson, Judith Jarvis. 1990. *The Realm of Rights*. Cambridge, MA: Harvard University Press.

Tuck, Richard. 1979. *Natural Rights Theories: Their Origin and Development*. Cambridge: Cambridge University Press.

Unger, Peter. 1996. *Living High and Letting Die: Our Illusion of Innocence*. New York: Oxford University Press.

Unger, Roberto. 1987. *False Necessity: Anti-Necessitarian Social Theory in the Service of Radical Democracy*. Cambridge: Cambridge University Press.

Waldron, Jeremy. 1981. A Right to Do Wrong. *Ethics* 92: 21–39.

_____ 1987. *Nonsense Upon Stilts: Bentham, Burke, and Marx on the Rights of Man*. London: Methuen.

_____ 1988. *The Right to Private Property*. Oxford: Clarendon Press.

_____ 1993. *Liberal Rights: Collected Papers 1981–91*. Cambridge: Cambridge University Press.

_____ 1994. Kagan on Requirements: Mill on Sanctions. *Ethics* 104: 310–24.

_____, ed. 1984. *Theories of Rights*. New York: Oxford University Press.

Wellman, Carl. 1995. *Real Rights*. Oxford: Oxford University Press.

_____ 1998. *The Proliferation of Rights: Moral Progress or Empty Rhetoric?* Boulder, CO: Westview Press (with bibliographical essay).

White, Morton. 1978. *The Philosophy of the American Revolution*. New York: Oxford University Press.

Wollstonecraft, Mary. [1790] 1996. *A Vindication of the Rights of Men*. Amherst, N.Y.: Prometheus Books.

_____ [1792] 1992. *A Vindication of the Rights of Women*. Amherst, N.Y.: Prometheus Books.

Index

act consequentialism
  and recognitional function of moral
    rights, 155–156
  see also consequentialism
act utilitarianism
  inconsistency with "active" rights, 73–74
  of Godwin, 46–47, 198
active right
  defined, 47
  Godwin's critique of, 47, 48
  see also permission; right to do wrong;
    right to "do as one lists"
alienability
  in Grotius, 19
  in Hobbes, 23
  in Paley, 37
  of dominion over one's body, in
    apologetics of slavery, 16
Amistad, The, 77–78, 79
animal rights
  adumbrated by Bentham, 58–59
  significance of, 200–201

Aquinas, Thomas, 8
American Revolution
  as experimental test of the value of rights,
    41
  French support for, 38
  see also expansionary period, first;
    Declaration of Independence
Anscombe, Elizabeth, 109
Aristotle
  as apologist for slavery, 34
  expounded to rebut relativism, 11, 197
Ashoka, Emperor, 11
assistance, right to
  as "positive" right, 97–98
  contractualist reconstruction of, 111–112
  in Bentham, 56, 57
  in Godwin, "passive" right to, 49–51
  in Grotius, 20–21
  in Paley, 37–38
  in Pufendorf, 25–26
  right to immigrate not classifiable as,
    184